The Trail of the Conestoga

by

B. Mabel Dunham

Contents

FOREWORD

Over one hundred years ago the Mennonites came from Pennsylvania to Ontario, in order that they might live under British laws, and there find homes for themselves and their families. To-day, due to the enterprise of these early settlers, Waterloo County is one of the banner counties of all Ontario.

Miss Mabel Dunham, in her book "The Trail of the Conestoga," has given an exceptional picture of the early immigration of these people. They came to this country to find it a wilderness, and almost within a generation, by their unceasing labours, they changed the landscape so that well-built and substantial homes found themselves surrounded by cleared land covered with abundant harvests. It is such literature that makes us realize the background of our country's story. We know and appreciate too little the initiative, patience and self-sacrifice which characterized the struggles of our forefathers in laying not only the material but also the political foundations of our country. If we go back to early days, we shall find that the problems which perplex us are no greater than those they successfully solved. In their example we should find alike strength and inspiration.

W. L. Mackenzie King.
Kingsmere, Quebec

CHAPTER I

It was a cold northwest wind that blew over Pennsylvania that first Sunday morning of, cold and blustery, driving the defenceless snow into every nook and corner, and covering the road that led from Brickerville to Lititz with a soft blanket of fleecy whiteness. Even the charred, ungainly stumps of the fences, which the day before had held up ugly, protesting arms to heaven, had been transformed over night into statuary of shimmering beauty. A marvellous sight!

Since daybreak Christian Eby had been standing at his kitchen window shivering. No thought of the wonder of the scene thrilled his stolid Pennsylvania Dutch soul. Away in the west he saw heavy clouds that betokened more snow, and down the chimney he heard the threatening howl of the wind. In his heart was discontent. Like the icy blast which seemed to penetrate even the thick walls of his ancestral home, cold dissatisfaction had blown in upon his life. His very soul shivered. Presently he turned to the wood-box for protection. Digging out the largest sticks he could find, he shoved them nonchalantly into the fire; then resumed his post at the window, and gave himself up to the cheerless contemplation of how like this winter's day his own wretched existence had come to be.

Meanwhile, Nancy, his wife, and the fountain whence all his wretchedness flowed, had entered the kitchen and was bustling about among the pots and pans of the fireplace preparing for breakfast. She was an industrious housewife, it must be confessed. Not even Christian could find fault with her on that score. She had another virtue, a rare one, they say, in women—she knew how to hold her tongue. There were volumes she wanted to say to her husband standing there at the window in utter dejection when he ought to have been out doing the chores, but she pressed her lips together and held her peace. To begin a conversation was a privilege she usually accorded her husband, whom the good St. Paul had set up in some uninspired moment as the head of the household. She was quite satisfied so long as she had the last word.

Still Christian did not speak, and Nancy began to cast impatient, reproachful glances in his direction. Just as she suspected, he was going off into one of those "fits" of his again. She knew the symptoms. A smile hovered over his features, a light sparkled in his eye. All of a sudden he seemed warm, buoyant, exhilarated. He was young again, dreaming dreams and seeing visions after the manner of men of half his years.

"Dumm!" muttered the exasperated woman, behind her teeth.

But patience was at last rewarded. Christian turned and began a little friendly conversation. "Nancy, I was chust thinkin'..."

He paused, but there was no answer. Nancy was pursing her lips, as though there might be something behind them that she wasn't quite ready to let out.

"I was chust thinkin'," Christian went on to say, looking about for something to increase his moral strength. He picked up the family comb and pretended to be giving his undivided attention to the care of his straggly beard, glancing furtively and apprehensively all the while in the direction of this thorn in the flesh that the Lord had sent him under the pleasing guise of wife. When he had mustered up a little strength, he completed his remarks with "mebbe till next winter we are in Canada already."

Nancy paid no attention. She did not so much as look up. She sat with a shilling crock set deep into her lap and "schnitzed" apples as though the lives of all her household depended upon the diligence of that moment.

Christian took courage, forgetting for the time being that silence is not always an evidence of consent. "Me and Isaac Brubacher are talkin' about goin' over till the spring when the roads get dry enough," he said. "Then we'll come back after a while mebbe and fetch her and you along over, too." He spoke as though it were not altogether a consummation devoutly to be desired.

Nancy jerked her crock around, and sharpened her knife ferociously on the edge of it.

But this visionary husband of hers did not see the storm brewing. He went stumbling blindly into it. "Isaac says he will buy him a new yoke of oxen," he continued, "and a new wagon, and..."

"That's your dumm notion," snapped Nancy, brandishing her knife in her good man's face like a regular shrew. "You needn't lay it to Isaac."

"But Isaac thinks..."

"Yes, I know. He always thinks what you tell him to. That's why you and him are so thick."

At this moment for some quite unaccountable reason Christian suddenly remembered the chores. He reached for his cap that hung on the peg behind the door, and wrapped his muffler about his neck. He lifted the latch—

But Nancy caught him by the coat-tail, and dragged him like a culprit into the middle of the room. "So now you want to run away, do you?" she scolded. "Them cows can wait till I get through with you. Feel for goin' to Canada, eh, and sixty years old till April."

"It's the last of April," interjected Christian, weakly. "Might chust as well be May."

"Whether it's April or May makes nothing out," Nancy assured him. "There ain't much time lost between them. You've got one foot draggin' in the grave already, for all you want to be so young. And you know it, but you're too dumm to let on. You can thank the Lord you've got a woman that's got sense enough to stop where she's got it good. He chenerally always hunts out a smart woman for a dumm man, the Lord does."

Christian kept edging towards the door. The moment Nancy released him he was off. A cold blast met him as he opened the door, a flurry of snow blew up his coat-sleeve. The glow faded from his face, the sparkle had left his eye. Nancy was right. He was an old man, trudging through life with one foot dragging in the grave.

"He ain't right in his head, he can't be," was the conclusion Nancy reached when she soliloquized over this latest dissension with her husband. But she spoke as though, in her opinion, Christian was more to be censured than pitied for his mental condition. It was the unfortunate people who had to live with him that deserved all the pity.

Nancy Eby was one of those stay-at-homes who are quite content to be tethered for life to a single spot. As far as she knew, or cared, the world extended very little beyond her own horizon. To her, the Hammer Creek community in Lancaster County, Pennsylvania, was the world, and its people the inhabitants thereof. It was on a neighbouring farm that she had first seen the light of day. Her wedding journey had been a walk hand in hand with Christian from the somewhat humble Bricker homestead to the Eby mansion on the adjoining hill farm, and when some day she should go to dwell forever in her Father's house of many mansions, her lifeless body would still remain among the scenes of her activity. So she hoped, and often as she stood at the window and gazed at the God's-Acre beyond, she had marked the spot where she and Christian would, side by side, sleep the sleep that knows no waking. This "dumm" notion of Christian's old age was directly opposed to her well-laid plans. But what of that? Everyone knew that he wasn't going to have anything at all to say about it. She would manage that—and Christian.

Christian Eby was proud of the home he shared with his wife. Little wonder that Nancy could not understand his desire to leave it. It stood on the summit of a hill overlooking the Brickerville road, and it was called, after a little stream that divided the farm, the Hammer Creek House. A lordly mansion it was for those days, two stories high, and built of clean gray sandstone that had been worn smooth with the rains of many years. Its spacious windows were all securely closed against the intrusion of any stray breath of fresh air, and behind the tiny panes of glass could be seen white linen blinds, half-drawn and adjusted with great precision, homespun without a doubt, and spotlessly clean. The front door was a heavy oaken one, and above it on a rectangular slab of red sandstone was carved a curious inscription:

> *John Eby   Elizabeth Eby*
> *Gott gesegne dieses Haus,*
> *Und alle was da gehet ein und aus;*
> *Gott gesegne alle sampt,*
> *Und dazu das ganze Land.*

The Hammer Creek House had long been something more than a dwelling. Many years had passed since the Lord had set His seal upon it and marked it for a Mennonite meeting-house. In the time of old Theodorus, the American patriarch of the Eby family, and the little log shanty in the heart of the virgin forest, this home had first been chosen as the place where the people should erect their altar. When Christian's father inherited the farm and built on it the stately house with walnut and oaken panelled partitions and a huge chimney providing for open fireplaces in all the rooms of either story, the Ark of the Lord had not departed from its wonted habitation. The legend on the name-plate over the front door bore silent but incontrovertible witness to the fact that in the hearts of the Eby family there was the same inborn piety as had characterized them in less prosperous days.

Christian Eby walked in the way of his fathers. His heart was as large as his home, and his reputation for piety and hospitality grew with each successive year. No one presumed to question his judgment in matters of agricultural import or in the ecclesiastical councils of the

Mennonite brotherhood. But this Canada talk! Everybody looked at everybody else when he began it. It was altogether too bad to think that at sixty and in apparent good health, the great and good man should have begun to show signs of approaching senility.

The chores were finished at last, and the object of the community's concern returned to the house, followed closely by his son, Hannes, a stalwart youth, who some years before had taken upon his shoulders the management of the farm. Several yards behind, two girls trudged through the snow, and found no end of difficulty in keeping to the beaten path, encumbered as they were with heavy milk-pails.

The younger one, who walked ahead, was still in her early teens. A woman of ideas for all that. She was calling out to her companion; "Why don't you call once, Susie, and tell Hannes he shall drag our milk in?"

Susie almost dropped her pails in astonishment.

"He's stronger than us," continued the young one, hearing no reply. "I'll tell him myself, if you give me the dare."

"Rebecca!" gasped Susie, in dire alarm, "if you do..."

Rebecca didn't.

During the few days her cousin had lived at the Hammer Creek House, Susie had been puzzling her brains over the child. Where had she picked up her ideas of life and conduct? Extraordinarily revolutionary they were for a girl of her age. When they had reached the shelter of the wood-shed, Susie put down her pails, closed the door and proceeded to learn what she could by that most direct of all means, interrogation.

"Wherever did you get such dumm notions, Beccy?" she demanded.

"What for dumm notions?" This, innocently.

"Why, to tell Hannes what he shall do."

"I didn't mean nothin'," Beccy made haste to assure her. "I only thought that he was stronger..."

"But Hannes is a man," interrupted Susie.

Beccy did not seem to understand, and Susie continued her investigation on another tack. "Was you ever in Lancaster yet?" she asked.

Beccy shook her head, wonderingly.

"Well, you didn't get it to home, that's sure," reflected Susie. "Us Mennonites ain't for leavin' the women rule it over the men like that. Your mam chumped every time your pop hollered, I know."

"But pop was sick."

6

"And now that he's went, she'll quick find another one to hop for," commented Susie. "She's set her cap for Israel Shantz already. She can have him for all I care."

What could Beccy do but sigh?

"That's what women are for," explained Susie. "It says in the Bible that women must obey their men."

"But I haven't got a man," Beccy made haste to remind her.

"And if you talk like that, you'll never get one," replied Susie. "Then what will you do, Beccy? Get an old maid." She served this ultimatum with an expression of disgust in her face and voice.

At this moment, Hannes opened the kitchen door and announced that breakfast was ready.

As soon as all the family, hands clean and faces shining, had gathered about the table, Christian gave a sign, at which every head was bowed in a silence at once prolonged and profound. It was a matter for each individual conscience to decide what thoughts they would think during those hallowed moments. Who was to know, but the All-knowing One, of course, if Christian took a return trip to Canada on the wings of his imagination, or if Nancy's thoughts grovelled about in the narrow confines of her kitchen? Beccy, perhaps, reflected on the awful calamity that awaits women who speak their minds, and forgot to thank the Giver of every good and perfect gift for the food she was about to receive. Who knows? But the marvel was that without any sign of warning, the wandering thoughts of all were gathered in at precisely the same moment, the concluding amens ascended conjointly on high, and the business of breakfast was auspiciously begun.

What a meal it was! The table fairly groaned with the weight upon it. Two heaping dishes of everything were set, one at either end of the table, so that even the children could conveniently spear everything their palates desired. Like all normal children the Eby off-spring desired all they saw. If any one of them didn't, the logical conclusion was that something was wrong and Nancy was ready with a remedy.

"Fetch the sulphur, Susie," said the observant mother when her eyes, having roamed about from plate to plate, fell upon a great round crust that Little Lizzie thought she had hidden successfully under her saucer on the side most remote from the maternal eye.

Susie brought a bowl from the mantle, and Nancy put some of the contents in a spoon and filled it with molasses from a jug on the table.

"Here, Lizzie," commanded Nancy, "take this."

Now although Lizzie was only seven years old, she had already formed a strong aversion to the particular kind of medicine which her mother offered her. She looked first at the spoon, and then at the crust that her mother pulled out ruthlessly from its hiding-place and exposed to public view. She was in disgrace and she knew it. If she could only wiggle out of it somehow. But there she was wedged in between her mother and Beccy on a bench as immovable as the rocks of all the ages.

Now Lizzie was a little Mennonite girl, and so she wore at table, as custom compelled all womankind of that faith to do, a covering for her head. A dark handkerchief of generous proportions was folded obliquely from ear to ear and tied under her chin. The distressed little girl now used it to hide her reddened face.

"Shame!" cried Christian. "Our Lizzie must be a little boy, eh, Bench, that she sets at the table with a bare head."

Benjamin, a shaver of nine, grinned with appreciation. He sat at his father's left hand and had an uninterrupted across-the-table view of the discomfited Lizzie, who never failed to laugh at him when he was in trouble.

Beccy was enjoined to cover once more Lizzie's rebellious head, whereupon the little one sat like a martyr, looking from the sulphur to the crust and from the crust back again to the sulphur. Her mother kept urging her to decision.

"Crusts give red cheeks, Lizzie," said Christian, encouragingly, "and strong teeth."

The kind word was all the child needed. She seized the crust, thrust it into her mouth and tried to swallow it at a single gulp. Nancy rescued it just in time and personally superintended its proper mastication.

When the last bite had disappeared, Lizzie essayed to look the world in the face once more. But to her surprise her mother's inexorable arm confronted her, and at the end of it, in close proximity to Lizzie's little pouting mouth, was the hated mixture of sulphur and molasses. She drew back, shook her head rebelliously, and began to cry.

"Ach, leave her be," urged Christian, whose kind heart was touched.

"Leave her be, did you say?" exploded Nancy. "That's the dumm way you have of spoilin' 'em. Here, Lizzie, don't make so slow."

But the little rebel made no haste to obey. War was imminent. The mother called into operation her strong right arm, and pushed Lizzie's defiant little head forward in contact with the spoon. Every eye in the room was centred on the scene of conflict.

"Take it, Lizzie," whispered Beccy, nudging her elbow. "I'll wash the dishes if you do."

At this, Nancy carried the battle into another quarter forthwith, and poured out the vials of her wrath upon the interfering Beccy. "What for did you do that?" she demanded.

"To make her do it," replied Beccy.

"And what do you think I am doin'?" Nancy wanted to know. "Ain't I makin' her do it? I didn't ask for none of your help."

"But she'll do it easier if you coax her," suggested Beccy.

"That's another one of them notions that grow in the Eby dumm heads," said Nancy. "They've all got them one way or another."

Then Christian, who had caught a glimpse of the self-satisfied smile that was hovering about Lizzie's little sulphur-dusted mouth, committed a fatal indiscretion. He laughed.

Nancy turned upon him reproachfully and demanded to know what he found so amusing in her endeavour to teach his child the rudimentary virtue of obedience.

"It's all!" cried Christian, quite unable to restrain his mirth.

"What's all?"

"The sulphur."

Nancy looked at the child who was the chief instigator of all this tumult of words. The sulphur had disappeared, and Lizzie was revolving her little red tongue around the circumference of her mouth gathering up with it all the stray particles of the dose.

"Is it good, Lizzie?" asked Hannes from across the table. He was laughing, too.

Lizzie made a wry face. It was clear that she was not too young to know the value of the gentle art of conciliation.

But Nancy was determined that Lizzie should pay the full penalty of her folly. "For that you can wash the dishes alone," she announced with decision. "I'll learn you to be actin' up behind my back."

Protests were useless. The crust, the sulphur, and the dishwashing had all unexpectedly fallen to Lizzie's lot. She had to eat not only her crust but also the bitter fruit of her disobedience. It was a disagreeable experience, but through it she learned a very valuable lesson of life and conduct.

No sooner had the dishes been cleared from the table and re-placed by the red tablecloth than Hannes took a book from his pocket, sat down at Christian's place and began to read.

Immediately Nancy was concerned. She bustled about excit-edly, and looked over her son's shoulder. Just as she expected. He was reading that useless story book of his. "He's at it again," she told her husband.

"Ach, leave him be," said Christian, not in the least alarmed.

"That's always the way," replied Nancy, in an aggrieved tone of voice. "You let me with all the trainin' to do. All them lies he is readin'! It'll ruin him body and soul!"

Christian was sufficiently interested in his son's spiritual wel-fare to put on his spectacles and go and look over his shoulder to see what was the nature of this pernicious literature that Hannes was im-bibing with such avidity. He was surprised to find his own name printed there. "Christian in the Slough of Despond," he read.

"It's all a pack o' lies," reiterated Nancy.

But Christian was absorbed in this namesake of his who seemed to have fallen into a terrible pit. He was so anxious to know if he got out again that he could hardly wait until Hannes had turned the page.

"You're readin' them lies, too," cried Nancy, consumed with that species of temper known as righteous indignation. She swooped down upon the table, seized the contaminating thing, and threw it into the fire. "There," she said with satisfaction. "Now it can't hurt either of you. Ain't the Bible good enough for you no more?"

Hannes was amazed, but he said nothing. It was no use, he knew.

"Where did you get it?" whispered Christian.

"From Jake Brubacher," replied Hannes. "He fetched it from Lancaster last week already."

Christian was keeping a watchful eye over Nancy's move-ments. At an opportune moment he drew out his purse, took out a number of coins, and said: "Tell him he can fetch you another one along over sometime when he goes again."

"It's a story-book," said Hannes, unwilling to spend his father's money for riotous literature without his knowledge and consent.

"A true story-book," replied Christian, shoving the money into the young man's pocket. "I read enough to know that. But you must hide it, Hannes, or it will come in the fire too." He glanced knowingly in Nancy's direction.

So the secret bargain was sealed.

Meanwhile, preparations were being made for the meeting. Fires had been kindled in the large front rooms, and little Benj was running about here and there arranging the chairs in rows. The Bible and the hymn book were placed on the pulpit table, and all was in readiness a whole hour before the time set for the meeting.

"Well, Bench," said Christian, entering from the kitchen, and patting the little fellow on the back. "Do you feel good to-day?"

Benj never complained of his health, but he was not a robust child. Like Jacob of old, Christian loved this Benjamin of his above all his other sons, and watched him anxiously lest, peradventure, mischief might befall him.

"You must grow big and strong or you can't come in Canada," continued Christian. "You want to go there some day, not?"

"I'm goin' with you along."

Of course he was. Christian would not think of going without his Benj. In all his visions of journey to the delectable land of the north, he saw his little son tramping along in his footsteps.

"We must have hope," said Christian.

"And faith," added Benj.

"Yes, and charity, too," replied Christian, thinking of Nancy in the kitchen. "It looks like you've got faith, Bench." He motioned to the rows of chairs. "Do you think somebody will come to meetin' on a day like this?"

"It's Sunday, not?" said Benj, into whose little mind had never entered the idea of the weather having any possible influence over the performance of religious duties.

"Yes, but the storm," answered Christian. "Roads will be all blocked. Nobody can get through."

A cloud of disappointment passed over Little Benj's face. He went to the window and stood there, trying to bolster up his faith with hope.

But the conversation which he heard from the kitchen did not bring him any assurance. "They won't come to-day," the mother was saying. "And if they do, who's to preach? Peter can't. He's sick."

Susie suggested a substitute, but Nancy shook her head. Not even the Bishop could preach like Peter, she said. But that was only maternal pride, for Peter was her eldest son, who years before had been married and was living happily on a farm near by. Early in life he had heard the call to preach, and although there were not being added to the church daily such as were being saved under his ministry, still he was an earnest, forceful speaker, and a very devout man. On Sundays he dug up the fallow ground in a figurative sense as diligently as he continued to do it literally on week days.

"Well, if Peter can't come," said Susie, "there'll be others that will. We can wisit anyway."

Beccy tittered. "Josiah Schneider?" she suggested, whereupon Susie turned her face to hide a suffusion of blushes.

"Who told you about Josiah Schneider?" demanded Nancy, making a mental note at the same time of Susie's confusion.

Beccy saw danger ahead and decided to hold her tongue.

"Did she tell you, too, how lazy he is?" asked Nancy, keeping her eyes glued upon the back of Susie's head. "Did she tell you that?"

"No——o," stammered Beccy.

"Well then I will. He's lazy and big-feelin' and most everything else. He won't make nobody a good man. Is it snowin' yet, Susie?"

"Yes," replied Susie, without so much as looking in the direction of the window.

"Well then nobody will come," decided Nancy. "Put the chairs back again on the wall, Benj," she called into the front room. "It won't give no wisiters to-day."

The words were scarcely out of her mouth when Christian Eby, in a loud voice that resounded through the house, made the joyful announcement that somebody was coming up the lane.

"On horseback!" cried Benj, turning from the chairs and running to the window.

"A Schimmel! Whatever!" exclaimed Hannes.

"A Schimmel!" echoed Susie, in derision. "What did he get a Schimmel for?"

"To ride on," laughed Hannes. "Looks like a good horse for all he's white. Think once, Susie, how you would feel if you was a nigger."

But Susie had not at that particular moment any time for ethnological problems. What concerned her was that Josiah Schneider had bought a Schimmel when she had in his hearing expressed a decided preference for bay horses.

"Can you make out yet who it is?" asked Nancy, a trifle anxiously.

"Sam Bricker, I think," replied Hannes.

Susie's expectant countenance fell suddenly.

12

"Looks around the head like the colt that kicked Daniel the dashboard out of the buggy," remarked Christian.

"It is Sam Bricker," decided Benj, dancing about in high glee at the prospect of a romp with his favourite cousin.

"Yes, it's Sam," was the general opinion. "He must 've bought Daniel's horse at the sale."

The great event of the week had been the disposal of all the household effects and farm stock of Beccy's father, the late Jeremiah Eby. From miles around the farmers had come in the early morning, had chatted and visited and eaten together; then bought what they could at a bargain and taken it home at the close of a perfect day.

For the bereaved family it had been a day of separation and sadness. The widow had to return in poverty to her father's home; the family was scattered. Daniel alone was to remain on the old farm, but in the capacity of hired man to the new owner. The girls were to be farmed out among the relatives; and Beccy was accounted lucky indeed when it was learned that it had fallen to her lot to drive back to the Hammer Creek House, sandwiched in between her new foster parents, Christian and Nancy Eby. Beccy herself was none too elated over her great fortune. She would have much preferred to remain on the dear old farm in the backwoods with all the associations of her childhood.

It was Christian who noticed first that Beccy was not with the others at the window. He had asked her if she recognized the colt, and she had not answered. He turned and saw her huddled in the corner behind the wood-box. He was about to go and console her; but Nancy, noticing, brushed him aside and went herself instead.

"What is it, Beccy?" she asked solicitously, drawing up a chair beside the girl and stroking her hair. It was the tenderest caress of which her undemonstrative Pennsylvania Dutch soul was capable. "Is it anything wrong?"

At these words of unexpected sympathy, Beccy sobbed aloud. She tried to speak, but a great lump in her throat choked her utterance. All Nancy could understand was something about wanting to go home.

"But you can't do that," she said. "He's went, your doddy, and he didn't let nothing behind him—nothing but debts. You must hire out some-place, and I'm sure you've got it good here. What did you have to home, eh, but a little log house way back there in the bush, and no wisiters or nothing?"

"But it was home," sobbed the child. She hid her face in her hands and her slight frame shook convulsively. Every word her aunt had spoken had cut her to the quick. It was as if she had poured acid into an open wound, mistaking it for oil.

"Rebecca Eby," said Nancy, and this time she spoke with some severity, "you ought to shame yourself for a cry-bubby to cry so easy. Stop it now and wash your eyes out. I'm goin' out now to see Sam's new horse."

She meant no unkindness; but she had her own ideas about the training of children, as well as about other things; and to indulge the child in a weakness would be, she maintained, to do her a lasting injury. So, admonishing her again to dry her tears, she joined the family at the kitchen door.

There everybody was asking innumerable questions, which had to be answered all over again when Nancy arrived.

"Where did you get him, Sam?"

"By the sale."

"So? Then, Christian, you had right for once. It is the colt that made so nasty that time with Daniel. How much must you pay for him?"

"Twenty dollars."

"So much? And the money? You lent that, I guess."

"I earnt it," replied Sam, a trifle impatiently.

"Well, you needn't get so cross about it," said Susie. "How do you call him?"

"Menno."

"Menno! A horse! Wherever did you get that name?"

All Sam knew was what Daniel had told him, that his little sister had been foolish about the horse, and had cried her eyes out when she learned that he was to be sold. It was she who had named him after Menno Simons, the founder of the Mennonite faith.

"Beccy!" whispered Nancy, nudging Susie's elbow, "We'll likely have trouble with that girl yet. She's got dumm notions, too, like all the Ebys."

Christian had waited only until his wife was too much engrossed with Sam and his horse to pay any attention to his movements, and then he had slipped into the house to see how Beccy was faring. He found her in utter dejection sitting in the corner.

"Come to the window once, Beccy," he whispered, patting her gently on the head.

"No, no," cried the girl, shaking herself.

"But Sam Bricker's there," coaxed Christian.

"Mebbe you don't know Sam yet, but he's in our 'Freund-schaft.'"

Beccy showed not the slightest degree of interest.

"He's got red hair, Sam has, curly, red hair," Christian went on. "He don't like it much, but I do. He's real smart, Sam is, and everybody likes him."

"I hate him," said Beccy, between her sobs. The tone in which she spoke gave credence to the words.

Christian stood back aghast. It was contrary to the Mennonite discipline to hate anything but the world, the flesh, and the devil.

"But what did he do to you, Beccy, that you hate him so?" he said. "Did you see him at the sale mebbe?"

"No."

"But there must be something."

"He's got Menno."

"Menno was your horse?"

Beccy nodded.

Christian Eby had long since learned from a rich experience that in dealing with women an ounce of compromise is worth a pound of coercion. And Beccy was a woman in the making. So he allowed that although Sam Bricker was far from hateful, he could at least understand why she might hate the man who owned her horse. He told her that he would see to it that she did not meet Sam until she was willing. He would stay with her until the others had come indoors, and then they would slip out through the front door to the barn, where they could see the "Schimmel" undisturbed by the presence of his new master. And Beccy at last allowed herself to be persuaded.

But it was not so easy to escape unnoticed. Sam saw them leaving the room as he entered, and he soon created an opportunity to inquire who the strange girl might be.

"Ach, her?" replied Nancy. "Why, that's only Beccy, Jeremiah Eby that had his funeral in the fall, his girl. We fetched her along over from the sale."

"Then Daniel is her brother?"

"Yes, and she's hired out by us now."

"So?"

"I and Christian thought we might chust as well take her," said Nancy. "Lizzie's too little yet to work much, and Susie will pretty soon be gettin' married now."

"It looks that way anyhow by Josiah Schneider," remarked Hannes.

But Nancy shut him up. Susie had too much sense to look at a lazy, good-for-nothing fellow like Josiah Schneider. If she only knew it, Israel Shantz would "make her a good man."

Sam did not appreciate the way the conversation had drifted to Susie and her matrimonial prospects when he was itching to hear about Beccy. But he was quick enough to make the best of the situation. "I know now why Susie don't like my 'Schimmel'," he said. "I and him passed Josiah Schneider and his stiff-jointed bay horse way back in the swamp already."

"Then he's comin'?" whispered Susie, in tense excitement. "He said he would."

"Yes, he's comin'."

"And goin'," added Nancy, grimly. "He's not goin' to set around here in my way all day."

Sam snorted. "If there's goin' to be a fight, I'll be goin'," he said. "Somehow or another I chenerally always get mixed up in it if I set around." And he arose to go.

"But you're not goin' yet," cried Susie. "Why, you've chust come."

Sam averred that he had only come to show his horse, and neither Susie's blushing entreaties nor the general protests availed to win him over. He put on his hat, pulled up his heavy coat around his neck, and went out.

Christian Eby started like a child caught in mischief when Sam opened the stable door. "Ach, you ain't goin' yet," he stammered.

Sam nodded, but he made no further move. Directly in front of him stood Beccy, the object of his interest, stroking Menno's face and head and ears, telling him that she loved him for he was her horse, her "Schimmel," own him who might.

"It's only Beccy," Christian ventured to explain, when he noticed how Sam gazed at her.

It must have been Christian's voice that startled Beccy, for the young man did not say a word. She looked up and saw the hated Sam Bricker standing there trying to smile at her. Immediately she bolted for the door.

But Christian stopped her. "You don't have to make strange, Beccy," he said. "It's only Sam Bricker, and he comes often here."

"And Menno comes every time along," added Sam, realizing that it was only through the merits of his horse that he might hope for any consideration at the hands of Beccy.

Instantly all hatred was banished from Beccy's heart. Sam Bricker held her small hand in his large one, and she was smiling through her tears into his laughing eyes.

CHAPTER II

Seven years and more had come and gone, and still Sam Bricker was pitching sheaves and feeding cattle on his father's farm. Seven long years they had been of hard work, little pay, and poorer prospects. Misfortune of one kind or another had dogged Elias Bricker all his life. Once it had come in the form of a bolt of lightning, destroying his barn and the season's crops. Again it was an accident to a valuable cow, or a pestilence that took his fattest cattle. Then the bank had failed, and the scant savings of years had taken unto themselves wings and flown away. Only the farm was left. A poor, god-forsaken farm it was, too. The little creek that a generation before had jogged along zig-zag fashion through the fields had changed its course, or ceased to flow—which, it matters not. The fact remained that it no longer existed for the Brickers. The buildings were small and in urgent need of repair, and altogether there was not a less desirable farm for miles around.

But that was not all. Elias Bricker's family had hampered him. His wife, whom he had married to be a help-meet, had for years been a confirmed invalid, demanding much attention and consideration, not to mention expense. His daughters were so numerous that it took nearly all he could save to clothe them, and the young men of the neighborhood seemed provokingly slow about relieving him of that responsibility. There were only two sons, the phlegmatic John, who had become a benedict early in life—married money, as he thought, only to find out when it was forever too late that he had made a mistake—and the red-headed, impulsive, energetic Sam. Two sons and only one farm. So it happened that when old age had laid the father on the shelf, John came by the farm; and Sam, for want of something better to do, became a sort of permanent, yet permanently prospectless, hired man.

The brothers were stabling their horses one evening at the close of a disappointing day's work in the fields, when Sam brought down his fist with a thud upon the stall, and announced that he was done with his job.

"Got a new one yet?" inquired John, tauntingly. He had heard his brother make just such statements before. He was always rash, was Sam. "Got a new one, eh?"

Sam did not answer. He ate his supper in silence, not so much as hearing those who had the temerity to address him. Everyone was relieved when he wiped his plate carefully with a piece of bread, signifying that he had finished his meal. Every eye was upon him when he pushed back his chair; then drew off his long boots with the aid of the boot-jack, and threw them and it into the corner. Whatever was wrong with Sam?

"He's took a piece of kindlin' wood along," observed the dowerless Annie, John Bricker's spouse. She got up from the table, ran to the window and peeked out. "He's settin' on the doorstep chust."

"What doin'?"

"Whittlin'."

John cleared his throat, a nervous habit of his when he was troubled. "It's chenerally always serious when Sam takes to whittlin'."

"Whatever it is, he's got it bad," commented Annie. "You'd best go and see once what's wrong."

John deliberated a few moments; then opened the door and went out.

He found Sam sitting on the top step surrounded by a mass of shavings. "What are you doin' that for?" he demanded, scarcely knowing whether to expect an answer or not.

"They'll do for startin' the fire in the mornin'," replied Sam, without looking up. "You can take them in."

But John did not intend to be so summarily dismissed. He had come for the express purpose of offering Sam some helpful advice—advice which this impetuous young brother of his stood in urgent need of. The worst of it was, he hadn't the faintest idea as to how he was going to impart it.

"If I was you, Sam,—" he ventured.

"You ain't."

"But if I was," he continued, overlooking Sam's curt reply, "I'd—"

"No, you wouldn't," replied Sam, without stopping his whittling. "If you was me, you'd mind your own business like I do."

It is an indication of the great perseverance with which the Creator had endowed John Bricker that he did not at this insult turn on

19

his heel and leave Sam unadvised. But experience owes a debt to importunate youth, and John Bricker was not a man to shirk a duty.

"How old are you, Sam?" he asked.

It was such an unexpected question that Sam looked up and replied civilly enough that he was twenty-six.

"There's Eliza Hoffman. She's twenty-four," John felt encouraged to suggest.

Sam sniffed.

"It's time you get hitched up," intimated John. "If you don't feel for Eliza, mebbe you can get somebody else with a farm along."

"Like you did," retorted Sam.

That was too much for John. He drew himself up, turned, and retired while he could with dignity.

"Can't do nothing with him," he told Annie, when he returned to the kitchen. "Stubborn as a mule. Always was."

"He must get married," said Annie. "Eliza Hoffman's soft on him, and she's rich." It sounded as though it might be a question of millions.

"That's what I told him," said John. "That's what everybody else has told him for months back. But no, he won't listen. There he sets mopin' when he has a chance to be runnin' with a girl like Eliza. And her pop has three farms."

Annie fully concurred with her husband in the idea that it was Sam's duty to retrieve the Bricker fortunes by contracting a wealthy marriage. And Sam could do it, if he would, for he was without doubt the most popular young man in the community. Sometimes in the middle of a stirring sermon, when her eyes were supposed to be closed in prayer, Annie had seen sly glances steal from under the snow-white caps of the young women of their Israel, and rest upon the red-headed Sam, the all-too-visible object of their adoration. And among them there was no one more ardent in her devotions than the wealthy Eliza.

"He'll come around all right yet," said Annie, hopefully, "Chust wait once and see."

Long into the night, Sam sat on the doorstep, whittling intermittently. The wind blew up, and the dark shadows of the swaying trees moved about him in the light of the moon like so many spectres from the nether world. A strange light played over the young man's features. Could it be that he had, at John's suggestion, arrayed before him in imagination the soft-eyed daughters of the landed fathers of the community, while he waived decision? Or was it to be Eliza and satisfaction all around?

During the rest of the week, Sam was strangely uncommunicative. If he talked at all, it was only to Menno, his horse, who seemed to nod his head from time to time and look very wise. In the evenings, he sat on the doorstep with his thoughts and a piece of kindling wood.

Annie was relieved when Sunday came. She had enough shavings to last the rest of her life, she declared. Besides, Sunday would surely bring some relief to Sam's agitation. She would keep her eyes open, and see for herself which way the wind was blowing.

No sooner had Sam gulped down his breakfast than he hurried upstairs to his room to put on his Sunday clothes. He was agreeably excited; conscious, no doubt, that it would be a day of momentous importance. Then, without a word to anyone, he took Menno from the stable, and started off on his Sabbath day's journey to the Hammer Creek House.

"He'll come there before they are et," remarked Annie, as she watched him going down the lane.

"And come back till we are all in bed," replied John. "He's gettin' awful thick with Uncle Christ these last couple Sundays back."

"Yes, I took notice to that, too," said Annie. "What does it mean?"

"We'll have to wait and see," said John.

Time had wrought many changes at the Hammer Creek House since the day when Sam had first brought Menno for the inspection of the Eby family. The house had been extended to nearly twice its former size, and there were now two front doors instead of one, so that it was to all intents and purposes a double house, without the customary dividing wall of solid masonry. In those days when the architectural possibilities of halls had not yet entered into the mind of man, room opened into room, bed-chamber into bed-chamber, and even house into house with amazing familiarity. The new part, they called "the doddy-house," and there lived the "doddy," Christian, with Nancy and the unmarried members of his family. Hannes, who had some years before taken unto himself a wife and the cares of a young family, now lived in the older part of the house; and upon his shoulders rested the responsibility of the farm.

The eventide of life had come for the old people. Christian had grown feeble, and when he walked, he leaned more and more heavily upon his cane. His chief occupation was to sit in silence hour after hour in his great armchair on the "stoop." Occasionally, when his face brightened with expectation and his eyes looked steadfastly into the distance, Nancy became alarmed at what she called the old man's "fits." But when Christian sank dejectedly into his chair, and dropped his chin upon his chest, his wife had no fears, for she knew that he was thinking of the past, as any normal old man might be expected to do. It was easy for Nancy to keep an eye upon him, since her chief occupation was knitting, and her wandering interest in Christian did not in any way interfere with the steadiness and accuracy with which the needles clicked over one another in rapid succession.

On Sundays it was different. Then Christian thought neither of the future nor of the past, but watched with interest the arrival of the friends for meeting. Nancy put her knitting aside, too, and bustled about in anticipation of "wisiters." As the years went by, the old people looked forward more and more to these weekly gatherings of old friends, and to the opportunities they afforded for the exchange of confidences and harmless bits of homely gossip.

When Sam Bricker arrived at the Hammer Creek House, he went straight to the "doddy-house." He found the Ebys still at breakfast.

"Ach, Sam, but you're early," exclaimed Lizzie, now a buxom lass in her teens, full of life and colour.

"Did you come to breakfast mebbe?" said Benj, with a laugh. His childish delight in his big, red-headed cousin had grown into the admiration of a worshipful hero. "Come, set down once by me."

So Sam helped himself to a plate from the cupboard, slid in beside Benj and prepared to enjoy a second breakfast. "Everything tastes so good here," he said. "From how it looks, you must have a pretty good cook."

"Beccy is our cook," said Nancy, thinking that Sam stood in need of information.

Lizzie giggled. "I guess you know that," she whispered to Sam. "You chust said that a-purpose. You're an awful teasy boy."

Nancy pricked up her ears. She saw Beccy leave the table hurriedly for no reason that she could see, and she noticed that Sam kept his eyes on his plate. She demanded to know what Lizzie had found to laugh at.

"Nothing," replied Lizzie, not without apprehension.

"You didn't suck it out of your thumb," said Nancy. "Out with it!"

From a childish experience with crusts, and sulphur, and dishwashing, Lizzie had learned the cardinal virtue of obedience. She glanced at Sam, beseeching forgiveness, and blurted out: "He wants to see Beccy get red at the cheeks."

Nancy grunted. "That's chust like them dumm Ebys," she said. "Poor Susie went like that, too. Thinkin' about that lazy, big-feelin' Josiah Schneider till she made him marry her. He'll never make her a good man, never."

"But Sam's not lazy, or big-feelin'," ventured Christian, who rather resented the way his wife had of laying all the stupidity she encountered at the door of the Ebys. "Beccy's pretty smart if she gets Sam."

"That's once you said right," replied Nancy, becoming somewhat agitated. "But she needn't be settin' her cap for him. He's took."

The red-headed young man on the opposite side of the table lifted his eyes from the plate and gazed in amazement at his aunt. "Took, am I?" he said. "And who do you think has took me?"

"Eliza Hoffman," replied Nancy, quite unconcernedly. "Her pop says he'll give her the best farm he's got the day she ties up with Sam Bricker."

"But——"

"And I told him he can get the papers ready," continued Nancy, without so much as noticing Sam's attempt at protest. "I said 'Sam's a Bricker. He ain't no dummhead.'"

At this juncture Christian decided that it was time to change the subject. He pushed back his plate and his chair, tilting the latter on its hind legs at a dangerous angle, and tucking his thumbs comfortably into the arms of his waistcoat. "I was chust thinkin'," he began.

As usual, he glanced nervously at Nancy and started again with greater assurance. "I was chust thinkin' about them days when we had the war, the Revolution, or what you call it," he said. "It wonders me that them soldiers didn't do me nothing. They were that mad."

"Because you wouldn't fight?" suggested Benjamin, pleased to find his father in a reminiscent mood.

"They thought I was for England," said Christian.

"And you was for England, not?" questioned Sam.

A merry twinkle danced in the old man's eyes. "Ach, you know it is in the rules that we shall not fight," he said. "Being Mennonites saved us a lot."

Sam laughed. A very handy rule, he said it was, allowing the "plain" people to sympathize, if they would, with their country's enemy, and at the same time protecting them from persecution as traitors. A very handy rule, indeed, and Christian agreed.

There could not be any doubt about the old man's sympathy with the loyalist party. Every day of his life he thanked God for England and Englishmen. There was a time when, as a child, his grandfather used to take him on his knee and tell him stories of the dark days of religious persecution in Europe. True tales, they were, too; such tales as only those who have lived through them can relate. His grandfather, old Theodorus Eby, was of Celtic extraction, born in northern Italy, and as a child he had roamed the barren mountains of Switzerland, a fugitive, enduring want and untold misery rather than forsake the doctrines of his fathers and assent to strange teaching. It was William Penn, a freedom-loving Englishman, who had delivered him. English ships, bought with English gold, had carried him, without money and without price, to a new England beyond the seas. Here, an English parliament had declared that he might live his simple life, here in every court of law his yea should be yea, his nay, nay, and here, in the event of war, other hands would wield his weapon and his need not touch the accursed thing.

Nancy was not listening, except in a general way. Christian's talk did not interest her. If he wasn't laying wild plans for his future—and hers—he was sure to be digging up and glorifying the buried past, while she was resolved to live wholly in and for the present. Above the hum of the voices she heard the slow, monotonous tick of the clock. Ah! it was getting late.

"I wonder how long youse would set here, if I would leave you," she said, spiritedly. "And what have you got to talk about anyway? Them days are past long already, and they don't come again neither, I hope. But the dishes is to wash, and the victuals is to put away. Come, Beccy, don't make so slow."

Beccy obediently began to stack the plates and Lizzie got out the dish-pan, while Nancy drove the men from the kitchen to the "stoop."

An interruption of this kind rarely disturbed the trend of Christian's thought. "We don't know how things would be if it would give another war," he continued when he was seated again. It must be remembered, he maintained, that the Mennonites had obtained their promise of exemption from the English. The United States, he was afraid, might claim their right to disregard a contract which they had had no part in making. It was quite possible that, in the days to come, the "plain" people might be required to bear arms in defence of the new republic.

"And if they was to?" asked Benj, anxiously.

"I dunno," replied the father. "They might take our farms away. We might even come in jail. Soldiers don't care what is your

24

religion. They only want you to fight." A deep sigh escaped the old man at these words of premonition. He could tell many a story of bitter persecution, meted out to his friends during the recent revolution, because they had refused to help drive the English from New England. A cloud of suspicion of disloyalty still hung over the Mennonites.

"And that's why you feel for goin' to Canada?" conjectured Benj.

Canada was the magic word which brought a glow to Christian's withered face. There the shackles of slaves were broken, and there men might live unmolested according to the dictates of their consciences. Englishmen had befriended the Mennonites in the past; would do so again in the future.

"But you can't go," said Sam, frowning unconsciously in the direction of the kitchen. It was maddening to think that a freedom-loving soul like Christian's should be held in such abject bondage to his own wife.

"No, I can't go," said the old man, resignedly enough. "If a woman wont, that's all the further a man gets. But if I was young yet, and not married——"

"You'd go?"

"Yes, I'd go. I hope you will go some day, Bench. I want that some day you will be a preacher in Canada."

Benj hung his head. He did not want to be a preacher; but to please his father he said: "mebbe." Then he turned to Sam and said, suddenly: "Why don't you go?"

It was now Sam's turn to look discomfited. "Me!" he exclaimed. "Ach, I'm not much worth."

"Not much worth!" ejaculated Benj. "Why, you're great!" and his face lit up with admiration for his hero.

But Sam didn't think so. "I'm not great like the Ebys," he said. "Peter can preach, and Hannes learns good, and Bench here has went far already with his book-learnin'."

"And you, Sam?" asked Christian, delighted at this laudation of the Ebys in the lips of a scion of the Bricker family. "Ain't you no good at all?"

Sam certainly did not think so at that moment, "It's the temper," he said. "I can't be nothing but a cucumber of the ground, like I read once in a book."

"A cumberer, you mean," laughed Benj, whereupon Sam looked more crestfallen than ever, until Christian patted him encouragingly on the shoulder, and said it didn't matter whether it was a cucumber or whatever kind of vegetable he was, nobody could say how much it was worth until it was ripe, "And it's a long time yet till your haulin' in day, Sam. It's a long time yet till your harvest."

It was no ordinary meeting that took place that day at the Hammer Creek House. Communion day came around only "once in so often," as Christian said, but when it did come there was sure to be a great aggregation of horses tied up all around the Eby farm. The Bishop always preached on this auspicious occasion; and for three years and more, the Bishop had been none other than Peter Eby, the eldest son of the family that grew up at the Hammer Creek Farm.

Everybody seemed to come at once, and at the appointed time all the available space in Hannes' house was filled. The men flocked to one side, the women to the other, with a distinct aisle between; while Peter and all the other preachers sat in a solemn row facing the congregation. A hush of reverence prevailed.

Eliza Hoffman was there in the seats set apart for the unmarried women. No one would have guessed from her dress and appearance that she was the wealthiest heiress in the community. Her little white muslin bonnet was no different from the others; its ribbons not a whit longer. Her dress was cut by the same pattern as her companions'; her shoes, like theirs, were of cow-hide.

And yet Eliza's little heart was fluttering and palpitating like no other maiden's heart in the room. Her soft eyes persisted in roaming to that section of the room where Sam Bricker's red head was conspicuous. The fact was that Eliza was experiencing that delightful sensation of being in love for the first time, and so infatuated had she become that it never entered into her silly little head to question whether or not there was any chance of her affection being reciprocated.

"Hasn't Sam Bricker got the nice hair though?" she whispered to Beccy Eby, who sat beside her.

Beccy declared that she did not like the colour. "It means temper," she said.

"And such nice brown eyes when he looks at you," continued the afflicted one, quite oblivious to Beccy's answer to her previous question.

Beccy knew what soft brown eyes Sam had when he looked at her, but she did not consider such worldly conversation in keeping with the solemnity of the meeting, and she did not reply. She was trying to expel from her mind all thoughts of Sam, and all other things mortal, while she centred her attention on things divine. Very devoutly she buried her face in her hands when she knelt in prayer. But ever and anon there crept into her thoughts the memory of Sam's little speech at the breakfast table; and when she least expected it, there flashed before the eyes of her mind the tell-tale glance that he had shot at her. Did Sam look at Eliza like that, too, she wondered? Was it just a little, meaningless way he had?

The time had come for the sermon. On days when the Sacrament was administered, the principal sermon was always delivered by the Bishop, but prefaced by an introductory discourse by one of the other preachers. The subject was comprehensive enough, being the whole range of Bible history from Adam down through the ages, with special emphasis on the events and prophecies pointing to the New Dispensation. This morning, the introductory sermon brought the Bible history to the time of Moses. It devolved upon Peter Eby to take it up at this point and continue it to the birth of Christ, His ministry on earth, and His final suffering and death. Old as the story was, the audience never tired of hearing it from Peter's eloquent lips. When he arose, all noise subsided into an almost painful expectation. After a few words of kindly greeting, he proceeded with the sacred narrative. Step by step he advanced, describing, explaining, illustrating, and sustaining his points, as he went along, with copious quotations from the Scriptures. Gradually he warmed up to his theme; and, when under full sway, his discourse moved along like some deep stream rolling oceanward without break or ripple, grand, majestic, irresistible. Most tenderly did he portray the acts and sufferings of the Christ during those last days upon the earth; the scene in Gethsemane; the sleeping disciples; the noise and tumult breaking the stillness of the night when the armed men came to take Him; the doings before the Jewish and Roman tribunals; the embarrassment of Pontius Pilate and his fruitless device to save Jesus; the message sent Pilate by his wife; his last resort, when he permitted the Jews to choose between Jesus and Barabbas; the cries of the infuriated multitude that pronounced his condemnation; the sorrowful train moving slowly up to Calvary; the preparation to carry the fearful sentence into execution; and, lastly, the finishing act in the sublime drama, the Saviour of Man nailed between heaven and earth, with parched lips in the agonies of death, crying to the Father to forgive His cruel tormenters, while the heavens darkened, the earth shook and the elements gave witness in thunders and lightnings to the divinity of Him of Whom the world was not worthy.

All this he portrayed so vividly that the speaker was lost in the subject. When it was over, Peter stood before his audience with tears streaming down his cheeks, his countenance glowing, as with uplifted hands he pointed the penitent sinner, as it were, to the foot of a visible cross.

There was no commotion anywhere, no loud demonstration of feeling, only the deep surging of a controlled emotion, a quiet tugging at the heart-strings, and a firm resolve to be more worthy of the great sacrifice. The holy elements were passed and partaken of with many a renewal of consecration.

The service of the Sacrament was always accompanied by the rite of feet-washing, a custom which the Mennonites observe religiously from time to time, believing that Our Lord taught it both by example and precept, so that His disciples might surely know that He expected it to be literally enacted. Humbling himself, as did his Lord, every man washed the feet of another, each woman washed those of a sister. Once more it was brought home to the little band of Christians that they were one family in the Lord, and that he that would be the greatest among them must be the servant of all.

The religious service over, dinner was the order of the day. Many went to their own homes, taking with them a group of friends; but the number that sat down to dinner at the Hammer Creek House was past modern belief. The women were kept busy most of the afternoon, setting tables and washing dishes. Nor did it occur to anyone that their observance of the Lord's day left anything to be desired.

Annie was keeping her eyes open for any indication of Sam's attitude towards the Hoffman girl, who with her parents had stayed to dinner. Eliza was very helpful in the kitchen. Chatty, too. She recounted to the assembled women all the wonderful things her father was willing to do for her husband, and she embarrassed Annie with her little attentions and inquiries about Sam. But there sat Sam, surrounded by a group of men, totally unconcerned about Eliza and the Hoffmans. Annie was puzzled, but she said nothing. That young brother-in-law of hers was an enigma she would never be able to solve.

As usual, Sam stayed for supper at the "doddy-house." Later he sat on the "stoop" with Christian and talked until it began to grow dark. No one had ever yet questioned the propriety of this, or thought it strange that Sam should have so much conversation with his uncle. But Nancy had had her suspicions aroused during the day, and she determined to investigate what she now held to be a very unnatural friendship. Accordingly, she bustled out to the "stoop."

"Why, Sam," she cried, affecting great surprise, "are you here yet? Your folks will look that you come so late home."

"It's not dark," replied Sam. "Full moon to-night."

"But it's late—most nine o'clock already."

Sam laughed and asked if she meant to send him home.

"Ach, no, not that exactly," said Nancy. "You can set as long as you otherwise can, but Christian must go in his bed." She caught the old man by the elbow and gently but firmly urged him to rise.

Christian yielded her passive obedience.

But Nancy changed her mind—a woman's privilege. She pushed Christian back into his chair and demanded to know what the two men had been whispering about. All the while she kept staring hard at Sam.

The provoking young man vouchsafed no reply.

"What is it?" she repeated, turning to Christian.

The old man had not the moral courage to hold out against her. "We wasn't whisperin'," he stammered. "I was chust sayin'."

"That's what I want to know—what you was chust sayin'," said Nancy, seizing Christian's arm to remind him of her strength.

Christian looked at Sam, questioningly.

"Tell her," said Sam, with resignation.

"I was chust sayin'," continued the old man, gaining confidence with each repeated word. "I was chust sayin' I'm glad Sam's got it in his head to go to Canada."

"So!" said Nancy, pursing up her lips in a way that betokened furious opposition. "And when are you thinkin' of goin', Sam?"

"Till the spring," replied the prospective emigrant.

"Sam Bricker, you're crazy!" exploded Nancy. "You must have took it from the Hallmans, for the Brickers ain't that way. And who will give you the money?"

"It will come," replied Sam, in a most provokingly indefinite way.

"Well, you needn't look to us for it," Nancy flung at him. "You won't get none here."

Sam flushed. He almost lost his temper. He drew himself up proudly and said he had not come to ask her for help—would not ask it if he were starving.

"But Christian—"

"Nor him," said Sam, to Nancy's infinite relief.

Nancy saw that she was not getting anywhere. Sam was such a stubborn-head that he could not be driven where his own judgment or inclination did not lead him. So she changed her tactics and tried to cajole him into a consideration of her own plans for his future. She reminded him that in a very private conversation with Eliza Hoffman's father—

"That makes me nothing out," interjected the obstinate fellow.

"But Sam you might chust as well have it," pleaded the importunate Nancy. "Then you can take it easy all the rest of your life. And Eliza's a nice girl, I'm sure."

But Sam didn't think so. He didn't want a woman with such a "strubbly" head as Eliza had.

"She'll comb it, if you'll have her, Sam," said Nancy, evidently with some conviction. "She'll do anything for you."

"Will she stick up her petticoat, too, that looks all the time a little out?" asked Sam, without the least attempt at hiding his sarcasm. "No, I don't want her and her doddy's farm."

But Nancy was persistent. "If you don't feel for Eliza, mebbe I could find somebody else with a farm along," she suggested.

"Don't want them," was Sam's emphatic reply.

"He's chose one hisself," blurted out Christian Eby. He was afraid lest Sam might yet succumb to Nancy's grilling, as he himself always did in the end.

Nancy looked at Christian and then back again at Sam. She knew by their faces that she had heard the truth. "And has she got the money?" she made bold to inquire.

"Not much," said Sam, "It's Beccy!"

"Beccy! Whatever!"

"And we're goin' to set up to-night."

Nancy's face was black as a thundercloud. "Well, you're not!" she blazed. "Beccy's in bed. So now you know."

Christian felt himself suddenly gripped by the shoulders and jerked off his chair. "Go off to bed with your crazy nonsense," he heard his wife say in a voice that betrayed anger at white heat. "And you, Sam,—well, I never sent anybody home yet, so you can set, as I told you before, as long as you otherwise can. I wish you good-night."

In a few moments there were evidences of a domestic altercation behind the closed door. Sam began to have grave doubts about seeing Beccy that night. Still he sat and waited.

It was no insignificant thing that he had asked of Christian when they sat together in the twilight of the hallowed day. He had practically made a proposal of marriage. Having gained her guardian's consent, the next thing to do was to ask Beccy herself. If she were willing, he would then be privileged to enjoy the exclusive rights of an accepted lover, to take the girl for a drive on a Sunday afternoon, to "set up" with her once a week, and to write short epistles proclaiming his love as often as he cared to between sessions.

The "settin' up" was a most auspicious occasion. Naturally, among so industrious a people, it was not to be thought of that the precious working hours of the day should be devoted to the billing and cooing of lovers. If lovers must coo, it must be at the expense of their sleep. So at nightfall the amorous youth, weary of limb yet light of heart, would take his way to the home of his lady fair, and when all her family had discreetly retired, they two would sit alone in the front room, gaze fondly into each other's eyes, and engage in pleasant discourse about the crops and the weather. The topic of conversation mattered little. What did count were the deep, deep sighs and languishing smiles that punctuated the sentences and brought out a richness of meaning not ordinarily associated with the simple words. So time would slip by all unnoticed until the sputtering of an over-spent candle in the socket, or the crowing of some insomnious rooster would remind them of the approaching dawn with its multitudinous duties. Then the fond lover would steal back home in the dim light, and all through the week, life would be for him one grand, sweet song, filled with memories and anticipations. Disinterestedly speaking, the "settin' up" was an ordeal that could scarcely be endured twice in the same week; but it was to the initiated the one event of an otherwise uneventful existence, a pleasant recreation breaking the dull monotony of life.

Still Sam sat and waited.

Nancy was haranguing her husband in the privacy of their bedroom—they slept in the room off the kitchen. Then all was quiet again.

Presently there was a noise. In his foolish infatuation Sam jumped to the conclusion that it must be Beccy coming down the stairs. He wanted to open the door and meet her in the kitchen; but Nancy had shut that door; and who was he, that he should presume to open what Nancy had shut? He listened, but all was quiet again. After all, it was only his foolish self imagining he heard because he hoped to hear, one of those silly, little tricks which the human heart loves to play upon itself, bolstering up hope with hope all for the love of hoping.

Half an hour longer the disappointed lover sat on the "stoop," torn between false hope and despair. Then he acknowledged himself outwitted. It was no use. Beccy was not coming. There was nothing to do but go home.

With drooping head and heart Sam walked towards the barn, where his faithful horse awaited him. But as he turned the corner of the house, he was suddenly confronted by the moon. It was large, and round, and red; and it was actually laughing at him,—as his Aunt Nancy was probably doing at that very moment. So would everybody else when they heard the story in the morning. Even Beccy, perhaps.

"Sam!"

He started. It was a woman's voice—Beccy's, if he could believe his ears. He looked closely in the direction from which it came. There she sat curled up in the corner of a little bench under the apple-tree, Beccy herself, and no mistake. Laughing, too.

"How did you come here?" cried Sam, even more surprised than he was delighted.

Her reply was very simple. Christian had told her to wait for Sam there. She wondered what had kept him so long.

Sam chuckled. He squeezed his great, manly form into the little seat beside the girl and began to talk in whispers. They must be careful not to disturb the slumbers of their Aunt Nancy, he said. Besides, he had something very important to say and he didn't want anybody else to hear it.

Beccy laughed again, this time a trifle nervously.

Sam was not practiced in the art of love-making, but he knew enough to slip his arm around the back of the bench and hold the girl fast. Girls had been known to run away under just such circumstances as these, and months afterwards the story would be told and retold with variations at threshings and quilting-bees all over the countryside. He wasn't going to give his friends an opportunity to joke at his expense.

In whispers, Sam told her his secret. He loved her. He wanted to marry her. He would never marry anyone else, if she refused him.

Beccy did not answer. She did not even laugh. She wanted to suggest Eliza Hoffman, but her tongue stuck to the roof of her mouth, and a great lump formed in her throat.

Sam went on to tell her his prospects. He had no farm and he had little money, but he had a great idea. In the spring he would go to Canada, where others of their people had gone before. He would go farther into the interior, where land would be cheaper, and there he would build his humble home, and hers, he hoped. He reminded her of the dangers, the loneliness and the labour it would mean, the privations, with only silent trees and howling wolves for neighbours, and field and river the only hope of sustenance. Would she be willing to go with him? Did she care for him enough to make the sacrifice?

For answer, Beccy dropped her head on Sam's broad shoulder, and quietly—very quietly, for fear of disturbing her aunt—she told him that she was willing to go anywhere in all the world with him. "With you and Menno," she said, "I am happy."

Long into the night the lovers sat and whispered, while the great moon beamed on them and lit up their happy faces. Not until it began to fade did Sam so much as think of Menno and home. He was "settin' up" with Beccy, and if he needed any justification for his dallying, he found it in his aunt's rather ungracious permission to stay "as long as he otherwise could."

Monday morning dawned, Beccy was usually up first, but for once Nancy was in the kitchen ahead of her, half-dressed and rummaging through the cupboards.

"Where's the sulphur, Beccy?" she asked, without looking up, "and the molasses. It ain't on the mantle."

"Is it anything wrong?" asked Beccy, solicitously.

"Christian ain't so good this mornin'," was the reply. "He chumped around a lot in the night."

"Where has he got the pain?" inquired Beccy, anxiously.

"No place. He's sick all over."

"Mebbe we kept him awake for all," said Beccy, and her voice was full of penitence. "We tried to keep quiet, and I made myself barefoot to come in the house, but——"

Nancy turned sharply and voiced all the surprise and curiosity she felt in a single syllable. "Huh?"

"Sam said you might come awake," Beccy ventured to explain.

"Then youse two was settin' up?"

Beccy acknowledged it.

"Where?"

"Under the apple-tree," replied Beccy. "We're promised already."

"And till spring, you're goin' in Canada, you think?"

Beccy nodded her head.

"Well, you're not!" announced Nancy, white with rage. She muttered something about the multiplicity of "dumm" people, with whom her lot had been cast, and made a lunge for the bedroom door with never a thought of sulphur and molasses.

CHAPTER III

When Sam Bricker came in from the harvest-field the next day at noon with his scythe over his shoulder, he was singing lustily.

Annie encountered him at the pump just outside the kitchen door. "You must be feelin' good, Sam," she said, quite at a loss to understand this young brother-in-law of hers. "'Taint for the good sleep you had neither. I and John heard you come awful late home. Till four o'clock you didn't have Menno in the stable already yet."

Sam stopped singing, but he hummed the tune to the end of the verse. He smiled knowingly, and thereby aggravated Annie almost beyond the limit of her endurance. "You didn't neither," she sputtered, "I can prove it by the roosters."

Sam laughed outright, and drank a great draught of water. When he had hung the tin cup again on its nail, he said; "What would you think, Annie, if I was to tell you I was settin' up?"

"Settin' up," exclaimed Annie, the expectation of news mitigating to some extent the heat of her indignation. "So it was that? I chust thought mebbe it was."

"Yes," admitted Sam, "that is what it was, and next Sunday can't come fast enough around again."

It was Annie's turn to laugh now. Sam was such an impetuous young man that she could not help being amused at the ardour of his love. She reminded him that she had always said that when the great passion struck him, it would strike him hard.

At this felicitous moment, John arrived upon the scene with his scythe, and Annie lost no time in telling him the news. "You had right, John," she said. "Pretty soon our Sam will be gettin' married now. Then you can look out for a hired man."

"Oho!" cried John, with delight. "And which farm will you get?" He confessed that he had no idea, when he made it, that his prophecy concerning Sam was capable of such early fulfilment.

"My farm is in Canada," replied Sam. "Till spring I'm goin' over to find it." He seemed unaccountably pleased about it.

"In Canada!" exclaimed John.

Annie had no words to express her amazement. She stood staring at Sam as if she doubted his sanity.

"You got that from Christian Eby," said John.

Sam acknowledged it, still with that provoking smile upon his face.

"But will she go in Canada?" asked Annie. "Did you ast her that yet?"

Sam's face was full of mischief. "She says she will go anywhere with me and Menno," he said. "I ain't worth it, I know, but she thinks I am."

"She thinks a lot of you, Sam," volunteered Annie. "She was talkin' to me out in the kitchen Sundays, and I could tell she was soft on you. But I didn't think she would go that far."

At this, Sam was fairly convulsed with laughter, but he controlled himself sufficiently to remark with much assurance; "She's goin' all the way to Canada. It don't give many women like my Beccy."

"Beccy!" exclaimed both John and Annie together. Was this another one of Sam's numerous jokes?

"Beccy," the rapturous lover assured them, and in spite of his laughter, they knew he was in earnest.

John's comment was short and pithy; "You're crazy." Annie's was just as discouraging, though she allowed herself a great volume of words to express it. In her opinion it was a good thing that there were others who would have something to say about the matter. Nancy, surely, would step in and save Beccy from this folly. And when the story of Sam's plans and Beccy's acquiescence spread from house to house during the week, these same sentiments were voiced everywhere. Sam was the fool to be censured; Beccy, the fond one to be pitied; and Nancy, the magnanimous deliverer, worthy of greatest praise.

Truly, Nancy made very earnest efforts to interfere with the plans of this amorous pair for their mutual good, but she was not altogether successful. Sam was too impetuous a man to be reasoned with, and Beccy held most sacred the promise she had made to Sam. Besides, there was old Christian to be reckoned with. He was sure to be aiding and abetting the young people, as opportunity afforded. Indeed, for a time it seemed as though there was danger that Beccy might become the innocent cause of a family feud, estranging husband and wife.

Beccy had become indispensable to Nancy. That was the rub. She had so long assumed the burden of the responsibility of the household that Nancy took it for granted that she would continue to do so until the end of the chapter. And if Beccy should go, who was there to take her place? Lizzie was only fourteen, and alarmingly undependable. Besides, Nancy had a theory that the claim she had on Beccy was greater than even that which she exercised over her own daughter. In her opinion, the obligations of adoption must always exceed those of birth.

Sam was the one who poured oil on the troubled waters and brought peace once more to the household. He was willing to compromise, he said. He would go to Canada alone, if need be; buy his land; and build his house and barn. In two years, he would return for Beccy. By that time Lizzie would be sixteen and, with practice, a good housekeeper.

"Then Jacob Brubacher will run off with her," grunted Nancy. She had not the least objection in the world to Jacob Brubacher—he was the one she had picked out for Lizzie years before—but she did not appreciate the idea of being left alone and uncared for in her old age.

Sam said no more. He had made his proposition. He would not argue the question further.

But as Nancy pondered over the proposal, she saw advantages in it that even Sam did not see. Two years was a long time. Many things might happen. There were a dozen ways that Sam might come to his death in the wilds of Canada. And if he escaped with his life, the chances were that his enthusiasm would have waned. He would probably be glad enough to settle down on a well-cultivated farm such as Old Jonas Hoffman would be willing to give him. Everything might yet come out all right in the end. So she gave her consent, not definitely and verbally, but gradually and tacitly with a sullen expression in her face. As Sam put it, she went around "all the time with such a long mouth on."

When winter came and the men left their fields to sit with the women about the fireplace in the kitchen during the long evenings, this insane idea of emigration to Canada began to spread like leaven throughout the whole community. Reports came in from different quarters of venturesome ones who had risked their all on a hazardous enterprise, and had not only survived but had sent back glowing accounts of the land of their adoption. It was a land of marvellous fertility of soil, they said, a land of civil and religious liberty, an ideal habitation for the people called Mennonites.

"What do you say, Annie, we go, too?" said John Bricker one evening, when another one of these enthusiastic reports had come in.

"Ach, I dunno," replied Annie, "It's not for me to say."

"Josiah Schneider is talkin' of goin'," continued John. "Susie don't fight it." He sat for a long time rocking himself in his chair and gazing steadfastly into the fire. "Would you go once, Annie?"

"If you want to," was the wifely reply. She held up a pair of diminutive trousers that she was mending, and added; "There's the boys to think about."

It was chiefly on account of his boys that John was considering the question at all. He had a promising young son of eight, his namesake, and the apple of his eye. Little Johnny, they called him. Was he to work year after year on the old worn-out Bricker farm, as John himself was doing, with nothing to look forward to but more work? What could the younger boys, Noah and Moses, expect of life in Pennsylvania but to be somebody's hired man? In Canada it would be so different. Land would be cheap. By the time the boys were grown up he might be able to give them a hundred acres apiece. Of course there would be plenty of hard work, but there never was a Bricker born that was afraid of work; though, like most sane people, they preferred it with some encouragement and emolument.

"And that's what they ain't got here," sighed John. "No prospects. Nothing to look forward to, and hope about."

"And there," observed Annie, significantly, "it's mostly all hopes and prospects."

"That's the best part of it," interjected Sam, who never lost an opportunity to urge John and Annie to decision. "Think once what fun it will be to dig a farm out of a bush yet."

"Yes," replied John, without much enthusiasm, "but there'll be more than fun, I think."

Sam persevered, and triumphed in the end. Before Christmastime John had decided to go, if he could sell his farm. Then Sam went around among the friends and relationship and finally succeeded in disposing of the farm to their own brother-in-law. The new owner would take possession in the spring, and the care of the old people in the "doddy-house" would pass into the hands of their own daughter. So everybody was satisfied, and none more so than Sam, through whose efforts and influence this great change was actually coming to pass.

At last preparations for the trip began in earnest. Sam bought a new wagon, a conestoga, and John painted his old one so that it looked like new. Annie wrapped her china carefully with her household linen, and packed it in boxes. Scarcely a day passed but somebody thought of something that must not be left behind, until the question arose as to whether the two wagons would hold it all.

Ever and anon the brothers consulted the almanac. It hung, as it did in all Pennsylvania Dutch homes, on a peg just underneath the shelf which supported the family Bible. As in the Scriptures the "plain" people sought the issues of life, so the almanac contained for them an infallible key to the whims and caprices of the weather. Not even the most venturesome among them would attempt the most trivial undertaking if the moon was unfavourable, and an enterprise so hazardous as the proposed migration to Canada demanded that all the signs of the zodiac should lend their benign influence and watchful protection.

The last Wednesday of April was the day that seemed best suited for the departure. Weeks before that time, not only on the Bricker almanac but on every other one in the community, the date was marked. Reference was made each Sunday in meeting to the intention of the Brickers, and prayers were offered on their behalf. The Brickers and the thing that they were doing became the chief topic of conversation and the most remarkable event of the season.

As the great day drew nearer, news of the land through which the travellers must pass began to come in, not reliable information by any means, but hearsay. Sam refused to despise even the scrappiest of assertions. He made a crude drawing showing the rivers and the mountains that were known to exist in their path; and on it he found a place for all the reports that came to his ears. Here were the all-but-insurmountable Alleghanies, and there the Niagara with its mighty waterfall. Between the two, someone had told him, was a boggy swamp that would mire them, if they were not careful. At any moment Indians might sweep down upon them with savage war-whoops, and they must be prepared to defend their scalps. It was a discouraging outlook, to say the least, but Sam refused to allow his spirits to be dampened. Some day, somehow, he believed, they would come through it all, and there would be an end to their journeying. He had pinned his faith to Providence, and Providence, he knew, was not in the habit of failing men who were strong of limb and stout of heart, and who had taken the precaution, as he had, to procure a mariner's compass in order to verify divine guidance.

At last the great day dawned. There was little work done in the Hammer Creek community on that eventful morning. The young men left the farm horses in the stables; forgot all about the ploughing. Immediately after breakfast they started off in the direction of Brickerville on horseback. At every gate along the road stood groups of young people impatiently waiting to see the procession go by, while at the doors of the farmhouses stood their elders watching just as anxiously, though perhaps with a greater show of composure.

At the Hammer Creek House there was a ferment of excitement. Benj had slipped away early, for he and the Brubacher boys had long since decided that for a few miles at least they would have a part—and a conspicuous part—in the procession. Lizzie Eby and Mary Brubacher wanted to go along; but their parents shamed them out of it; and they had to be content to sit, one on either gatepost, each dangling a pair of restless, bare feet.

Nancy was decidedly out of sorts. She kept reminding Christian that this was what had come of his "dumm" notion, and if anything happened to the Brickers, he could take the blame. As for herself, she did not intend to countenance what everyone knew she did not sanction. Not one step farther than the door would she go. Not that she wished the Brickers any harm, but.... And if Christian had any sense, he would stay away, too.

For Beccy, it was a time of much anxiety. She endured Nancy's predictions and maledictions as long as she could; then beat a hasty retreat out the back door. There stood the little bench of tender memories, which every autumn was brought from its place under the apple-tree into the shelter of the "stoop." She dropped into it, and gave herself up to a flood of memories that rushed in upon her mind. That little bench! How often she had sat on it with Sam, when they had told each other their love. Now she sat alone; from now on she must sit alone; and tell her love to the silent stars. Perhaps forever.

The procession was coming. She could hear the horses' hoofs on the gravel road, and the voices of the riders. How happy they seemed to be. But her heart was breaking.

Old Christian Eby, in defiance of his wife's protests, had reached for his cane and was calling for Hannes to help him down the lane. Hannes' wife and the children went too, but Beccy outstripped them all in her haste and evident agitation.

The sight was an imposing one. There were two conestogas, each drawn by two span of heavy draught horses, and covered with a white, linen, bonnet-shaped top which was supported by a half-dozen or more narrow, curved staves extending the full length of the wagon, and protecting its contents from rain and sun. The gearings were a brilliant red, presenting a striking contrast to the sky-blue of the wagon-box. There was something so whimsical, yet so substantial, about the conestogas that they seemed admirably to suit the quaint, puritanical and thrifty Pennsylvania Dutch souls they bore.

"We're on our way to Canada," sang out Benj Eby, who as they approached the Hammer Creek House, spurred on his horse that he might be in the vanguard. "Will you go along, Mary?" This he addressed to the barefoot Mary Brubacher, for whom he had long entertained a tender regard.

"Ach, you," replied Mary, somewhat abashed.

"Well, then, Lizzie, you come," Jacob Brubacher cried out. "You ain't got a-scared."

But Lizzie shook her little head. She hadn't forgotten that her mother had forbidden her so much as to think about Canada. She cast at Jacob a look of scorn and told him to "go on with his nonsense."

Then the wagons came up. The first was John's. In it were packed innumerable boxes and household effects, until there seemed scarcely room for Annie and the children. Annie was sad and tearful; but the little ones were blissfully happy, the baby sound asleep, and Noah and Moses so engrossed with the antics of a pair of kittens which it would have broken their hearts to leave behind, that they were quite unconscious of the significance of this event in their young lives. Upon the seat beside his father rode Little Johnny, cracking the whip for effect, and pretending that he alone was responsible for the good behaviour of the horses. Perhaps he was, for when he cried "Whoa," they stopped short, all four of them, in front of the Hammer Creek House.

Unfortunately he forgot to give the command to the cow, which trudged along behind the conestoga, frisking her tail with the utmost indifference. The result was a collision which caused some injury to the jersey's sleek-looking nose.

"Back you!" cried Sam, who was following in the second conestoga. He had a great deal of regard for that cow, for she had a very important rôle to play in the little drama which was about to be enacted. It was her duty to provide not only milk but butter for the journey. The leather bag, which hung from the back of John's wagon, and responded to its every motion, was the improvised churn, and for once in her life Annie did not need to assume any responsibility for the churning. All she had to do was to remove the particles of butter when the motion of the wagon had made it "come."

Sam's cargo was principally livestock; a number of chickens whose males kept up a constant clatter; a pair of pigs, scrubbed to a cleanliness almost beyond recognition of the species; and a few frightened sheep huddled into the farthest corner. Sam himself sat upon a barrel of potatoes, and used as a foot-rest a peck-measure of apple-seeds, which he had secured gratis, but with much labour, from the pulp of a cider press. By careful grafting and budding he hoped to grow from them an orchard superior to the best in Pennsylvania. But of course that was only one of the many evidences of Sam's unbounded optimism.

John and Annie did not alight when the horses stopped before the Hammer Creek House, but they leaned over the wagon-box and held out their hands in farewell. The parting was harder than they expected. Tears blinded their eyes, and they could scarcely speak.

"Good-bye, Uncle Christian," they succeeded in saying, and "good-bye" they waved to Nancy.

"Make it good," said Christian, deeply moved. "You won't see me no more. It don't go long now till I am over there." He motioned to the graveyard across the way.

"And we don't come back no more," sobbed Annie. The consciousness that never again would she see her friends on this side of the black river had dawned upon her as never before in this last hour of farewell.

"But we'll meet over yonder," the old man reminded her. The bright hope of the expectancy of that happy day lit up his face and made it shine as the angels' must shine. "It gives another world at the end of this, thank God."

"And Beccy will pretty soon come over," said John, seeking to offer his disconsolate wife some consolation which would be more immediate and more satisfying in this vale of tears. "Till two years only, ain't it, Sam?"

Sam had jumped from his wagon to take his farewells. While John drove on, he lingered for a few moments, shaking hands with everybody, leaving Beccy to the last and holding her hand only a little longer and a little tighter than the others.

"Will you be ready till I come back?" he whispered.

"Ach, Sam, if I was sure you will come back—"

"Till two years, Beccy," he assured her. "That don't go long."

"A week is long if you don't come," sighed Beccy, remembering how interminable it always seemed from Sunday to Sunday, from one "settin' up" to another.

"But every day I'll think about you and wonder does everything go good with you, and nights when the moon is shinin'—there's something about the moon always makes me think about you, Beccy."

"Me, too," said Beccy, and looking into Sam's eyes for one ecstatic moment, she smiled a sickly smile.

"We'll have it for a sign between us," suggested Sam. "It's the same old moon shines in Canada as here. And if it's a full moon, we'll set up. Will you, Beccy?"

Such a foolish question! Of course she would.

He took her to the back of his wagon and showed her how securely he had tied Menno's halter. For a few happy moments he feasted his eyes upon her as she stroked the horse's long, white mane, and patted his sleek neck. His thoughts wandered back to the day when he had first seen her caress him, her "Schimmel," and his. And now they must part.

He was gone before Beccy realized it. Once more the heavy wheels of the conestoga were revolving, this time away from her. Hundlie, the collie dog, was running behind yelping with indecision and protest at the strange proceedings. It was all over.

She had been brave, Beccy was glad of that. Not a tear had she shed and not a sigh had escaped her in Sam's presence. That would have made it so much harder for Sam. As for herself, it didn't matter— nothing mattered. She would steal off somewhere alone, where she could cry to her heart's content. No one would ever know how unhappy and anxious she really was, and how empty her life had suddenly become.

But her tears did not bide Beccy's time. First a few warning splashes, and then a great flood like water when the dam is broken. Her whole body shook with emotion, and yet she could not tell definitely what moved her. Sorrow at parting with Sam, to be sure, and fear for his safety, a twinge of disappointment, too, that she could not go with him; but more than anything else an overwhelming mistrust that her farewell had seemed so cold, so constrained, when, if Sam only knew it, every word she uttered had been a heart-thrust.

"If he was here now," she wailed, "he'd know how I feel it."

Old Christian dismissed Hannes with a significant wag of his head and hobbled over to the spot where Beccy stood sobbing out her troubles into the elbow of her sleeve. "Better so," he said, as he put his arm consolingly about her, "better for both."

Beccy buried her face on her uncle's shoulder and continued to sob.

"We'll stop here a while, Beccy," said this comprehending friend who had come to her aid. "We don't want her—I mean you'd best be where there ain't so many goppin' at you."

Beccy knew what he meant, and she was glad enough to sit with Christian by the roadside listening to his words of comfort and sympathy. All too soon they would both have to return to the cheerless atmosphere of the kitchen. Even now Nancy's portly figure stood in the doorway, restless with impatience, pronouncing upon them, no doubt, the old familiar epithet.

Meanwhile Lizzie Eby and Mary Brubacher had clambered down from their exalted positions when the excitement was over, and were sauntering off in the direction of the Brubacher farm. They were chatting volubly. There never were two such inseparable friends as Lizzie and Mary. Day by day they shared their petty joys and sorrows, strengthening the bond of good fellowship between them. They never spoke of or analyzed their love. Perhaps they would never realize, until they were separated, how sweet and helpful had been their youthful companionship. At times they quarrelled and foreswore their friend-ship, but invariably cemented it again with tears and riveted it with all sorts of atoning sacrifices interchanged between them. People said they grew more and more alike as the days went by. Some even avowed that they began to look alike. Certainly they felt alike, for if Lizzie had the tooth-ache, Mary would not eat; and if Mary chanced to stub her little barefoot toe, Lizzie's chubby, little foot must needs be bound up too. So subtle was the relationship between them.

But the greatest bond of all was their common interest in the Brickers. Annie was Lizzie's cousin by marriage, but she was also Mary's aunt, being a younger sister of Mary's mother. In Pennsylvania Dutch parlance, they all belonged to the same "Freundschaft."

The farewell of Sam and Beccy was the topic under discussion on this morning of great events.

"He didn't give her good-bye different to the rest," Mary was saying.

"And think once how she cried," replied Lizzie. "I wonder did she want him to kiss her, or something like that."

Mary was sure of it.

"Mom says they won't get married ever," continued Lizzie, with awe-stricken voice and countenance. "And mom she chenerally always knows."

"Eliza Hoffman?" Mary raised quizzical eyebrows. Little pitchers, they say, have big ears, and Mary's had evidently been large enough to absorb the gossip that was thought to be beyond her understanding.

Lizzie blinked her eyes and nodded her head with emphasis. "'Taint no use to fight mom," she affirmed. "And Sam he don't need to think he's any different to the rest of us."

Then they began to talk, as growing girls will, about the future of their own lives.

"What if Bench will go some day?" suggested Lizzie.

"But he won't."

"You can't never sometimes tell, Mary," said Lizzie. "Pop wants him to. What if he will go and let you here?"

A soft pink suffused the area of Mary's round cheeks and crept down her neck. She protested that Benj would not do such a thing.

"But if he would?" persisted Lizzie, determined to have a direct answer to a rather pertinent question.

"Then I'll have to go, too," replied Mary. The pretty pink deepened into a purplish red and she turned her face away.

"Whatever!" cried Lizzie, in utter disgust. "Jacob's got to run with me."

"But he says he's goin' too."

"Leave him," replied the dauntless Lizzie, with her head in the air. "I guess he'll pretty soon come back again."

Mary gasped at the highhandedness of this friend of her bosom.

"And here he'll stop," added Lizzie, with such an air of finality that the journey was continued in silence to its destination.

Oh, the innocence of childhood, playing on the sands of the shore when the tide is low! How little did they know what was in store for them and for Beccy, when the great flood of waters should come in and on its bosom carry them out to the deep, broad, boundless sea of life!

CHAPTER IV

The journey upon which the Brickers had set out was full of danger at every turn and tiresome in the extreme. There seemed no end to the hardships and discomforts they were forced to endure on their way to the land of hope and promise. Each new day brought a repetition of the privations of yesterday; every night meant another succession of anxious, sleepless hours. Days passed into weeks, and the weeks slipped by with little more than the darkness and the dawn to mark the monotonous flight of time. Nor did they have the satisfaction of knowing what progress they were making; nor when their journey would have an ending. It was an unknown trail they were following, and no one had yet travelled it on schedule time.

On all their previous expeditions into the great world that existed beyond the confines of their own community, the Brickers had always travelled towards the south. To the south lay the city of Lancaster, which had recently become the capital of the county. It was also a commercial centre, and to its market the Brickers took their produce, exchanging it for such luxuries as sugar and tea. To the north, however, everything was new and strange. It was an unknown region.

The same was true of the west. Never once had any one of this little party of emigrants been far enough in that direction to see the Susquehannah, but what they had heard of it caused them no little anxiety. It was the great river which carried the waters of their own Hammer Creek and of all the streams of Eastern Pennsylvania down to the ocean. How they were to cross this mighty body of water they could not even conjecture.

They came to it before long, and found that it was even mightier than they had anticipated; a mile wide, it was said; and it seemed as if an eternity of space lay between them and the farther shore. When with hearts full of misgiving John and Sam looked at each other, they were approached by a man, who came to offer a solution to their difficulty.

A little man he was, with a freckled face and a shock of dark hair curling over the edge of his cap. His coat was open to the wind displaying an inner garment of many colours. In his hand he carried a heavy stick, which he waved about in a most conspicuous fashion.

"Is he crazy?" whispered Annie, genuinely alarmed. She caught her baby in her arms and held her tight.

"Want to go across?" asked this strange specimen of humanity, drawing nearer.

John assured him that they did.

"Well, Mike O'Neill will take you over before you can say Jack Robinson," was the comforting piece of information the man offered.

"And where is he?" John inquired.

The Irishman, for no one could mistake his nationality, tossed his cane into the air and laughed uproariously. "The smartest man in these parts, this Mike, if it is meself as has to say it."

Sam looked at John and John looked at Sam. Whatever did the fellow mean by giving such a left-handed answer? They had asked a civil question. Why couldn't he have answered it in a straight-forward way?

"Sure I'm Mike O'Neill meself," said the stranger, when he saw their embarrassment. "It's from ould Ireland I come, and that's the way we talk over there. Me business is runnin' back and forth on the river, and I'm at your service."

"Runnin' on the river!" ejaculated Annie. "He must be crazy."

The Irishman smiled. "Wid me ferry," he added, pointing to a great flat-bottomed scow, whose cargo was being unloaded at the wharf. "She didn't think I was doin' it in me boots, did she?"

Sam hastened to assure him that Annie was nervous and begged him if he was really the ferryman to lose no time in taking them across the river.

But the Irishman did not intend to be hurried, "Go on wid you," he said, with well-feigned indignation. "Would you deprive poor ould Mike O'Neill o' the pleasure o' talkin'? Is the missus scared? Does she want to do it herself perhaps, and give me a holiday? Well, I've took a lot like her over, and if I don't take her, too, safe and dry, I'll give her lave to crop the two ears off the side of me head."

Annie recoiled at the suggestion of such an infamous bargain, and had no more to say.

The men drove down to the wharf and inspected the ferry. It was at least thirty feet long and about half as wide. Never could the

Brickers have imagined such an ingenious contrivance; yet there it was before their eyes, an accomplished fact. It was propelled by a dozen large oars—sweeps, the men called them—which the oarsmen said they plied by treading mechanically backwards and forwards until the distance was covered.

John was encouraged to drive his horses on deck and put himself and his possessions in the care of the ferryman. He did it with reservations, however. Neither to the right nor to the left would he look, but he kept his seat and his hand upon the reins, ready for any emergency. Not even Little Johnny's exclamations of wonder and excitement could tempt him to take his eyes off the horses. As for Annie, she was sure they were all going to be drowned; and she clasped her little ones to her breast, determined that if her fears were to be realized, they should at least all find themselves in the same watery grave.

To Sam, the passage was nothing more nor less than a high adventure, which he was prepared to enjoy to the full. He had no responsibility for any life but his own, except, of course, those of the animals, whose noise and filth were ever with him. He was glad enough for an opportunity to climb down from the wagon to get away from these companions of the lower order and give himself up to the enjoyment of the hour.

When at last they landed on the western shore, and could look back over their shoulders at the river, even Annie laughed at her fears. It was only the dangers that were still ahead that troubled their minds.

For days, yes, for a whole week, they dreaded the Alleghanies. By day they saw, or thought they saw, the blue mountain-tops ahead of them far on the northern horizon; and at night they saw them again in their dreams. Utterly insurmountable they seemed, whether they appeared in fact or in fancy; and the nearer the travellers approached them, the more formidable did they appear.

They came at last to the foothills, and there they halted to rest. Their horses would need all the strength they possessed to pull the heavy wagons up the long, steep grade to the summit of the mountain.

But that night occurred a memorable experience. The children had been put to bed at sunset, and their elders followed soon after. They were all tired, and cross, and downhearted. They had been so long upon the way and had covered so little ground. And now the Alleghanies were before them. It was a prospect that did not inspire even Sam with abundant hope.

Little Johnny always slept with Sam and the animals, and for safety and mutual encouragement the two conestogas were usually drawn up side by side during the night. After the horses had been un-hitched they were fed and watered, and tied by their halters to some near-by tree, and blanketed for the night.

All was quiet. Sleep had come to all but Sam, who lay upon his back tossing this way and that, wishing that sleep would come to him, too. He closed his eyes and counted ten at least a hundred times; then watched innumerable sheep jump over an imaginary stile; but it was all of no avail. In spite of all he did to court sleep, he was wakeful and restless.

Presently he heard a strange sound. He sat up on his bed of boards, cocked his ear and listened. He heard it again. What a peculiar sound! Or was it only Annie snoring in a minor key? Very quietly, Sam lifted one corner of the linen covering of his wagon and peeked out. Directly under John's wagon he saw a large, dark animal, walking about with an air of proprietorship, gnawing and crunching the bones that remained from the evening meal. A bear, no less, and no cub either!

Sam's heart was in his throat. It would have been bad enough to encounter the brute by day, but to find him encamped under a wagon of sleeping people in the dead of night was quite another matter. He decided at once that nothing could be gained by sounding an alarm, or awakening anybody. He must be especially careful that Little Johnny should not be disturbed, lest he should scream with terror. But how was he going to get the intruder to remove himself and leave them and their animals alone?

A bright idea suddenly flashed through Sam's uneasy mind. Climbing carefully over the sleeping boy at his side, he reached a box, opened it, and took from it a ham, which the provident Annie had placed there for their own consumption at a later day. He would present this as a peace offering to the enemy. In this tangible way he would pay his respects to Mr. Bruin, and ask him if he wouldn't please go away and leave them and their horses unharmed.

Leaning over the edge of the wagon-box, Sam dropped the delectable leg of savoury meat to the ground. He saw the monster sniff at the crumbs which lay under John's conestoga, and turn towards the feast which Sam had spread for him. With gruff, gutteral gurglings of relish the beast devoured it, and then, to Sam's infinite relief, walked slowly away.

"Is it anything wrong?" whispered John, poking his head out of his conestoga, and catching Sam in the act of withdrawing his.

"Ach, nothing," replied Sam, as indifferently as he could.

"That's what I told her," said John, "but Annie is sure it was a bear."

Sam tried to laugh. "Only a dog," he told his brother. "It was at her boiled ham, tell Annie."

John turned to give his wife this comforting message, and soon all was quiet again. But Sam did not sleep; did not try to sleep. He spent the rest of the night on guard against another unwelcome nocturnal visit.

The ascent of the Alleghanies on the following day was an experience not soon to be forgotten. It took more than nine miles to travel the first three miles of the incline. At that rate, the men reckoned, they would never get there at all, so they tried hitching eight horses to one wagon, and at that they could advance only from ten to twelve rods before the horses needed rest to gain strength for another long, steady pull.

John was utterly discouraged and ready to turn back to Hammer Creek, while Annie wished devoutly they had never come. Even Sam's spirits had fallen and he began to entertain serious doubts about ever seeing as much as the other side of the mountain, not to mention their ultimate destination in Canada.

Suddenly John gave a triumphant cheer. He had discovered a road that promised a short cut through the rocks to the other side. With hope revived he entered it and followed it as it wound its devious way through masses of solid rock. So narrow was the road at times, and so perpendicular its walls, that the wagon grazed the rock now on one side and now on the other. At no point was it possible to see more than a few yards ahead.

Quite without warning, John suddenly found himself face to face with a stranger from the opposite direction,—a rough, bold fellow who announced with a mouthful of profanity that he had the right of way. John hugged the rock, but still there was no room for the man to pass.

"Back up there, you fool," demanded the imperious fellow. "What do you mean by blocking the road with your Noah's Ark?"

John bit his lip and held his ground.

"Back up, I say," repeated the bully. "If you don't, I'll soon make you."

"Back up yourself," shouted Sam from around a bend in the road. "You can do it easier. There's two of us."

At this intimation from Sam, the burly fellow became at once more conciliatory. He deigned to get out of his wagon to view the situation. "Now by all that's holy," he exclaimed, when he had peeked into the conestogas, "what do you think you are doing? Moving?"

John nodded. That was at least what he was trying to do.

"Going far?"

"To Canada," replied Sam, with a confidence that he himself knew was quite unwarranted.

The impertinent fellow laughed loud and derisively. "Canada," he said. "You'll never get there. You might better turn around now than wait till later. The bears and wolves will eat you up. They like the kids best." He wagged his head in the direction of Little Johnny, who was standing with his hands in his pockets and surveying the situation with all the sagacity of his elders.

John put his arm protectingly around the boy's shoulders and drew him close.

Sam grunted.

The man proceeded to present proofs to substantiate his warning. He knew a family that had tried to go over, he said. A pack of wolves fell upon them in the middle of the night and ate up two of the children besides all the provisions. The parents escaped with their lives but died later of starvation. They never mentioned Canada after that. The United States was good enough for them.

"What you say, Sam, we go back," said John, horror-stricken at this tale of woe.

But Sam pushed John and his suggestion aside with a gesture of impatience. He was busy telling this teller of tales that he and John would help him take his wagon apart and carry it piece by piece to the other end of the conestogas.

"Then drive on and leave me with my mess," grumbled the man. "Curse you anyway, why don't you turn back?"

"Because we're goin' on," replied Sam, heatedly. "We're only wastin' time by talkin' here." He moved off towards the man's wagon.

But the insolent fellow would not listen to reason or to persuasion. He would take his wagon apart only on condition that the Brickers would likewise dismantle both of theirs. They wrangled for half an hour to no purpose, and finally each man set to work to unhitch his horses and unpack his wagon. One by one they carried the boxes overhead on their shoulders. It took hours of time and much labour. Much cursing, too, on the part of the stranger, who was determined not to carry his last load across until the Brickers had taken their wagons to pieces, as he had his. He wasn't going to take any chances on those confounded Dutchmen getting away before he did.

When it came to setting up the wagons and packing them again, the Brickers had a decided disadvantage. Long before they had completed their work, the stranger had bidden them a scornful farewell and was off again on his way.

"What for a man do you call that now?" said Annie, quite overcome by her fears and her exertions.

"Ach, him," said John, shrugging his shoulders.

In Sam's opinion the fellow was a good example of an unregenerated man, an inhabitant of that unhallowed place which they termed "the world."

Annie's only reply was a deep sigh. Was Canada in "the world," she wondered. Did men of that kind live there?

It was nightfall when the Brickers at last reached the summit of the mountain, too tired of body to exult in this great accomplishment. They hastened to set up their beds, but they could not sleep. All night long strange noises fell upon their ears. The woods seemed filled with wild animals whose weird cries echoed and re-echoed from every side. Even the children were restless and glad to see the morning dawn.

The descent of the mountain was scarcely less arduous and decidedly more perilous than the ascent had been. The weight of their wagons now gave them momentum, and it was all the men could do to hold in their horses. Again and again there was danger that the whole caravan might go tumbling over some precipice to certain death. It was night before they could breathe easily, knowing that at last they had passed the dreaded Alleghanies, and all the dangers that threatened them there.

A level stretch of country lay ahead but it was covered with dense forests and drained by innumerable streams, some little more than creeks and others great swift-moving rivers. There was at times only a blazed trail—and Sam's compass—to point the way; but the Brickers went bravely on. Each day was like the one that had passed; the second week was like the first. Trees, trees on every hand, a narrow path before and behind.

Some of the streams through which the trail led were treacherous and almost impassable. The western branch of the Susquehannah was not deep, they thought, but when they had ventured into it, they found that the water rose over the wagon-boxes, flooding the floors of the conestogas and saturating much of the baggage. The Tonawanda presented another difficulty. The banks were not high but quite steep and very muddy. There was no bridge, and no possibility of getting across without one. So on both sides of the stream the men felled small trees and brushes, casting them into the water and constructing with them a temporary passage-way for their heavy teams and wagons. A sort of corduroy bridge it was, and it had all the discomfort and none of the security of an ordinary road of the same variety.

Day by day the road-weary travellers were nearing the Niagara River. Of all the dangers of the entire journey there was none that loomed up before their terrified imagination like that mighty river with its swift currents and its mighty waterfall. So many stories of its treachery had reached their ears that they spoke of it in a lugubrious sort of way as the River of Death.

But, like death, the Niagara lost much of its terror upon approach. They came upon it suddenly near its beginning, where the waters of the lake push into the river and flow towards the north without noise or tumult, blue as the skies above. There was no sign of waterfall, no evidence of danger anywhere. On the farther shore they saw Canada, the land of their dreams. Then their drooping spirits were revived, and discounting all the trials and discouragements of the journey, they looked forward hopefully to the future.

"Look once, Johnny," cried Sam, with ecstatic joy. "There's Canada!" He lifted the little fellow to his shoulder and pointed across the river.

But Little Johnny looked blankly about him. "Where?" he cried, demanding more explicit information.

"Why, there!" replied Sam. "Can't you see? All that bush on the other side of the river, that's all Canada."

A shade of disappointment passed over the child's face. "It's all the same as here," he said tragically. "I thought it would be different."

"It is different," insisted Sam, as he let the child down again. "But you can't see it with your eyes, the difference. Wait once till you are as old as me. Then you'll know what I mean."

With this decidedly vague and protracted promise of explanation Little Johnny had to be content.

The question now was how the Brickers were to be transported across that great expanse of water to the fair shores of Canada. The river was both wide and deep. There was no ferry, no sign of human life. Could it be that with infinite pains they had come this far only to be turned back within sight of the land of their dreams?

People with indomitable wills laugh at difficulties and say it must be done. Sam Bricker was just that sort of person, and it was not long before he had solved the problem, to his own satisfaction at least. Since there were no boats to be had, they must make them, he said.

John turned and looked at him sharply. What mad notion was this that Sam was entertaining? Boats!

"The wagon-boxes, you dummhead," said Sam. "Make them loose from the wheels, and they will float."

"Drown, you mean," muttered John. "The water will leak in through the cracks."

"There ain't goin' to be no cracks," replied Sam, trying to be patient. "There's lots of moss here, I'm sure."

"And the cow?"

"She can swim with the horses," Sam decided. "That's what she's got them four legs for."

It seemed to Sam that John's mission in life was to throw a wet blanket over any scheme that he proposed. Here he was ready with another objection. "There's the current," he said. "Look how strong it is, and like as not it's worse underneath. We'd all go tumbling over the Falls. No, Sam, we can't cross here."

"But look how close we are," urged Sam. "The Falls is miles away."

John would not listen. In no uncertain tone he told Sam that he would go back to Pennsylvania rather than risk a crossing there. Annie added her protestations. Sam was not convinced, but he finally consented to bottle up his effervescent enthusiasm and listen to the counsel of his elders.

Travelling along the banks of such a river as the Niagara was a new experience for the dwellers of the plains of Pennsylvania. Again and again they exclaimed at the massive rocks and the majestic scenery along the way. The water, too, fascinated them, rumbling and tumbling, as it did, in its headlong course. Never had they seen such wild beauty before.

But the climax came when they reached the great waterfall. Speechless they stood and gazed at the spectacle, too wonderful for words. For the first time in their lives they understood the emotions which must have surged through Moses' breast when he stood before the burning bush in the presence of God. It seemed that they, too, stood upon holy ground.

Little Johnny was not impressed with awe and reverence as he ought to have been. His little mind was filled with questioning. He kept prancing about from one to another of his elders, demanding to know where all the water came from, and where it was going, and why it made such a noise, and why it rained when the sun was shining.

"Be still," whispered his mother, in precisely the same tone of voice as she used to admonish him to behave at meeting.

The child obeyed. He went quietly and stood beside the men at a spot which commanded an excellent view of the Canadian Falls. He looked at the great horseshoe, which his father pointed out to him, and soon his young heart, too, was filled with wonder and silent awe.

The Brickers camped that night within sight and hearing of the waterfall. They could think and talk of nothing else but the miracle of nature which had stirred the deepest emotions of their souls. It was beautiful, and wonderful, and majestic, to be sure, but—of what use was it? This was the question which arose in the minds of these people who all their lives had been trained in strictest economy. What was this waterfall anyway? Nothing but an insurmountable barrier to navigation on the lakes for all time to come, a useless as well as an exceedingly dangerous piece of nature's furniture.

Was it going to bar them forever from Canada? That was what the impulsive Sam wanted to know. They had had one chance to cross, he reminded John, and they had allowed it to pass. If they had taken his advice, they would have landed long since on Canadian soil.

John urged patience, and presently he had the satisfaction of pointing out a group of redmen running the rapids in their canoes. He held out the hope that a few miles farther on they would find water calm enough to venture across it in their conestogas.

The prophecy was fulfilled, for when they had passed the little Indian village, from which the fleet of canoes had set out, they found not only still water but a convenient landing-place from which to launch their improvised boats.

Then the brothers set to work with a will to overcome this great obstacle which alone lay in the way of their fondest hopes. The wagon-boxes, it must be confessed, made admirable boats, as far as size and shape were concerned, and it was not an impossible, although a laborious undertaking to caulk their seams with moss and pitch, so that they might also possess that most essential feature of a good boat,—sea-worthiness.

As they worked, the brothers regaled themselves by recounting the various occasions when they had been tempted to turn back to Pennsylvania. The contemplation of the discouragements which they had successfully overcome seemed to magnify the greatness of their achievement and to encourage them in the adventure which they were about to undertake.

"That time in the Alleghanies was the worst," said Sam. "I was afraid you would go back."

"Sometimes I wish I did," John confessed.

"The bears would eat you when the hams was all," commented Sam, with a twinkle in his eye.

"Bears!" shrieked Annie, who sat near by, quite unnoticed, but watching every movement and hearing every word.

"Dogs, I mean," said Sam, hastening to cover his indiscretion.

But Sam had no skill in the art of prevarication. Annie knew the truth, and she allowed her imagination to run riot with it. Bears had been in his conestoga, in close proximity to Little Johnny. They had actually opened the box and stolen a ham from under Sam's very nose. It was a mercy that they had not all been killed and devoured piecemeal at the brutes' pleasure.

In vain did Sam avow that it was not so bad as Annie thought. There was only one bear and it had never been inside the conestoga. He himself had opened the box and stolen the meat. If he had deceived her, it was only that she might not be troubled. But Annie refused to believe a word of it, preferring to pin her faith to the lurid creations of her own imagination.

The two men exchanged worried glances, and finished their work in silence.

And now all was ready for the great adventure. The conestogas had been made water-tight; their canvas tops, which had been removed to facilitate the work of caulking the seams, had been replaced to serve as sails. Every inch of available rope had been brought out and spliced into one length. Holes had been bored into the topmost planks of John's conestoga, back and front, so that it might be secured at one end to a huge oak tree on shore and at the other to Sam's conestoga. The cow bawled out her wonder; the horses snorted with excitement.

"Git up!" cried Sam, brandishing his whip.

"He's goin' to drownd," shrieked Annie, hiding her face so that her eyes might not witness the horrible catastrophe.

The plan was that Sam was to have the much-coveted privilege of landing first on Canadian soil. If he failed to get across, it would be an easy matter to pull him back to shore; if he succeeded, he was to tie the rope to a tree on the farther shore, and give John a sign to advance.

Yard after yard of rope was uncoiled as the distance widened between Sam and the shore of the homeland. A strong northwest wind stood the adventurer in good stead, and his horses played well their important part. There were anxious moments when Sam's heart seemed to stand still and when John and Annie watched anxiously in the distance. But at last the goal was reached. With a whoop of victory Sam leaped to the shore and secured the rope to a sturdy maple tree.

Then John felt encouraged to make his venture. It was not long before he found himself out mid-stream battling with wind and wave, but anchored all the while to Sam's rope. He landed, too, in safety, in spite of his wife's forebodings.

So there they were at last, a little group of weary immigrants in a foreign land, dumped, as it were, with their livestock, their furniture and all their worldly possessions in one heterogeneous heap on the inhospitable shores of Upper Canada. The trees waved indifferently in the breeze, and the water murmured monotonously by.

CHAPTER V

It was Saturday evening, and already the shades of night were beginning to fall when the Brickers landed so unceremoniously on Canadian soil. Time and light sufficed only to rearrange the contents of their conestogas for the night. Then breathing a prayer of thanksgiving, they stretched their weary limbs, watched the new-sprung foliage of the trees sway in the breeze and listened to the weird music of the water, until both eyes and ears were closed in the sweet unconsciousness of sleep.

The Brickers, of course, never travelled on Sunday. That was their day for rest, meditation and worship, though not by any means an excuse for late rising. Sam and John were up with the sun. They fed their stock, killed a number of black rattlesnakes which seemed to infest that region, discovered a spring of fresh, sparkling water to make their oatmeal porridge, and returned to see what else Annie was going to give them for breakfast.

"It's the Promised Land," cried Sam, laughing good-naturedly and swinging the water-pail. "Look once, there's the Jordan River,"—he pointed to the Niagara—"and back there's the wilderness. We was forty years in it, not?"

"It seemed so," thought Annie.

But John was determined to be literal. "Forty days, it was," he said, "forty days exactly, for I counted them. And what for a river do you think the Jordan is?"

"Too hungry to tell you now," replied Sam, refusing to be depressed by his brother's prosiness. "Come, Little Johnny, fetch the dishes, and me and you'll set the table."

The table was a deal one of the drop-leaf variety, which folded into a tiny corner when occasion demanded but spread two broad, obliging wings at meal-time. Around it the little company gathered for their first breakfast in Canada.

It was when Sam was drinking the last draught of coffee from his saucer that there was borne in upon his mind the importance of this day in the history of the Bricker family. Even in old age they would recall this first morning in Canada and all the events which should transpire in it. He proposed that they should celebrate it in some appropriate way.

John ridiculed the idea at first. "We don't have to shame ourselves for what we do any time," he wanted Sam to remember.

But Sam was not satisfied until he had persuaded Annie to take off her dark handkerchief and put on her little white muslin bonnet in honor of the occasion. He told Little Johnny to set the benches in rows, and get out the Bible and hymn-book. He induced John to read the account of the crossing of the Jordan, and then they all knelt together and said "Our Father."

And how they sang! Sam started the tunes as well as he could, while John and Annie and even the children joined in. Soon the silent woods reverberated with the long-metered hymns of their primitive faith. The birds gathered from all directions, perched on the lower branches of the trees and shook their tiny heads critically, while the squirrels frisked about from tree to tree in wild alarm.

All day Sam's thoughts kept wandering back to Hammer Creek and the homeland. Sometimes he sat with Christian Eby on the "stoop" at the "doddy-house," just beyond Nancy's hearing; and again he talked with his own parents and his sisters in their humble home at Brickerville. But most of the time he walked at Beccy's side, or sat with her on the bench under the apple-tree, listening to her sweet confessions of love. Quite exaggerated they were, these whispered conversations, but none the less delightful on that account.

The evening and part of the night he spent with Menno. Beccy was with them in spirit, for the moon was full. Only once since they parted had it reached its zenith, and on that occasion a storm had hidden it from view. But to-night there was scarcely a cloud in the sky. In all its glory the great orb of night looked down at Sam and smiled. And Sam looked up into its fat, benign face, and stayed "as long as he otherwise could."

At daybreak on Monday the journey was resumed. A corduroy road followed the course of the river, and this the Brickers took, trusting that it would eventually lead to the Mennonite settlement, which was said to exist somewhere along the shores of a great lake called Ontario.

By nightfall they had reached a little village situated at the junction of the Niagara River and Lake Ontario. Newark, the people said, was the name of the place, and although there were only a hundred houses, more or less, it boasted of some important public buildings, including Navy Hall, where only a decade before the Parliament of Upper Canada had held its first session. The seat of the government had recently been removed to York, across the lake, but the glory still hovered about the historic spot.

At Newark the Brickers turned towards the west. They were told that if they would follow the road along the shore of the lake for twenty miles, they would come to The Twenty, a settlement of people as like themselves as peas in the same pod.

Encouraged by this information, they passed on their way. The road was passable, but progress seemed very slow. Night came and went, and again the journey was resumed. Every hour the excitement grew more intense. John declared that they had travelled at least forty miles since they left the Niagara—and still no Twenty.

Then suddenly Little Johnny emitted a joyful cry in the very moment of his father's discouragement. "Look," he cried, "Look at the smoke!"

Sure enough, there it was—a little blue curl mounting heavenward above the trees in the distance, the first visible sign of the long-expected Twenty. John stopped his horses, poked his head out of the conestoga and motioned to Sam. No sooner had the din of the wagon-wheels died away than there fell upon their ears the joyful, if monotonous sound of a well-swung axe. Chop! Chop!

"Are we here?" cried Annie, a bundle of nerves and excitement.

If John replied at all, his answer was lost in the volume of noise that Sam was making through a funnel that he had formed with his hands.

"Oo! Oo!" rang the echo.

The chopping suddenly ceased, and the snapping of twigs gave warning that someone was breaking his way to the road. The next minute there stood before the expectant people a tall, well-built, muscular man, who bore all the marks of a Mennonite, a broad-rimmed hat pulled down to his ears, a shaggy beard, and a closely-clipped upper lip.

"We're here," cried Annie. "We're here at last." She heaved a great sigh.

"And where do you come from?" asked the wood-chopper, advancing to meet the men, who had jumped down from their wagons.

"From Hammer Creek," answered Sam. "It's in Lancaster County."

The woodsman's face beamed with delight. "So?" he said. "Mebbe you know Christian Eby."

"Christian Eby!" exclaimed all the Brickers in one breath. "Why he's uncle to us!"

"Rachael she belongs a little in that Freundschaft yet," the man informed them. "She's my missus, Rachael."

"And who are you?" demanded John.

"Levi Moyer, from Berks County over."

"We are Sam and John Bricker," said Sam, indicating which was which. "John, he's married already," he added, by way of introducing Annie and the children, whose heads were protruding out of the back of John's conestoga.

There was no more woodchopping for Levi Moyer that day. He insisted upon taking the whole party at once to his home—and his Rachael.

It was a very humble home to which he led the way, only a little log shanty with layers of white plaster between the logs and a coat of whitewash over all. A pioneer shack in the heart of the virgin forest, but a happy home for all that.

Rachael stood at the doorway to welcome the strangers, shading her eyes with one hand and supporting her baby on a hip with the other, a bit of Pennsylvania in Canada. She was a typical Mennonite woman, short and stout, and dumpy. Her dress was of homespun, and made in a style so universally followed by the women of the sect that it might almost be called a uniform. A tight-fitting bodice clung to her natural figure and buttoned conspicuously down the front. The skirt was long, and full, ungored, and gathered in copious folds around her unstayed waist. Over her shoulder she wore a sort of shawl of the same material as her dress, and the tips of it were fastened at the centre of the waistline, back and front, while a large, dark apron protected the skirt. The usual coloured handkerchief, folded diagonally, covered her head and was secured with a knot under the second fold of her undulating chin.

It was a hearty welcome that Rachael Moyer accorded Annie. She seemed almost as glad to see her as Annie was to have reached this stage of her journey. A woman with a bonnet she did not see every day. Occasionally she saw a squaw, or a woman who wore a hat, but they were, like men, different.

And yet Rachael's greeting was not effusive. Being a Mennonite, she had been trained to restrain her emotions. When she had shaken hands with the men, she took Annie to the table in the corner of the front room, where she might lay aside her black bonnet and her heavy outer shawl. Then she put Annie's baby and her own into the cradle and helped Noah and Moses extricate their little limbs from their many garments. "It's a cold day for this time of the year," she remarked by way of opening the conversation.

Annie looked up and began to blubber.

"Ach, don't go and cry," said Rachael, patting her on the back.

But the admonition was too late. Annie had lost control of herself. She cast herself with abandon on Rachael's breast and sobbed as if her heart would break.

Rachael straightway forgot her predilection to restraint. She threw her arms impulsively about the weeping Annie—at least as far as they would reach—and mingled her tears with those of her new friend. "I know," she kept repeating. "I know it all."

"I'm so tired," wailed Annie.

"I know. I don't forget yet what like it was when we come over." It was five years, she said, since she had left Berks County and all her friends there to come to this strange land as Levi Moyer's bride. The trip still stood out in her memory like a horrid nightmare. She knew exactly how Annie felt.

Presently it occurred to Rachael that a cup of tea would do them all good, and she hurried away to the kitchen to prepare it. Annie picked up her baby and followed. She could not bear to allow Rachael out of her sight.

"And to think I musn't make it yet," said Annie, watching the busy housewife at her work. "I got so tired with the cookin' all the way over."

"I know," replied Rachael.

"And never nobody else's things to eat."

"Yes, I know," comforted Rachael. "But now you can chust set, and eat, and rest."

The men were called in from the barn and together they had their cups of tea in the middle of the afternoon with enough accessories to provide a regular noon-day meal.

At last the time had arrived for the discussion of a subject that was foremost in the minds of all. No Pennsylvania Dutchman can be quite happy, even at table, so long as back somewhere in the recesses of his mind there is a lingering doubt about how everybody is related to everybody else. Levi had said that Rachael was "a little in the Eby Freundschaft yet." The time had come to ferret it out.

Rachael introduced the subject by remarking that Levi had told her that the Brickers were related to Christian Eby.

"He is uncle to us," replied John. "She, Nancy, is sister to our doddy."

"So!"

"Yes, and we know them as good as anybody," added Sam.

Annie had a piece of interesting information which she was anxious to impart to the Moyers at this time, and when she had asked and obtained Sam's permission she blurted it out; "Sam's gettin' in thicker with them yet. He's runnin' with Beccy Eby."

"Christian's girl?"

"No, Jeremiah, his. He is dead already. He went with the consumption. He was brother to Christian."

"So," said Levi, genuinely interested.

"And why didn't you fetch her along over?" inquired Rachael.

So Sam had to explain the situation at Hammer Creek. He spoke hopefully of Nancy's promise to relinquish her claim on Beccy in two years.

But Levi shook his head mournfully. "You can't tell what will happen all in two years," he declared. "She might go with it, too. It's ketchin', consumption."

At this juncture Sam found it convenient to change the subject of conversation by inquiring if Rachael, too, might be an Eby.

"No," replied Levi, "Rachael is a born Cressman, and her mom was a Shantz. Her mom's oldest sister was married with a man that had a brother, and he was a hired man once to Christian Eby. Ain't that right, Rachael, how it goes?"

But Rachael had a different version of the connection. According to her tell, it was her mother's youngest sister that had married a man, whose sister had married the hired man himself. But whichever it was, they were agreed upon the personnel of the hired man in question. He was a Baumann. Black Ephraim, they called him, for he was of a swarthy complexion.

"Baumann!" exclaimed Annie. "What for Baumann would that be now?" She knew so many by that name.

"His mom was a Bingeman, or a Sauder," replied Rachael, "or was it a Wissler? I can't think. But anyway he hears a little hard."

"Ach, him," cried John, discovering a flash of identity in the midst of diversity. "I mind him. He was at a funeral once—"

"That's him," interjected Levi, with an air of finality. "He chenerally always likes to see folks get buried."

And so the identity of the hired man was established and the bond of friendship strengthened between the Moyers and the Brickers. "It seems like we are long friends already," observed Levi, "knowing Ephraim Baumann together like we do."

From the Moyers the Brickers learned much that day about Canada and its people. It was five, long, lonely years, they said, since they had come from Berks County to their new home in the wilderness. Visitors were few, as distances were great. Every year had brought a few conestogas. The Kolbs and the Albrights had remained at The Twenty, but the majority had pushed their way farther west. Far inland, they had said they were going to a marvellously fertile region drained by a great river—the Heasley Tract, they had called it—but whether they had so much as found the place the Moyers did not know. They had never seen nor heard tell of them again.

From the very first mention of this fertile valley in the interior, Sam was intensely interested. He wanted to hear more about the Heasley Tract and the people who had gone to settle it.

The Moyers told them all they could remember. In the fall of, two conestogas had come to their shanty late at night. Sam Betzner with his wife and five children were in one, Joseph Sherk and his wife, Elizabeth Betzner, in the other. They could not be persuaded to settle at the Twenty, but in a few days they had pressed resolutely on.

"And got buried in the mud, like as not," sighed Annie. She did wish that Sam and John would be content to take up land somewhere near the Moyers, and leave the Betzners to their unknown fate.

But Levi Moyer was as interested in telling his narrative as the Brickers were in hearing it, and Annie's sighful comment escaped him. He went on to tell how in the aged parents of Sam and Elizabeth Betzner had come over, too, with all the rest of the family. How they had enjoyed Old Man Betzner's visit! He was a pleasant man, fond of talking, and he had a wonderful life story to tell. Left an orphan in Switzerland, at the age of four, he had been adopted into a childless family, and had grown up as the prospective heir to an estate worth thousands of dollars, only to find, at sixteen, that a child had been born to his foster-parents and that he was no longer welcome. At seventeen, he had run away to America. Landing at Philadelphia, he made his way inland on foot, sleeping at night in barns, or on beds of straw in the fields. He had settled in Franklin County; had won with great diligence a farm and a wife; and enjoyed a good name among his neighbours. But the wealth he had lost in the old world did not come to him in the new. A curse rested upon the United States, he declared.

What else was to be expected of a nation born in the throes of a bloody war? And now he had come to Canada, bag and baggage, with all his children and his children's children. If anybody wanted him, they would find him in the bosom of his family somewhere on the Heasley Tract.

"It makes it easy when they all come," commented Annie, thinking of all the friends she had left behind.

But Levi did not intend to be side-tracked. He went on to tell of the coming of the Gingerichs, and the Bechtels, and the Biehns, and the Kinzies, and the Rosenbergers, and of the complications and ramifications of relationship existing among them. He told, too, of the Suraruses and the Livergoods, and the Shupes, who had gone through just a few weeks before.

"They will break the road for us," remarked Sam.

Annie heaved another sigh and drew her baby closer.

"Tell them about George Clemens," urged Rachael, revelling in these pleasant reminiscences. "That George had such a way with him."

He must, indeed, have been a young man of an enlightened mind and of an engaging manner, although, unfortunately, still a bachelor. Levi said it was while George Clemens was visiting friends in Montgomery County that he had first heard of Canada and of an impenetrable bog, called Beverley Swamp, through which would run some day the shortest route to the Heasley Tract, although as yet no man had ventured through it with a team of horses. Immediately he made up his mind that he would go to Canada and drive through the terrible swamp. He wanted the honour of doing it first. So he got all the information he could about the new land in the hope of persuading his father to let him go and settle there. The father was a man of much experience, a commodity which he was willing to impart to George on easy terms. He warned the boy not to believe all he heard, but to go first and see the land for himself before deciding to settle there. George was overjoyed at his father's attitude. He joined a party at once, and offered to drive one of their conestogas. He wanted all the practice he could get, he said, before tackling the Beverley Swamp.

"And did he get through?" asked Sam. He was anxious to meet this George Clemens in whom the spirit of adventure was so strong.

"Ach, he got through all right," Levi was convinced, "but I didn't hear nothing. You don't know George yet. It wouldn't come in his head that he could turn back."

Sam gave his head a decisive nod. "If George Clemens could do it," he concluded. "Sam Bricker can too."

"And so can John," said the other, not to be outdone in courage by his young brother.

Annie did not say anything, but a thoughtful, far-away look stole into her sad eyes.

Levi Moyer did not encourage this adventurous spirit in the Brickers. He advised them to heed the admonition Old Man Clemens had given George, to go first and see the land before buying. If they found it all they desired, they could return to The Head of the Lake where the owner, Robert Heasley, lived, and make their bargain. It would be an easy matter to find Heasley, as he was a man of wealth and influence at The Head of the Lake, and a member of the Parliament of Upper Canada.

"We'll go till morning," announced Sam.

But in the morning Annie could not hold her head. The unusual exertions of the past weeks, the care of the children, and the preparation of meals under all sorts of adverse circumstances had overtaxed her physical strength. Then there was the added excitement of meeting the Moyers. She needed a rest, she said. In a few days at most she would be ready to continue the journey. So Rachael bestowed upon her sick guest what attention her multiplied duties allowed her. She tucked her into her own bed and experimented on her with all the homely remedies she knew. Whenever she could spare a moment, she spent it at her bedside.

Still Annie did not improve. The men worked in the field with Levi, but impatiently, for every day in his service meant one less that season on the Bricker clearing that was to be evolved somewhere on the Heasley Tract. Annie had been sick a week when Sam suggested that he and John should take Old Man Clemens' advice; go on horseback to spy out the land; make their bargain with Heasley, if they were satisfied with the Tract; and then return to the Moyers for Annie and the children. This arrangement offered the additional advantage of giving the men an opportunity to become acquainted with the road before venturing over it with their conestogas.

The proposal met with John's approval, and next morning Levi Moyer went to his work alone.

CHAPTER VI

It was a fortnight before the brothers returned, but they came in high spirits. They had made a bargain, a really good bargain, to judge by their faces. Sam in particular was bubbling over with enthusiasm. He kept patting his bulging waistcoat pocket, the top of which was secured by a procession of pins. "So it won't lose out," he explained.

"And what have you got all in that pocket?" Annie wanted to know.

"The deed," replied Sam. "Do you want to see it once?"

Of course they wanted to see it. So the little company gathered about the Moyers' kitchen table, while John and Sam unfolded their precious papers and smoothed out the creases.

"Read it," demanded Annie, on the very brink of expectation.

The words were long and unfamiliar, but the meaning was apparent. It was not in vain that John and Sam Bricker had skimped and saved on the old farm in Pennsylvania. With the earnings of those lean years they had each bought three hundred acres of land at the ridiculously low price of a dollar an acre. Landed gentry, they were now, Sam took the pains to inform them.

What pleased John most of all was the nature of the soil. It was of a rich, black quality, he said, and the claims that they had staked were covered for the most part with giant timbers the like of which he had never seen before. He was thinking of the wonderful crops he and little Johnny would raise one day on land of such amazing fertility.

Levi Moyer was greatly impressed with the price. He was sure that Robert Heasley had no idea of the value of the land that he was selling at such a figure. Perhaps he had never seen it; but Sam assured him that he had it from Heasley's own lips that he had visited the tract many a time, and that he knew it to be the best land in all Upper Canada.

"There must be something wrong with it," insisted Levi. "He wouldn't give it away like that unless he's crazy."

"Heasley ain't that," interposed John. "He can't be. He's a member of Parliament."

Levi sniffed.

"That's chust it," Sam proceeded to explain. "He has to be all the time in York with his hands in the Government, he said, and he can't get no time to sell the tract. Us Mennonites come all together to buy, and that makes it easy for him. So he can sell it cheap."

"Oh, that way?" returned Levi, who had the grace to pretend that he understood both Sam's laboured explanation and Heasley's business acumen.

"He must be smart though," said Annie, whose interest was centred in the deeds. "Look how good he writes—so good I can't read it even."

Levi laughed. "Them lawyers," he said, sagely, "they chener-ally always learn to write so nobody can read it."

"But I thought Heasley wrote it," said Annie. "His name is at the bottom."

"And John's is, too."

"But John can't write like that—nor Sam neither."

"Annie has right," said Sam. "Heasley did write it. It seems he is such a lawyer, too, along with all the other things he does. It saves him a lot of trouble, he says, and till he goes to York again he takes the papers along and puts them in the Government House."

"But—" began Levi, then stopped.

At this moment his attention was attracted to John who was sitting in a rocking chair romping with his boys. Noah and Moses sat one on either knee shrieking with delight while their father bounced them alternately up and down. Little Johnny sat on the "doddy's" feet, demanding his share of attention and elevation. When they were all wearied with excitement and exertion, John gathered them all into his arms and told them wonderful tales of the land that was to be their home and of the bright hopes he entertained for them.

"What you think, Little Johnny," said the happy man, "there's a school there already, and a teacher that can learn you good."

But Little Johnny was not at all interested in schools and schoolmasters. He wanted to know if there would be any little boys for him to play with.

John refused to be lured away from the great subject of educa-tion. Old Sam Betzner had engaged a teacher for his grand-children, he said, and John had agreed to pay a portion of the salary so that Little Johnny could go, and Noah, too, and even Moses, when he was big enough.

"And we got good news for you, too, Annie," said Sam. She would be near the Betzners, he said, next-door neighbour to Young Sam's with Old Sam and Joseph Sherk a short distance up and on the opposite side of the river. He had visited every home on the tract, and there was not a woman but had sent Annie a friendly greeting, a welcome in advance.

"And did you see George Clemens, too?" asked Rachael, while Levi clapped his knee and said; "That George!"

"He got through the swamp," said Sam. "He's that proud he was the first."

"And is he married?"

Sam laughed. So did everybody else when he told how George had likened his own unhappy state to a poor, wizen-faced frog, sitting on his doorstep with his mouth wide open waiting for a fly to pop in. It was just like George to talk that way, the Moyers said.

When the men asked Annie how soon she would be ready to start, she declared that she would go in the morning. She had forgotten all about the strange, undefined hallucinations that for a week or more had seemed to overshadow her soul, and rend it with conflicting hopes and fears. Now it was a deep-seated yet unspoken terror for the safety of her husband, augmented from time to time by visions of crouching bears. Again it was—but this she would not acknowledge even to herself. In spite of herself, there crept into her heart a dread that John would return and carry them all off to certain death in the jungle from whose horrors he had himself miraculously escaped. Whether John returned or not, the prospect was none too pleasing. Then suddenly and unexpectedly the adventurers had returned, unscathed, and fired with enthusiasm. Instantly Annie's every fear was allayed, or forgotten, and in her heart there reigned only hopes as buoyant as those of her husband.

Nevertheless, when the hour of departure came, and the horses were hitched once more to the conestogas, Annie's heart experienced a certain twinge of regret at leaving the Moyers and The Twenty. Rachael knew exactly how Annie felt. Indeed, she was feeling very much the same herself. It seemed too bad that the Brickers could not be satisfied at The Twenty, she confided to Annie, as she helped her pin on her shawl and tie her bonnet-strings.

The impatient men were calling her to hurry.

"I won't see you no more," said Annie. There were tears in her eyes and sobs in her voice.

"Don't go and cry now, Annie," implored Rachael, clasping her by the arms and holding her tight for a minute. "Look! I picked you some geranium slips off." She pressed into Annie's hand a little bundle tied with a moist rag. "You must plant them till you are there once. Flowers make always such good company. I found that out long already."

Annie took the bundle, stifled her emotions, and hurried to the door. John had called again, and Little Johnny sat at his side cracking the whip in anticipation of the departure. Even the cow bawled out her impatience.

"Make it good," Levi was saying to the men.

Rachael followed Annie to the conestoga, and watched her climb over the wheel into the wagon. Then she lifted the children one by one.

John had gathered up the reins. Little Johnny had said good-bye a dozen times.

"Thank you for the wisit, Annie," cried Rachael, remembering her manners in the very nick of time. Among her people it was a very negligent hostess, indeed, who failed to thank her guest for the privilege of extending hospitality.

"If you could only come and wisit me back—" said Annie.

The heavy wheels began to revolve. A wave of the hand, a glance of the eye, and they were off.

For several days the little company travelled on their monotonous way along the southern shore of Lake Ontario towards The Head of the Lake. One day was as wearisome as the next. The people they met were few and far between; for the Indians and the men who travelled on horseback used the narrow trail that ran high and dry along the crest of the mountain, while the Brickers with their wagons were compelled to use the road along the shore. Journeying with a conestoga loaded to capacity they found to be an experience which grew more and more laborious and more perilous the farther they advanced. The roads became worse and worse, in some places almost impassable. Length and breadth a good road should have, but these had a third dimension, a depth that was uncertain, irregular, and oftentimes profound.

Not only the horses but even the drivers were tired when at last they had emerged from the marsh at The Head of the Lake, passed within sight of the palatial home of Robert Heasley, and come at last to a little village which bore the euphonious name of Coote's Paradise. A small, inconsequential town it was, to be sure, in comparison with the towns of Pennsylvania, but a place of no little importance in Upper Canada in the early days of the nineteenth century. Indeed, it was something of a metropolis to which the people of a wide area came to have their varied needs supplied. It boasted, first and foremost, a tavern, and in the doorway of this pretentious building stood a leering, bottle-shaped man advertising his wares. The blacksmith's sign hung just across the way, and the path between it and the tavern was narrow and well-beaten. A decent church topped the neighbouring hill, and under its windows the village cows pastured peacefully. There was a mill, too,—the only one, the proprietor claimed, within a radius of thirty miles.

Past all these buildings John drove until he came at last to the village store, directly in front of which the progressive storekeeper had installed a pump and a watering-trough for the convenience of his patrons and as an incentive to trade.

"Better buy what you want all," suggested John to Annie, as he alighted from the wagon and began to pump. "It don't give many more stores now."

"Then we are soon there?" said Annie, hopefully.

John did not answer. He was too busy pumping.

Annie climbed down as well as she could with her baby in her arms, then turned and put the question to Sam who stood by watching her. "It seems we are soon there?"

Sam grinned.

"Not?" demanded Annie, suspiciously.

"Twenty-five miles yet," replied Sam. "Forty, if we was to go by the river."

"You're not goin' through that Beverley Swamp," cried Annie, filled with apprehension.

Sam nodded. That was the intention, he said.

Annie's heart sank. Why would Sam persist in going through that death-trap, she wanted to know. She reminded him of the rain that had fallen during the past week. The roads would be in a terrible state. They would never come through alive.

But Sam had another point of view. This was the first of many trips he would have to make with the heavy wagon between Coote's Paradise and the Heasley Tract, he said; and he intended to take the shortest route possible. Each trip would make the next easier.

"And what must you come so often for?" inquired Annie.

"Flour," was Sam's laconic reply.

"Twenty-five miles to a mill yet!" scoffed Annie.

"And sugar and tea," added Sam, disregarding the woman's aspersions.

"Twenty-five miles to a store! And if I want to sell my butter and eggs?"

"Twenty-five miles," said Sam, stoically.

"Whatever!"

At this juncture John came up, and beguiled Annie into the store.

It was a wonderful emporium, that store, where on one floor and from a single clerk could be procured anything from a plug of chewing-tobacco to the finest homespun linen. The proprietor had an eye to business, for he met them at the door, shook hands with them affably and inquired the name and age of the baby, before handing them over to the tender mercies of the clerk.

Now when John had told Annie to buy what she wanted "all," it was with the expectation that her wants would be few. He did not intend that she should spend his hard-earned money for anything that was not absolutely necessary. So Annie passed by the many commodities which the salesman spread temptingly before her, and selected a few candles to replace some that had been lost on the way, a half-dozen shilling crocks to use in case of emergency, and a bale of dark-coloured print which, the clerk glibly remarked, wouldn't show the dirt.

Sam, meanwhile, was bent on adventure. For several days he had been promising himself a novel experience, and a delightful one, when he should reach Coote's Paradise. On his previous trip through the village he had noticed behind one of the small panes of the store window an interesting paste-board sign. "Post-office" it had spelled, and it was around that magic word that his secret hopes of adventure clung.

For once in his life Sam was nervous. But he found it a delightfully pleasant sensation, notwithstanding. He slunk past the proprietor, evading his outstretched hand, and passed John and Annie in the aisle of the store without noticing them. He stood first on one foot and then on the other at the end of the counter, and finally darted into an obscure corner behind a barrel of salt. Stealthily he drew out from the self-same pocket which contained his precious deed, a sheet of paper. He looked about cautiously. He was alone, and unobserved. Then he reached for the quill and for the bottle of ink which stood on the proprietor's desk near by, and as fast as his unskilled fingers could convey the words to the paper, he wrote:

"Dear   Beccy,
I must write a cupple lines so that you know we live yet and goes everything good so far. Annie was sick by Levi Moyer's but she is good again. I bot akers and John the same. It is on the Grand River. Last night it was a full moon,

Your Sam."

It was done, and it looked well, his first love-letter. And such agreeable palpitations of the heart as it produced!

Sam replaced the articles on the proprietor's desk, folded his letter, and secured the ends of it with one of the numerous pins which had been doing duty on the top of his waistcoat pocket. With the precious epistle clutched safely in his hand, he came out from his hiding-place and proceeded to look for the post-master.

He found the officer he sought, but it proved to be a woman, a proud, scrawny, newsy-looking creature, who sat at a desk near the back of the store, knitting industriously. When he had screwed up his courage to the sticking point, Sam accosted her and pushed the letter somewhere between her nose and her work.

"What's this?" demanded the haughty dame.

"A letter," replied Sam. "I thought I would chust give it to you now."

"But what is it?" said the post-mistress, putting aside her knitting and removing the pin that secured the paper.

"Oh—" cried Sam, in alarm. "Don't read it. It's my letter."

Then the woman became positively insolent. She shrugged her angular shoulders, emitted a sonorously expressive groan and said; "You want to mail it?"

Sam nodded. "That is if you please," he added, in confirmation, striving with all his might and main to be polite.

"But it has no address," objected the lady. "Where do you want it to go?"

"To Beccy—I mean to Rebecca Eby," stammered Sam.

"And where under the sun does she live?"

"In Pennsylvania, by Hammer Creek in Lancaster County."

"Then write it down," snapped the civil servant, most uncivilly. "Of all the stupid people that come to this post-office."

Sam's face flushed as red as his hair. It was a long word—Pennsylvania—but he did his best. He did not like that post-mistress.

She had nipped for him in the bud all the rosy romance of letter-writing.

"Where's your money?" the woman was saying, and she held out an expectant hand. "You don't expect me to pay for it, do you?"

"Not unless you read the letter," retorted Sam, whereupon he pulled out his purse with great deliberation, and produced a coin.

"A dollar!" demanded the shrill voice of the woman.

"A dollar!" echoed Sam, weakly.

"A dollar," was the uncompromising reply.

Sam hesitated. Finally he held out his hand and said; "I think I'll take it back. It ain't worth that much."

The outraged post-mistress flung the letter at him, muttered unutterable things, and resumed her knitting.

Poor Sam! With a heavy heart he picked up his document of a thousand loving thoughts, and slunk his way out of the store. When John and Annie returned to the conestogas, they found him sticking a row of pins into the top of his waistcoat pocket.

"Looking at the deed again?" asked John.

"No," replied Sam. "I chust put a dollar in safe, so it won't lose out."

Two hours later the Brickers had turned their backs on Coote's Paradise, and were on their way to the Heasley Tract, with Sam's conestoga now in the van. As usual, Sam had had his way. In spite of Annie's fearful protests, they were going by the direct route through the Beverley Swamp. They were about to be buried alive, if Annie was any sort of prophet, in a grave twenty-five miles long and as wide and impenetrable as the confines of the terrible bog. The worst of it was nobody would ever know when or where the final struggle had been.

Poor John had to listen to these complaints and prognostications day after day, and he soon grew weary and utterly discouraged. Before long he was fully persuaded that he had been very foolish to allow Sam to lead them into this quagmire of unknown troubles. Perhaps, after all, Annie was right. As like as not, they would all be swallowed up alive.

Sam led on, blissfully immune to the influence of Annie's fears. Only the grunts of the pigs and the cackle of the hens disturbed the peace of his conestoga. He carried his compass in his pocket, and every day he consulted the almanac, which predicted sunshine and great heat. What more could he ask for his pilgrimage through the Beverley Swamp?

But the almanac proved not altogether infallible, for day after day turned out cloudy and damp. On the third day an interminable rain set in, and soon the Beverley Swamp was a veritable bog, in which it seemed quite probable that the whole caravan would be overwhelmed. Even Sam began to look serious and wonder if their days were, indeed, to be cut off in the flower of youth, before they had reached their destination. On three different occasions the men had to take their conestogas apart and carry the pieces and their baggage upon their backs for long distances to more solid ground. They were in constant danger of losing their way. The vegetation was so luxuriant that it hid the path in many places, and on every hand there were yawning death-traps half-concealed by shrubbery, where insects and reptiles grew and multiplied. Even the trees entered into the dark conspiracy, intertwining their heavy branches to exclude the light. Not only Annie and the children but even the men were tired, and chilled, and in imminent danger of contracting disease. The men lost their tempers times without number, and Annie kept reminding them that she had told them so. Oh, why had they ever left Pennsylvania? If only they could go back to it now! Oh, to be able to go anywhere in the whole wide world—anywhere, so long as they had the assurance that they would never again hear of the Beverley Swamp!

But there is an end to every road and it comes at last with patience. For two weeks the Brickers had followed the trail through the Beverley Swamp, but they came at length to firmer ground. The sun shone once more with warmth. The worst was past. Immediately their flagging spirits began to revive. They forgot their aches and discomforts, controlled their turbulent tempers, and with fresh hopes pressed on.

Directly ahead flowed the Grand River. Quite unexpectedly Sam sighted it one day and very soon he found the trail along the river-bank. They were now within a few miles of their destination. The day of the realization of their hopes was at hand.

Young Sam Betzner's house was the most southerly of the settlement, and there was great joy when the Brickers saw it through the trees on the opposite side of the river. With all possible haste they crossed where the water seemed lowest, and cast themselves upon the hospitality of the Betzners.

A right royal welcome awaited them. The Betzners opened their hearts and their homes and showed them a thousand kindnesses. When Sunday came, it proved a day of great rejoicing. From far and near the Mennonite people gathered at Old Sam Betzner's, two miles farther upstream on the east bank of the river, and there the Brickers met all the people of the settlement. The Sherks came from the adjoining farm, and the Bechtels and the Gingerichs from across the river, the Reicherts, and the Livergoods, and the Shupes, and the Suraruses by a short cut through the woods from the more northerly shores of the winding river. From the east came the Rosenbergers and George Clemens, still cheerful in spite of his loneliness. Annie met the women who had sent her kindly messages, and little Johnny met his teacher, David Rittenhouse, and some of his future schoolmates. Everyone had a hearty hand-shake and a cheerful greeting for the new-comers. What did it matter if it was a little late before they could settle down to worship? Joseph Bechtel preached all the better for their coming, and with greater zest the little company sang the praises of the great God who had made them, as well as their fathers, to lie down in green pastures and beside the still waters.

Autumn had come, and winter was fast approaching. The tall trees that all summer long had been swaying lazily in the breeze bestirred themselves and put on for a few days their gayest attire, as if they would do honour to the latest arrivals, then gradually, piece by piece, their splendid garments fell from them, disclosing to view dark, unsightly, naked limbs.

The Brickers knew the seasons well enough to realize that they must lose no time in making preparations for building, unless, indeed, they wanted to live all winter long in their conestogas. So they went to work with a will. Day by day there resounded through the empty forests the sound of the axe and the crash of falling timbers. The indignant owls began to hoot in wild alarm; the sombre evergreens mourned with many a sigh the fate of their luckless companions; in the distance the hungry wolves howled for vengeance; the river hid its fish; and all nature seemed to frown upon the intruding disturbers of the woodland peace.

But not even the rigours of a Canadian winter could dampen the ardour of the dauntless pioneers. If nature was unfriendly, hope was strong and buoyant, and day by day as they toiled with axe and saw, the echoing forests resounded with cheerful song.

The site that John had chosen was near Young Sam Betzner's, and there they made the first clearing. They built a stable for the horses, a primitive building with vertical logs for the framework and sashes, horizontal logs for the walls, and spliced logs slanted at the proper angle for the roof. Bark and twigs filled each chink and cranny. Then they built John's house—like his barn, but with a long, projecting roof supported by pillars over the front door. As soon as it was finished, the great boxes were lifted from the conestogas and emptied. Beds were set up in one room, kitchen utensils were hung up in the other. A cheery fire blazed in the fireplace, and on the floor were laid strips of rag carpet and hand-woven mats. Crude furnishings, to be sure, but the hearts of our forefathers beat high with hope.

It was February before anyone but Sam himself had time to think of Sam's house. The younger and more adventurous of the brothers had chosen a spot on the east side of the river farther north than anyone had yet ventured to settle. It was three miles from the Betzner settlement, as the crow flies, and twice as far following the course of the river.

Day after day the brothers trudged their way through the snow to this place, which Sam called his "Bauerei." All day long from dawn till sunset they felled the timbers which were to find a place in Sam's forest home. They were tedious days for Annie. Breakfast and supper, and ten, long, lonely hours between, with only the prattle of the children to break the silence. Many a silent tear she shed, and turned her back to wipe it away before the little ones should see. It was hard—nobody knew how hard it was. But she must be brave.

The winter of 1802-1803 brought terrible anxiety and no little suffering to the Mennonites on the Heasley Tract. The crops had been poor and the winter was long and bitterly cold. More than one family faced starvation. But theirs was a community of brothers; and brothers, they knew, were born for adversity. They shared even their last crust. The potatoes were so scarce that the peelings had to be saved for planting in the spring. Annie brought out all her provisions and sent them wherever the need was greatest, bemoaning always the hams that Sam had surreptitiously dropped to feed the bears of the Alleghanies. There was much relief when spring came at last, before anyone of their number had succumbed to the exigencies of winter.

There was no end of trouble about the building of Sam's house in the spring. It was all Sam's own fault, for he kept changing his mind about the plans every other day. When he had chosen the site, he found that a huge oak of marvellous girth had years before staked that claim. John laid his axe to the root of the tree, but Sam stopped him. Part way up the trunk, he wanted it cut. It was to be Beccy's table, and the house must be built around it. Every log had to reach a certain standard aesthetically, or Sam would reject it. No knotty, misshapen logs should house his Beccy.

John had to put up with it all. His brother's notions first wearied; then angered; and finally amused him. "You would 've saved yourself a lot of bother, Sam," he said one day, "if you would 've fetched her along over. Till you are married once, you don't have to ask her where she wants the chimley set, or how high the table must be. She'd chust take what you give her all, and be thankful."

These and similar taunts Sam bore with commendable good nature, and before summer came, Beccy's house was ready, awaiting her coming.

The spring of 1803 brought more settlers to the Heasley Tract. With each successive week came new conestogas, and there was a welcome for all. The older settlers offered timely advice and assistance, and these overtures of friendship were all gratefully received and reciprocated. A new Pennsylvania was emerging in the heart of Upper Canada, a new Pennsylvania with the same people, the same traditions, and the same religion as the old.

CHAPTER VII

Ever since coming to Canada Sam Bricker had secretly entertained a great ambition, aside, of course, from the dominant one of having Beccy with him, and that was to see Muddy Little York, the capital of Upper Canada, where the people lived in even greater luxury than Robert Heasley at The Head of the Lake. He had a sneaking desire to see the world, the world that his religion taught him was to be shunned like its boon companions, the flesh and the devil.

It happened opportunely enough that John also had an overwhelming ambition, but a very respectable, God-fearing one, namely, to possess another cow. Sam decided that this dream of John's must be realized; he offered to go to York to buy the animal. John demurred at first, thinking he could buy more cheaply and more conveniently at closer range, but Sam would not listen to excuses, and in the end he had his way. John's ambition was to be realized—and incidentally, Sam's.

Sam's first intention had been to take Menno and go on horseback, but thinking that he might have one animal too many on his return trip to suit his convenience, he decided to leave Menno at home. He would walk.

It was a bright September morning when Sam found himself in a tavern in the village of York, in the very heart of the great, outside world, and sixty-odd miles across country from the Heasley Tract and all the restraining influences of his own people. It had been late when he arrived on foot the night before, too late to get anything to eat, and now he had a voracious appetite, and a thirst for adventure. He appeased both at the breakfast table.

Sam Bricker was not the sort of man to keep his eyes upon his plate when a novel world lay unfolded before him. As he shoved his food into his mouth at the end of his knife, he watched for an opportunity to increase his store of knowledge about the great unknown universe by which he found himself surrounded.

A chromo of brilliant colour hung on the wall opposite this armchair explorer, and held his attention. It was a likeness of a pompous gentleman, adorned with a row of shining medals, a scarlet waistcoat, and a rosy complexion. Before it, all the rest of the room paled into insignificance.

Sam Bricker had never heard of the socratic method of eliciting information, but he knew how to practice it. All he needed was a victim. He found him in the person of a tall, distinguished-looking young man in military uniform, who was standing indifferently in the doorway. Catching his eyes, Sam beckoned him with his fork.

The soldier with the dignified bearing looked in another direction.

Sam persisted.

The young man stared.

"Come here once," called Sam, and he had the satisfaction of seeing his victim pocket his dignity and come slowly towards the chair which Sam had pushed out in anticipation of his approach.

"I want to ast you something," began the inquisitor.

The soldier replied with all politeness that he would do his best to answer.

Sam pointed to the picture on the wall. "Who might that be?" he asked.

The stranger glanced casually at the picture in question, then turned again to Sam and scrutinized his face very closely. A suspicion of a smile was playing about his mouth. "That, sir, is your sovereign, George the Third, King of England," he said, speaking the words distinctly and emphatically, as if he hoped by so doing to impress his interlocutor with the dignity of His Majesty's station in life.

Sam was gratified with the information and encouraged to continue his investigation. "So?" he said with the rising inflection. "Then he will be related with the tavern-keeper, not?"

The young man smiled and, not unkindly, asked by what process of reasoning he had arrived at that conclusion.

"His picture," returned Sam. "He wouldn't send that over, such a big one anyways not, if they wasn't connected somehow."

The soldier looked at Sam long and earnestly. "Where do you come from, sir?" he said at length.

"From Heasley's Tract over on the Grand River," replied Sam. "I am there a year already."

"And where did you live before you came there, may I ask?"

"In Pennsylvany."

"Pennsylvania. That accounts for your failure to recognize our king," said the stranger. "He hasn't been your king very long."

Sam hastened to contradict him. "He was always our king," he said, "but I never saw his picture yet. Mebbe he found out we was Mennonites and wouldn't have none to give him back."

"You don't sit for portraits, then, your people?"

Sam shook his head and referred him to the commandment which forbids the making of a likeness of anything that is in the heaven above, or in the earth beneath, or in the water under the earth. "We want to live right," he assured him.

This doctrine was new to the stranger. Never had he heard such a literal interpretation of the Scriptures. This new Canadian interested him, fascinated him. He straightway forgot all about the man whom he was to meet by appointment, and gave himself up to the study of Sam and his idiosyncrasies. "You said a moment ago," he continued, "that our king has always been yours. Do you mean to say that there are people in Pennsylvania who have been loyal to the British crown all these years since the Colonies broke from the Old Country?"

Sam nodded his head, smiling knowingly.

"And is that why you are coming here to live?"

"Ach, we have all different excuses," Sam had to confess. "Some for that and some to get land cheap."

"Tell me about your people."

No one knew better than Sam Bricker the marvellous story of the Mennonites. On many a Sunday afternoon when the young men of his age were standing in groups talking about the crops, their horses, and the weather, or lounging in some obscure corner whispering sugary nothings into receptive ears, he had preferred to sit with the old men on the "stoop," or about the fireplace to listen to their tales of the long ago. And now he could recite, backwards or forewards, as desired, the generations of all the families of his acquaintance with equal speed and with greater precision than most of the old women. Like every Mennonite in good standing, he knew all the articles of their creed with biblical allusions to substantiate them, and unlike many an older one, he had estimated how much of ridicule, of persecution, of poverty, and of bloodshed the tenets of their simple faith had cost, from the time that Menno Simons had presumed to oppose the well-established doctrines of the Papacy.

All this Sam told the soldier—and more. When Sam saw with what unfeigned interest the man listened, he could not refrain from digging deeper into the illustrious history of his people. He knew the traditions of his ancestry long before the birth of the founder of the Mennonite faith. He told how authentic records had confirmed the fact that most of their families were of Celtic extraction, and had been brought in primitive days from heathendom to Christianity under the ministry of the Waldenses; how the mighty Church of Rome, not deigning to notice this spurious race until it had begun to threaten her supremacy over civilized Europe, had harassed them with bitter persecutions during the fifteenth century, compelling many to leave the fertile plains of northern Italy and take refuge in the highlands of Switzerland; how in the days of the Reformation they had endured the persecutions meted out to all Protestants, and when Menno Simons had raised his declamation against infant baptism, they had rallied with Germans and Lowlanders to his standard; and how for years they had been the butt of Catholic and Lutheran alike, wandering homeless and dejected up and down the Rhineland, enduring in silence the sneers of society, the buffetings of the bigoted and the oppression of governments because, forsooth, they claimed a right to religious freedom, objected to military service, and refused to take judicial oaths. Then had come the invitation of William Penn, and gladly they had left behind them the old life with all its wretchedness and entered into their Elysium in another world, where swords were to be to them forever as ploughshares and spears as pruninghooks, where the only oath required was continued allegiance to the God of their fathers. But into this paradise had come a disruption. Its quiet fields had been turned into battle-grounds, its churches into thundering forts. The inoffensive people, steadfastly abstaining from arms for conscience sake, had been misunderstood and adjudged a menace to the new commonwealth, and there had seemed a grave danger that sooner or later the Mennonites would be deprived of the consideration they had so long enjoyed, immunity from legal courts and exemption from military service. In their embarrassment, the more fearful ones were turning their eyes to far-off Canada, where, they had been told, the old conditions were still maintained, where the unturned soil offered unstinted rewards to the diligent, and where they might live, they hoped, unmolested by the world and its conventionalities, its wars and rumours of war.

At last the long story was told. Sam pushed back his plate, leaned back in his chair and sighed. The contemplation of the ills his people had borne in the ages that had passed made him realize that this mortal life of ours is at best a burden, a vale of trouble and of tears.

The stranger was silent for a moment, but presently he grasped Sam's horny hand and shook it heartily. "You have every reason to be proud of your ancestry," he said. "Martyr blood of the centuries flows in your veins. That is better than riches and worldly honour. I think I can understand your feelings. It often takes more character to turn the cheek than to strike the blow. I am a soldier—"

"You! a soldier!" exclaimed Sam, starting back and springing to his feet in excitement. In all his wild speculations of adventure in York he had never dreamed of encountering a man who had fallen so low in the scale of moral existence as to blandly acknowledge that his business in life was to fight—and to kill—his brother-man.

The soldier laughed and drew his sword. "Don't be afraid," he said, when he saw how Sam shrunk from the slightest contact with the weapon.

"You! a soldier!" said Sam, incredulously, "and soldiers make all the wars in the world."

"Not at all," was the reply. "They stop wars. No true soldier will use his sword except as a last resort. He must use every power he possesses to preserve the peace of the nations."

This statement did not coincide at all with Sam's preconceptions about the function of military men, but for the sake of the individual soldier who had won his heart, he was willing to let the matter drop.

The soldier seized Sam's hand and shook it whole-heartedly. "If there were more people like you in the world," he said, "there would be fewer wars."

Sam was prepared to answer the challenge. "The Mennonites are doing all they can for peace," he said. "There are folks in Pennsylvany that have eighteen and nineteen children already."

While the soldier laughed, a young civilian who had been standing for some time behind his chair, tapped him familiarly on the back.

"Why, Jim Wilson, you here?" cried the soldier. "My apologies. I got so interested in this man's story that I forgot all about our appointment."

"So did I," was the laughing reply. "I am afraid I must apologize to you both." He included Sam by a wave of the hand. "I have been eavesdropping."

"Well, we wasn't tellin' lies," replied Sam.

"And it never hurts anybody to hear the truth," added the soldier.

That was precisely what Jim Wilson had been thinking as he stood and gazed into Sam's earnest, honest face during the recital of the story. Behind the Mennonite's frank, open countenance there could not possibly lurk any hidden sin or dishonesty. No need for such as he to cover his misdoings with a cloak of respectability. He was what he seemed to be, an honest man with a guileless heart and a conscience void of offence towards God and his fellowman.

The pleasant conversation ended. Sam now turned his attention to the real mission that had brought him to York—the cow. He put on his hat preparatory to going out into the streets to seek out the dealers in livestock.

But Mr. Wilson stopped him with the question; "Do you live on the Heasley Tract?"

Sam said he did.

"And you have come to York to lay in a supply of provisions, I suppose?"

"No," replied Sam. "I came to buy me a cow for John, my brother that is. I chust walked over."

"Walked!" ejaculated both the men at once.

Sam laughed. "That's nothing," he said. "I'm good friends to walkin'. I don't get easy tired."

"Round by The Head of the Lake?" inquired Mr. Wilson.

Sam nodded.

"Ninety miles. When are you going home?"

"Till morning," said Sam. "I must not stop so long away. The harvest."

"Of course," said Mr. Wilson. "Well, I'm coming around to see you off. Don't go away without seeing me." And he was gone.

Life in York was certainly proving very novel and interesting. Two acquaintances before he had left the breakfast table was something for Sam to boast about when he got back to the tract. And Jim Wilson was coming again to see him off. It was all very pleasant and entertaining, this little excursion of his into "the world."

The cow! He must tear himself now from his own pleasures and devote himself to the more serious occupation of bargaining for a cow.

But no sooner did our adventurer get out upon the street to inquire where such a purchase could be made than he fell in with a very obliging wag of a fellow, who volunteered to conduct him to an auction sale in the afternoon and show him the sights of the place in the meantime.

Here was luck beyond Sam's greatest expectation. An auction sale was always a sort of holiday at Hammer Creek, where everybody within a radius of twenty miles went, if for nothing else, to hear the jokes and see the fun. To buy a cow at an auction sale in York would be nothing short of a pleasant diversion.

"If you've got the money," Sam's new friend observed, with a curious twinkle in his eye, whereupon Sam drew out his purse and disclosed the fifteen silver dollars that John had entrusted to him.

His name was Peter Potter, this new acquaintance of Sam's with the twitching eyes. He made a precarious living, he said, by selling ideas to people who didn't have any. Sam had never heard tell of such a calling in life, but it sounded very romantic, and he could not help but feel somewhat elated that fortune had provided him with such an agreeable companion.

They started off at once upon a sight-seeing tour. As they walked down the main street of the village, the guide poured into Sam's ears an enthusiastic forecast of what York was to become in another quarter of a century. Reared, as he believed it to be, by enchantment in the midst of a wilderness to become a great metropolis, it was remarkable what strides it had already made towards that happy consummation of his hopes. Only recently it had been made the capital of Upper Canada. He would take him first of all two miles into the wilderness to see Castle Frank, the home of the Governor.

Castle Frank impressed Sam not so much on account of its beauty but because of its association with the great and mighty people of the earth. It was a low, rambling, frame building of a single story, with a huge verandah in the middle of the front elevation. It was a much more beautiful home than he had built for his Beccy, but by no means as pretentious as Robert Heasley's at The Head of the Lake.

The relative importance of these two presumably great men troubled Sam as he walked with Peter Potter along the road which led through the wilderness from Castle Frank to the next point of their itinerary, the Place of the Government. He would see what Peter had to say about it. "Did you see Robert Heasley's house yet?" he asked.

"Heasley? Him that lives at The Head of the Lake?" said Peter.

Sam said that was the very man he meant. He encouraged him to continue.

"I didn't see his house yet," said Peter, "but I've seen him." Here he indulged in one of his characteristic squints. "Little bit of a fellow with a swelled head. Rich as Croesus—"

"Who's that?" interrupted Sam, determined to learn as much as he could.

"Croesus? Oh, a rich old Jew, descended from Judas Iscariot. You want to watch them rich fellows. They cheat you every time they get a chance."

"But Heasley is a Member of Parliament," objected Sam.

Peter Potter laughed so hard that he had to hold his sides. "Ha! Ha! that's good! So you thought they are a pack of angels with wings all sprouted, them politicians. Did you never hear about wickedness in high places?"

Sam's faith in British law and government sustained a jolt. He ventured to inquire whether the Governor was that sort of man, too.

"They're all alike," said Peter Potter, waving his arms dramatically to include the whole countryside. "Everybody's trying to get rich and nobody wants to work. The Governor he's a Sir, and he never learned how, and Heasley he don't have to now."

"You mean—?"

"Yes, I mean he's got enough of other people's money to live on the fat of the land for the rest of his days."

Sam bit his lip and said nothing.

"He takes it out of poor people like you and me," continued Peter Potter, blinking both eyes together by way of variety. "Makes laws to suit himself. But us poor people have to skimp, and save, and go hungry. I'm hungry now."

"There, there," said Sam, "don't tell me any more, and I promise you all you can eat for dinner." He was growing weary of Peter Potter and the disturbing ideas he peddled. "Look! what place is this we are comin' too?"

"The Place of the Government," replied Peter Potter, whose optimism and national pride revived with the promise of a good square meal. "I can tell you us people of York are proud of them there buildings."

In the middle of a small clearing stood two edifices of equal dimensions about a hundred feet apart and connected by a covered colonnade. Peter was ready with the information that when the large centre structure should be built, as it was proposed, these buildings now standing would be mere wings to the most imposing building in all Upper Canada.

"Yes, yes," said Sam, "but I want to look at what I see with my eyes, not what I see in your mind. If the men that make the laws in Canada are all bad, like you say, they won't need no big building in the middle. With cheats in the government, Canada can't grow. Put that in your idea-bag once."

Peter Potter was silenced for the moment, and Sam was left in peace and quietude to enjoy the scene before him. Turning his back upon the buildings, he looked towards the west, down the only real street of the embryo city, out to where the flat roofs of the garrison dotted the landscape. To his right was a grove of oak-trees, their heavy branches tossing to and fro, the forest primeval. Near by, on his left, stood an old block-house, and within a stone's throw a sheet of calm water, with a long arm of land thrown protectingly around it, danced in the noon-day sun. Far beyond, the tumultuous waves of the lake rolled in interminably from some distant region beyond the blue horizon.

It was that distant horizon that held Sam's interest. Somewhere in that direction the noisy Niagara tumbled its way to the lake. Farther still to the south was Pennsylvania. Many miles separated him from Beccy, the girl of his dreams, but he was with her in thought. He sat beside her on the narrow bench beneath the apple-tree. He held her hand; he whispered in her ear. Was she ready to go back with him to Canada? Ah, what a wonderful girl was Beccy. At last they were married. The time had come for them to say farewell to Pennsylvania. She was climbing into the conestoga; they were off. Slowly they were trekking their way to the north, climbing the Alleghanies and crossing the Niagara. They were in the Beverley Swamp. He was telling her once more about a certain little log house on the Heasley Tract—

Something jarred Sam's elbow at this felicitous moment. His happy dream faded. "It's only me, boss," Peter Potter was saying. "You didn't forget about the dinner, did you?"

All the way back to the tavern Sam walked as in a trance. He heard his loquacious companion discourse on all the places of interest they passed upon the way, but he was weary of York and its possibilities. What did he care about the jail with its high stockade outside and its stocks and pillory within? What did it matter to him how many hops the people of York amused themselves with, or how late they danced? He was tired of the world, ready to go back home. This life was not for him and Beccy.

Peter Potter noticed the change, the absentmindedness, which had come over his client, but he was not at all disturbed by it. He had an idea which experience had proved to be very efficacious in just such a situation as this. He piloted Sam to the dinner-table, and ordered a pint of rum—just enough, he explained, to cool them off after their morning's exertion—and although the garrulous Peter confessed that he was himself very partial to the beverage, he saw to it that Sam emptied his mug. It was his treat, he said, but Sam paid the bill.

After dinner they went to the sale. Already a great crowd which must have comprised most of the male population of York, had gathered about the auctioneer, and soon the fun began. He was a jolly fellow, that auctioneer, and wonderfully persuasive. Before Sam knew what he was doing, he had bought a piece of china, which fell and broke on the toe of his cow-hide boot, and a dash churn, which he could never hope to transport from the premises, let alone to the Heasley Tract.

There was only one cow for sale, and it was the last on the list. Shrieks of derision greeted it, when it was led up to the block.

"How much am I bid for this fine muley?" cried the auctioneer.

"Fifty cents," jeered one of the bystanders.

"Ah, come on," the auctioneer called back. "Give us a decent bid. How much for the muley? Here's a man that wants a cow, don't you now?" He fixed his large persuasive eyes on Sam. "How much do you bid?"

There was no resisting that auctioneer. "Five dollars," replied Sam.

The auctioneer began his song. "Five dollars I am bid. Make it ten! Ten! Ten! Ten is not too much. Who'll make it ten?"

"Seven," called some unknown competitor whom Sam could not see.

The crowd had made the amusing discovery that two men were vitally interested in that old skate of a cow that nobody else would look at, and they pushed in on all sides to see the fun.

The auctioneer straightened himself up for another flow of oratory. "Seven I am bid. Seven dollars for this fine muley! Who'll make it ten? ten! ten! Thoroughbred and fresh! Going at seven dollars, going—" Then he paused, looked at Sam and winked a knowing eye. "If you're wise, young man, you won't let it go at seven. Make it ten."

He was such a persuasive fellow, that auctioneer, and Sam couldn't do anything else but nod consent.

Then the volume of persuasion was diverted towards Sam's rival bidder. "Make it fifteen," he coaxed. "A fine healthy muley, and I'm bid only ten dollars. Fifteen I want, fifteen! Make it fifteen!"

"Fourteen."

"Ah, fourteen," said the auctioneer, turning his attention again to Sam. "Now make it fifteen. Fourteen I am bid. Fourteen dollars, going at fourteen dollars!" All the time these wonderful eyes of his were fixed upon Sam's excited face.

"It's the only cow they have," Peter Potter reminded him, elbowing his way through the crowd to offer his friend a bit of advice in his hour of need. "Better take her. She's cheap at that."

Sam knew better. He had examined the animal before she came to the block, and even his poor, rum-befuddled judgment told him that she was dear at half the price. But there he was, the hero of the moment, with the auctioneer's eyes upon him, Peter Potter at his elbow, and the crowd hanging upon his answer. Was he going to disappoint them all? He looked up and said the magic word.

"Fifteen!" cried the auctioneer, in a voice resonant with exultation. "Thank you, sir. Sold for fifteen dollars!"

A hearty laugh resounded on every hand, the sale was over, and the crowd dispersed.

Sam went around to where the cashier sat, and paid his money. Then he led his cow about the barnyard in search of his friend, Peter Potter. He wanted to say good-bye to him. But Peter was nowhere to be seen, and nobody had ever so much as heard of anyone by the name of Potter.

Gradually it dawned upon Sam that he had been swindled, that the man whom he had banqueted had not only raised his bid but pocketed his money. And so this was how Peter Potter made his living, peddling ideas to people who hadn't any. He spent the evening tramping the streets for some trace of the peddler, but all in vain. Thoroughly ashamed of himself, he crept into bed at last, and made up his mind to leave York and its worldliness as early as possible in the morning.

After a sleepless night and a scant breakfast, Sam started to the stables for his cow. Such a bundle of skin and bones as she was! He slapped her lean flank, and jerked her impatiently towards the door, this fifteen-dollar muley that he had bought with John's hard-earned money. When he had led her out in the yard, he wanted to kick her. How he was ever to present her to John he did not know. He only hoped he could slink away from York without seeing anyone he knew.

But there at the gate was Mr. Wilson lifting the latch as Sam approached.

"You don't have to make open for me," said Sam, embarrassed beyond measure at the unexpected attention.

"But I want to," replied Mr. Wilson. "I want a word with you."

Sam was relieved to note that he did not even glance at the cow.

"I want to tell you that there is a mortgage on your land."

Now to Sam and his co-religionists a mortgage was nothing short of anathema. They believed that the Great Apostle had that particular legal transaction in mind when he enjoined upon the early Christians to owe no man anything. To be accused of having a mortgage on his property was equivalent to an insult, and Sam was on the defensive at once. "You lie," he said, coldly.

"I do sometimes, I acknowledge it," replied Mr. Wilson, "but I swear to you that this time I am telling the truth."

"I am an honest man," said Sam, quite at a loss to understand this turn of affairs. "I have paid for my land, and I have the deed to home. I thought you and me was friends."

"So we are," affirmed Mr. Wilson. "That is why I am telling you that the Heasley Tract is mortgaged for twenty thousand dollars. Your deed is no good. Heasley wrote it himself. He has cheated you. Go to the Registry-Office and look up the records."

For a moment Sam stood as if stupefied, turning white and red by turns. Finally he struck his muley upon the flank, and told her to go on.

But Mr. Wilson stopped him, protesting most emphatically that he was telling the truth, and begging him not to leave York until he had investigated the matter thoroughly.

"If I was you," said Sam, turning a pitying glance at the man beside him, "if I was you, I'd get my head charmed once. I know a man that was awful bad with it that way, and he got it straight again. He was smart, too, and all. If I was you,—"

"Thanks for the advice," said Mr. Wilson, with quiet dignity. "Perhaps I'll make use of it some day." He closed the gate, and walked slowly and thoughtfully towards the tavern, while Sam and his muley jogged along on their homeward way.

CHAPTER VIII

As Sam Bricker trudged his way along towards The Head of the Lake, the seeds of suspicion that had been sown in his mind suddenly took root and began to grow into a haunting conviction. He had paid little attention to the babbler Peter Potter of infamous memory regarding the dishonesty of Robert Heasley, but here was Mr. Wilson, a reputable citizen, not only confirming the statement but dragging it around like some foul skeleton and leaving it at Sam's own door. "A mortgage! Twenty thousand dollars! He wrote the deed himself!" These were the odious fragments of conversation that kept ringing in Sam's unbelieving ears until at last they seemed to ring true.

Heasley had written the deeds himself. Sam had seen him do it. He could picture him now sitting in his armchair at his desk with his quill between his fingers, pausing occasionally to look up and smile, or to make some thoughtful inquiry. False smiles they were and purposeful thoughtfulnesses, if Mr. Wilson had spoken the truth.

But there was the possibility that Mr. Wilson was mad. Perhaps he had himself been defrauded by Heasley and imagined everyone else in like predicament. Even if it were true, what object could the man have in appointing himself the bearer of such bad news? Undoubtedly the man was insane.

Then Peter Potter entered into the argument. He knew nothing about Sam's dealings with Heasley, and he had given him a reputation for dishonesty. Sam remembered the old adage about the ability of a thief to catch a thief. The world seemed full of thieves who were going about like ravenous wolves seeking whom they might devour. Peter Potter had succeeded in extracting a good chunk out of Sam's pocketbook. Could it be possible that Robert Heasley had stolen from him all he had in the world?

No. Sam would not believe it. He could not persuade himself that a man of education, a lawyer, a Member of Parliament, could stoop so low as to defraud an innocent and inoffensive people who had come as strangers to a land where justice and equity were said to prevail.

"Thieves are no respecters of persons," suggested that other suspicious mind of his.

But Sam still refused to listen. Heasley had been grossly misrepresented, he decided. His accusers had forgotten that he was a lawyer, competent to draw up his own deeds, thereby saving unnecessary expense. They did not know that he had taken copies of the papers to York and deposited them in the Registry-Office.

But had he? Poor, demented Mr. Wilson had told him to go to that very place to discover Heasley's treachery. The proofs were there evidently, and Sam must go and find them. He owed it to himself, to Heasley, and to the little company of Mennonites away back on the tract.

So back to York went Sam with his cow. He found the Registry-Office without any difficulty. It was one of the buildings that Peter Potter had pointed out to him when they were returning from the Place of the Government. Sam had seen it, but paid little attention to it—a low, rambling, log-house, surrounded by a picket fence. Sam tied the muley securely to the post, then strode up to the door of the office and knocked.

No answer.

Louder and louder he rapped, but no one heeded his summons. Nobody paid the slightest bit of attention except two half-grown boys who stood near the gate and tittered, exulting, no doubt, in the prospect of a novel entertainment that a lucky chance had brought them.

The next minute a tall, dignified soldier swung down the street past the little, low log-house with the picket fence.

Sam shouted a cry of recognition. "Hi there! It looks like you are in a hurry."

The soldier glanced up and stopped immediately. "Oho! What are you doing here? I thought you would be on your way home by this time."

"I was," replied Sam, "but I had to come back. I want to make sure." He looked the very personification of perplexity.

The soldier advanced to the door where Sam was standing. "What's the matter?" he said. "Can I help you in any way? Remember you will always find a friend in Isaac Brock."

Sam's heart warmed. Here was a man whom every instinct of his being bade him trust implicitly. He opened his heart and told his trouble.

The soldier led the way into the Registry-Office without the ceremony of knocking. "We'll look it up," he said.

Meanwhile the two adolescents who had laughed at Sam had been feasting their eyes upon the manly figure of the soldier. It was only when he had disappeared from their sight that they could find words to express their admiration.

"It's him!" whispered one of the hero-worshippers. "It's Colonel Brock. Ain't he straight though?"

The other looked at the muley and thought of Sam. Queer specimens these were to be associated with his hero.

"He's helping him," said the first, "not a bit proud, is he, Charlie?"

"He wouldn't be great if he was," replied the other. "Say, Bill, when I'm big, I'm going to be a soldier like him."

Charlie's eyes twinkled mischievously. "You'd better start by helping people instead of poking fun at them," he said. "Look what he did."

"What about yourself, Charlie?" said Bill. "You don't need to try to preach to me."

Inside the Registry-Office Sam Bricker was having an anxious time. The soldier found Mr. Ridout hidden between the pages of a ponderous tome which lay open on the desk, called him out and introduced Sam. He was a very courteous man, that registrar, and eager to please. He must have been very efficient, too; for, in an incredibly short time after he had retreated again to his hiding-place, he had the desired information. The Heasley Tract was mortgaged for twenty thousand dollars.

"And are there no records of sales of any portion of the Tract?" asked the soldier.

"To Sam Bricker?" suggested the Mennonite.

Sam's hopes died with the answer; "No, sir."

"None whatever?"

"None whatever."

"But this man bought three hundred acres over a year ago and has his deed. He knows nothing of any mortgage."

The registrar shrugged his shoulders. "If he has a deed," he said, "it isn't worth the paper it is written on."

Sam actually staggered under the blow.

"You see Heasley has only half interest in the Tract," continued Mr. Ridout. "Jim Wilson owns the other half, and he knows nothing of any sales. He was telling me only yesterday that he wished he could get his money out."

"Wilson!" cried Brock. "Why it was Wilson that told him about the mortgage!"

"Strange," commented the registrar.

"Not at all. You see Wilson heard him tell his story. He's made up his mind to spoil Heasley's little game. Jim's straight. But I'm wondering what's to be done. Mennonites, you know, never take the offensive."

If the two men had been watching Sam, they might have been better prepared for what happened next. Was it a sudden clap of thunder that set all the quills a-waltzing and bounced the clerk off his chair as if he had been shot? Oh, no. Only a man in a temper, darting lightning from his eyes and thundering with his clenched fists.

Like lightning, too, he was gone, and all the little group that had rushed to the door of the Registry-Office could see was the dim outline of a man dragging behind him with herculean strength a slow-moving cow, an operation which raised between the picture and the spectators a mitigating cloud of dust.

"I thought you said that Mennonites don't take the offensive, Colonel," laughed the registrar, balancing his quill behind his ear. "I hope he gives Heasley time enough to say his prayers."

"That's more than he deserves," replied the soldier. "But I must hurry on. There's trouble over at Fort George. Mutiny. I was on my way to the dock but I couldn't pass that Mennonite in distress."

"Going around by The Head of the Lake?"

"No, across by water. They're rigging up a boat for me now. I'm not going to lose any time getting there."

"And not much in getting back, I warrant," said the registrar, digging the colonel in the ribs. "She's a fine girl, and we are always thankful for the glimpses she lets us have of you. Good luck to your oars. Hope to see you again soon."

The colonel strode to the gate; then turned to wave his farewell. "Be good to the Mennonites if you get a chance," he said. "There's something rotten in the state of Denmark."

Charlie and Bill had been shamelessly eavesdropping.

"Mutiny!" gasped Charlie, with eyes as big as saucers. "At Fort George!"

"Where are your ears?" retorted Bill. "He said it was in Denmark."

Whether the trouble was across the lake or across the seas mattered little to Charlie and Bill. Both were equally inaccessible to them. Their limit was the dock, their one concern in life to arrive there in all haste. They raced each other down the middle of the street.

So the great world of Muddy Little York went about its business and forgot about Sam Bricker and his muley. Sam was having a sorry time of it. He had dragged the cow outside the village when she suddenly decided to change her tactics. Instead of doing all in her power to retard her own progress and that of her conductor, she now ran as fast as she could, tugging behind her at the end of her halter a greatly distressed and exceedingly wrathy man, whose frantic appeals to "so easy now" were worse than useless.

This tug of war between man and beast did not tend to improve Sam's humour, but it did help him to control his temper. He was boiling with rage, yet he had sense enough to know that he would do well to hide his passion and resort to cajoling words and gentle pats on some of the animal's bony angles, in case he should be fortunate enough to get within arm's reach of her again. He believed that a soft answer might turn away the wrath of a cow.

He was right. The animal gradually slackened her speed, and looked back at Sam with a half-frightened, half-remorseful expression in her eyes. In a short time there was a silent but none the less well understood pact between them that for the time being each would relinquish all claim to leadership and be content to jog along beside the other after the manner of all self-respecting men and cows.

When evening drew on, Sam was so wearied with the exertions of the day that he was glad enough for an opportunity to rest. A similar predilection possessed the cow, and she needed no admonition to lie down under the trees of the roadside. Sam found a resting place for himself near by in the hollow of a fallen tree. There he would spend the night, not sleeping, of course, but thinking and planning for the future.

With his temper under control, Sam soon saw that there was nothing to be gained from his first mad impulse to hurry to The Head of the Lake, to pounce upon Heasley and confront him with his duplicity. Heasley was only half a man physically, but in dishonesty and hypocrisy he was a veritable giant. To meet him alone on his own ground would mean dismal failure; to turn back and put his case in the hands of a lawyer would never do. It was not his affair alone, and no matter how ready he himself might be to entangle himself with the law, and legal courts, he knew that the others away back on the

Heasley Tract would rather lose all than voluntarily subject themselves to such contamination from the world.

Sam cut off a twig from the tree and began to whittle. What if he should lose all of his hard-earned three hundred dollars, the savings of years of toil? What if he had to give up the three hundred acres that he had bought with the money, the new house that he had built on mortgaged land? He kept whittling harder and harder. What if he should lose Beccy? If she should consent to marry him, homeless and penniless as he was, what was he to do with her? They might starve together. Was that all the consolation life held for him?

Presently this exceedingly worried young man snapped the twig in two, slipped his knife into his pocket, stood up and shook himself. He had reached a decision. He would not starve. He would meet Robert Heasley alone—yes, even on his own ground, in his palatial home at The Head of the Lake—but never with the enemy's weapons. With a little sling and a few pebbles that he hoped he would find at the opportune moment, he would meet and slay this Goliath and deliver his people, and he and Beccy would live to tell the story to their children's children in the very valley of Elah.

It did not enter into Sam's impetuous head that it was necessary to ask divine coöperation in this newly-conceived plan of his. Of course he believed in prayer, but after the manner of impulsive people, it was his habit to act first, to think next, and to pray last. Then if the outcome had been anything like satisfactory, and if he happened to be thinking about the achievements of the day when he was conveniently on his knees at his evening devotions, he might insert a few words of laudation for the aid he did not solicit, and so add a saving, grateful note that could not help but please the ear of the Almighty.

But Sam did pray before he lay down that night, not the mechanical phrases he was accustomed to repeat—he never even thought of them—but a real petition that came from the depths of his burdened heart. "Oh, Lord, help me!" he cried. "Help me, oh, Lord!" He could say no more, for a great lump filled his throat and choked his utterance.

The muley heard the cry, started in alarm and bellowed. A night-owl heard it, and uttered an agonizing shriek that startled both man and beast. Through the woods the echoes sounded and resounded until it seemed a full chorus of unseen demons joining in a mocking laugh.

Sam looked up. He did not see the bird in the darkness, but through the branches of the trees there shone in all its glory a full, fat, harvest moon. Beccy's moon! But even as he gazed at it thinking of the girl, the plaguy screech of the uncanny owl made him think more of Beccy's aunt. Just so she would laugh when she heard the news, and wag her head to affect a sorrow she did not feel. With just such an ill-concealed note of exultation in her voice she would tell all the countryside; "I told them so." So between reminiscences pleasant and unpleasant, Sam tossed to and fro in the hollow of the tree he had chosen for his bed, until sleep finally came and drew the curtains of forgetfulness between him and his worries.

In the morning the muley was dead. There lay her gaunt form quite motionless on the grass with her long tongue protruding from between her teeth. Already a swarm of great black flies had congregated in anticipation of a feast.

Sam kicked the hated carcass contemptuously and sighed. Another cloud had appeared in his stormy sky, but this one had at least a silver lining. It was very gratifying to think that the death of the muley made it possible for him to suppress the whole story of Peter Potter and the auction sale. For the sum of fifteen dollars with which, sooner or later, he must reimburse his brother, he could keep both his secret and his reputation.

Empty-handed, he journeyed on, stopping occasionally for food and sleep. It was late in the afternoon of the third day when at last he came within sight of Heasley's house at The Head of the Lake.

A well-built, commodious building it was, in comparison with a certain log shanty on Heasley's Tract in the backwoods. Sam remembered how he and John had marvelled at it the day they had sealed their bargain. Such extravagant furniture they had never seen, such beautiful curtains, and carpets, such highly-polished brass andirons. But what interested Sam most of all was the spinet—music-box, he had called it. Before it had sat a lady in costly apparel, and with apparently no effort at all she had produced strange, jerky sounds, like, yet wholly unlike, the long-metered tunes he loved so well. She had sung a song to entertain them while Robert was writing the deeds. It was a gay sprightly thing that had tickled Sam's fancy at the time, but now the memory of it and of the affluence of the Heasleys filled his heart with deep, resentful gloom, as he walked resolutely up the path that led to the front door.

The Heasleys were aware of his approach. There was no question about that. He saw one of the curtains of the second storey move, and he could not help hearing the same gentle, well-modulated voice which had sung so sweetly, announce with a snarl; "Another Dutchman, Robert! Be sure he wipes his feet before you let him in. And whatever you do, don't ask him to stay to supper. I don't know why I should have to feed all those clowns from the backwoods. Do you hear?"

"Yes, dear," Sam heard the husband reply.

But when Robert Heasley came to answer Sam's knock, he totally disregarded his wife's commands. Quite effusively he drew the despised Dutchman over the threshold into the house without so much as a glance at the door-mat. "Yes, Heasley's my name," he said, before Sam had time to open his mouth. "From Pennsylvania, I judge. What part?"

"Lancaster County," replied Sam, as soon as he could regain his composure.

"And your name?"

"Sam Bricker."

"Bricker!" exclaimed Heasley. "There were two brothers by that name went up—let me see—it was in the spring of last year, I believe. One was married, he said, and a decent sort of fellow he was, too. The younger one had red hair. Looked a lot like you. A brother, perhaps?"

"No."

"A cousin, then?"

"No."

"But surely you know him. You Mennonites all seem to be connected in some way or another."

Just at this moment our David picked up his first little stone. "I know him better than most people," he said. Then in a voice pregnant with meaning, he added, "He cheats easy."

"You don't say so!" exclaimed Heasley, bristling with suspicion at the unexpected discovery he thought he had stumbled upon. "I must say I found him honest enough. But do sit down. This armchair. Let me take your hat. You'll stay for supper. There's always room for one more."

But Sam, to the infinite delight of Mrs. Heasley, who was listening intently at the top of the stairs, declined the invitation, and pulled his hat just a little farther down over his ears.

"Well, I won't urge you against your better judgment," said Heasley, "but what you have to say about this young Bricker interests me. Now that you have mentioned it, he did look as though he might be crooked. Something of a devil, I should say, if things didn't suit him."

"A devil!" shouted Sam. "Is that what you call him?" It was with difficulty that he kept his hands off the man.

"Not yet," said Heasley, laughing nervously. "But I don't suppose I'll be having any more dealings with him. He's back on the Tract in his little shanty, no doubt, and happy as a clam."

"A happy home, you think?" said Sam, from the depths of his burdened heart.

Heasley appeared a trifle confused, and suggested that they proceed to business. He got out the plan of the tract, unrolled it and spread it out on his desk for the inspection of the prospective buyer.

"That can wait," said Sam, thrusting it aside. "I don't want your mortgaged land." He paused and gazed steadily at Heasley until he had the satisfaction of seeing the colour come and go upon the face of the guilty man. The second stone had struck its mark.

"My word!" exclaimed Heasley, pulling himself together. "Who are you that you dare speak so to me?"

"I am the devil!" was the defiant reply.

"I don't doubt it for a minute," returned Heasley, affecting indifference. "You are that young Bricker, I suppose?"

"I'm the devil."

"Yes, yes," mocked Heasley. "You roar like one. I wasn't contradicting you."

Sam had only one stone left, a sharp one of accusation. He put it in his sling and hurled it vehemently at his enemy. "Give me back my three hundred dollars. You stole them!"

"Stole them, did I?" stammered Heasley. He was beginning to waver.

"The devil will have his own!" shouted Sam. He sprang from his chair and strode with determination to the other side of the desk where his enemy stood leaning against the spinet for support.

Heasley sank into a chair and sullenly watched the movements of the Mennonite out of the corner of his eye. Weakly he ordered Sam to leave the house. He might have saved his breath for Sam continued to stand with his back against the door, his arms akimbo, with teeth clenched and eyes afire, greedy to reap the spoils of victory.

At this moment a frightened female voice was heard calling: "Robert, dear, come here at once. I want you." Just so did the goddesses of mythology come to the aid of their heroes, when they found them overtaken in deadly conflict. "Come, Robert, I want you."

Under the spell of that voice, Heasley darted to the staircase and banged the door after him, evidently with some misgivings lest the Mennonite might include himself in his wife's timely invitation.

But Sam did not follow. He had, as they say, other fish to fry. He let himself noiselessly out of the front door and ran to the back. This he secured on the outside against any hope of Heasley's escape. Then he returned, and having taken the precaution to close all the windows, he resumed his stand before the front door, the one remaining exit to the ground floor of the house. Barring a jump from some upstairs window, a rather dangerous alternative for even the bravest of men, Heasley must sooner or later meet him there.

Fully half an hour Sam waited before he had the satisfaction of hearing a pair of heavy, masculine heels clanking down the stairs. When Heasley opened the door and entered the room, he wore an air of offended dignity. Something like that King John must have worn when his nobles forced him to sign the great charter.

"Here's an order for your three hundred dollars," said Heasley, shambling over to the desk and signing his name with the flourish that Sam had so often admired. "Here!"

But Sam would not touch it. "I want the money," he said stolidly.

"You have only to take this to York to get it," he said. He kept urging the paper upon the Mennonite, and finally in desperation he pushed it into his hand.

Without so much as looking at it, Sam tore it to ribbons.

"But I have no money in the house," protested Heasley. "You will have to give me time."

It sounded very plausible this excuse that Heasley had invented, and Sam suggested that he would be willing to go back to York to get the money if Heasley would go with him.

"Back!" exclaimed Heasley. "So you have been there?"

Sam acknowledged it.

"And was it there that you heard about the mortgage?"

Sam stated that he had been to the Registry-Office.

Heasley suppressed a sigh. "So you went as far as that, did you? Who sent you there? That's what I want to know."

Sam satisfied the man's curiosity with the information that it was Mr. Wilson who had told him.

"What! Wilson!" cried Heasley. "Not Jim Wilson?"

"Yes, him."

Heasley uttered a whole series of deep, sonorous groans interspersed here and there with muttered curses. "And who sent you to Wilson?" he demanded. "I'll get at the bottom of this."

"He came to me," replied Sam, and he told in detail how it came about.

Heasley was dumbfounded. He could scarcely believe his ears. "Opened the gate for you, did he? No, he's not crazy. He's no fool, but shrewd—shrewd as the devil." He stood piecing the threads of Sam's remarkable story in the secret recesses of his mind. Suddenly he started. He thought he saw a straw of suspicion floating, as it were, on his sea of trouble, and like a drowning man he clutched at it. "Where's this cow you were leading out when you think Wilson opened the gate for you?" he sneered. "Tell me that."

"She went dead."

"Went dead, did she? Where?"

"On the road."

Heasley laughed outright. "A very convenient death. Ha! Ha! Why don't you start writing stories? Too bad to bury an imagination like that in the backwoods."

Sam had to defend himself. He felt bound to substantiate his statements. Before Heasley had finished with him, he had dragged from him all the sordid details of his adventure with the infamous Peter Potter.

Heasley's spirits revived with the telling. A wicked gleam shone in his eyes. "What gullible people these Mennonites are," he thought, but aloud he said; "I am wondering how you are going to earn that fifteen dollars to pay your brother."

Sam said he did not know. It was worrying him considerably.

Heasley leaned towards the Mennonite and whispered his suggestion. He would give him back his three hundred dollars—and fifteen to boot—if he would go back to the tract and keep his mouth shut about the mortgage.

Sam straightened himself up and threw his head back proudly. "I would rather lose all I have—I'd rather die—than do that," he said.

Heasley sneered. "You decline my offer, then?"

"I want my money," said Sam, simply.

"And when you go back to the tract—?"

"I'll tell the others."

"And if I return the money to all of them, what then?"

Sam thought a moment and supposed they would all have to go back to Pennsylvania, or buy land somewhere else in Canada.

Heasley was a shrewd man. He did not propose to allow another man to reap the benefit of his dishonesty. He did not want a pack of Mennonites to bespatter his fair name, not, at least, until he had all his money out of the tract. He deliberated a moment, then made another proposition. "Raise the twenty thousand dollars," he said, "and I'll lift the mortgage and give you a clear title to the whole tract. Twenty thousand dollars for sixty thousand acres is not a bad bargain."

Sam gasped. Twenty thousand dollars was a fabulous sum to a man who was worried over fifteen dollars with which to reimburse his brother.

"Your friends in Pennsylvania have plenty of money," continued Heasley. "Go over there, get them to form a company and buy the tract. When the bargain is closed, you shall have five hundred acres of land in any unoccupied part of the tract you may choose. That's the best I can do."

Sam's eyes fairly danced with excitement. This was good news to take back to the tract. Here was the solution to their troubles, and an opportunity for Sam himself to come into possession of property in an honourable way. "I think I'll stop to dinner so we can talk about it," he said, to Mrs. Heasley's infinite disgust. "I couldn't eat much long already. The mortgage upset me so."

Because there was nothing else to be done about it, the disdainful lady of the house came downstairs and set an extra plate on her supper table for Sam Bricker. But whatever may have been her innermost feelings, her manner left nothing to be desired. Sam was much impressed with her dignified bearing, and his eyes followed her everywhere about the room. He was delighted when after the meal she sat down before the "music-box," and sang a lively tune.

Robert hovered near and tried to make himself agreeable. "She is very clever, my wife," he ventured to remark, seeing how Sam admired her.

"Ach, she's all right for you," was Sam's quite innocent reply. "But I have to have somebody that's a good cook."

"Did you ever hear the like?" sputtered Mrs. Heasley, when she stood with her husband at the front door speeding their parting guest. "He wants a good cook. Did you hear that, Robert?"

"Yes, and nearly exploded over it."

"Well, that settles it," blazed the irate lady. "That's the last Dutchman I'm going to feed."

"Cheer up, dear," said Heasley, as they entered the house. "It's not so bad as all that. He didn't seem very grateful, I know, but he paid you the compliment of eating everything in sight."

CHAPTER IX

When Sam Bricker reached the Heasley Tract and told his story, a terrible consternation fell upon the poor, deluded people. Was this the reward of the labours and sacrifices of many years, this the boasted justice and security they might expect at the hands of the British people? Would to God they had stayed in Pennsylvania where they might eat bread to the full. Why had they ever come to this foreign wilderness, this Canada of their dreams, now the land of blasted hopes?

But in spite of the desolation all about him, Sam Bricker refused to be dejected about the matter. He proclaimed the gospel of a better day. Heasley had made an excellent offer, he said. Twenty thousand dollars for sixty thousand acres, more or less, and two years to raise the money. If only the friends in Pennsylvania could see the land, it would be an easy matter. But even so, it was not impossible. A little information and a little persuasion was all that was necessary to transplant half the population of Pennsylvania into the narrow confines of the Heasley Tract.

Sam was, of course, naturally of a buoyant disposition. He never lost hope so long as he could control his temper, and there was no limit to the effort he would exert to realize his hopes. But never had he experienced such an opportunity as this to anchor his hope and determination on the promise of a wondrous reward. He had not forgotten that Heasley had offered him five hundred acres of land, if he would bring about the consummation of the bargain. A challenge had been thrown down. Sam decided that he would take it up. He would not only deliver the defrauded people, but he would wrest this great reward from the hands of the defrauder. He would win the five hundred acres, and incidentally he would enjoy another smack of adventure.

The first thing to do was to have himself appointed a representative of the dwellers on the Heasley Tract with a commission to go to Pennsylvania to solicit twenty thousand dollars. That was not as easy as it first appeared. It meant that he had to try out in Canada all the latent powers of persuasion from which he hoped at a later date to produce such phenomenal results with the people of the homeland. And Sam was too impulsive a man to adapt himself readily to the practice of so conciliatory an art.

With this secret motive in view, Sam called a meeting at John's house. Nominally it was for the purpose of discussing how the little company of deluded people were going to pull themselves out of the trap into which they had fallen by reason of their credulity. From every part of the tract they came, these victims of Heasley's roguery, the Betzners, the Gingerichs, Joseph Sherk, the Reicherts, the Livergoods, the Shupes, the Suraruses, the Rosenbergers, and George Clemens. Some waved their worthless deeds in noisy protest; others sat sullen and dejected, overcome with alarm too deep for words.

Sam stood up and told the story of his terrible discovery, the rumours of which had already spread like wildfire throughout the tract. For a very good and substantial reason, he suppressed all mention of certain events which loomed up large in his memory, but he enlarged upon his visit to the Registry-Office and the revelations which awaited him there. He told in detail the story of his encounter with Heasley, and ended with a glowing account of the wonderful bargain he had forced Heasley to offer because of his importunity.

"But Sam," said Old Sam Betzner, with bated breath. "Twenty thousand dollars! I never had that much money in all my life."

Sam insisted that it was a bargain. A chance to buy three acres for a dollar was worth looking into.

"But you can't buy even a bargain without money," argued the old man. "We haven't a dollar. He's took everything!" He sat in an armchair looking as if he had just interred the last remnant of hope.

Then Sam suggested the people of Pennsylvania. They would help, he was sure.

But the men shook their heads and refused to follow where Sam's optimism would lead them. "We mustn't look to them," they said. "They don't throw their money away."

Nothing that Sam could say influenced them in the slightest degree. They had settled down to a state of utter dejection. Some even talked about returning to Pennsylvania that fall. Still Sam refused to be discouraged, and clung obstinately to the secret hope that he cherished in his breast. In his heart of hearts he had made up his mind that it was he, and not they, who was going to Pennsylvania, and that right soon.

The following day a party was organized at Sam's instigation to explore the Heasley Tract from end to end. They spent a week tramping back and forth through the wilderness, and yet there were sections that they did not cover. No one could doubt but that it was a land of marvellous fertility of soil, a forest of inestimable worth, a goodly heritage.

"All for twenty thousand dollars," said Sam, significantly.

"But—"

"And we have two years to get the money."

But the men shook their heads again. If they had a lifetime it would still be utterly impossible.

Still Sam refused to be disheartened. He called another meeting to listen to a proposition which he was prepared to put before them. When they were all gathered in John's kitchen, he asked them to provide him with the names of twenty of the wealthiest and most influential of their friends in Pennsylvania. When the list was completed, he held it up before his audience and reckoned. "A thousand dollars from each, and they can buy the best tract in all Upper Canada."

"Ach, you, Sam—."

"And I'll go and fetch the money."

"What, you, Sam? Alone?" The tone they used was certainly not designed to be conducive to any dormant seeds of vanity that might have been lurking in Sam's palpitating breast.

"Nobody will go along," replied Sam, overlooking the implied lack of confidence. It had never entered his head that there was any need to share the responsibility—and the reward.

Joseph Sherk had been sitting on the wood-box listening intently to all that was going on, but saying little. It was he who shared with his brother-in-law, Young Sam Betzner, the honour of having been the first to penetrate into the wilds of the Heasley Tract. He was also the first that had stumbled into this pit that Heasley had dug, and he was deeply concerned about how he was going to get his young family out of it. He had come to the conclusion that Sam Bricker was right. There was no hope for them, unless help came from Pennsylvania. He heard Sam's equivocal reply, and he took the liberty of putting on it quite a different interpretation to the weak defence that Sam had intended. To the amazement of everybody, he stood up and said; "You don't have to go alone, Sam. I'll go along."

It was surprising to see how quickly the general opinion changed with this new turn of affairs. Those who were loudest in their declarations to return to Pennsylvania that very autumn now decided that they would "wait and see once if Joseph Sherk could make anything out." The two men were duly delegated to go to Pennsylvania and solicit help in the name of the dwellers on the Heasley Tract. Joseph Sherk was named first, and to him the helpless, hopeless people pinned all their faith. Sam was to accompany him, if he wished, but only with the understanding that he must at all times and in all things submit to the will of his superior.

It was a heavy blow for the impetuous youth, but he bore it manfully. He shook Joseph by the hand cordially enough, and said he was willing to agree to the terms as laid down by the men. He bore no malice; for then and there he told of Heasley's magnanimous offer of five hundred acres of land to the man who would consummate the deal; and he promised that when Joseph and he should come riding back to the Heasley Tract with the money, Joseph should not only have half the land but first choice of location. But the prospective recipient of these concessions—and, indeed, all the others—only smiled grimly at Sam's effervescent optimism. They weren't looking for rewards, they said. They would be thankful to their dying day if only they could get a clear title to their land, or failing that, the amount of their original investment.

And now the time had come for Sam to make a certain confession to his brother John. Sam had, quite intentionally, alas, given the impression that he had heard the calamitous news about the mortgage before he had thought of buying the cow. Nobody dreamed but that he still had the fifteen dollars safe in his possession, if, indeed, this greater anxiety allowed them to think of it at all. But Sam knew that some day the story of the muley that died by the wayside would break upon the community with a horrible stench and her hated skeleton would haunt him through the long avenue of the years. With confusion and shame he acknowledged his sin, but begged John to keep his secret at least until he was well upon his way to Pennsylvania. That and a little patience was all he asked. As soon as he could earn the money, he would pay him his fifteen dollars with accrued interest.

John sighed and shook his head. Was there ever such a fellow as Sam? Oh, why had he ever listened to the babbling of this scatter-brained brother of his? Through him he had lost everything. Here he was stranded, penniless, in a strange land with a delicate wife and a troop of children on his hands. Where in the world was it going to end? "Ach, Sam! Sam!" was all he could say.

Sam knew the thoughts of his heart. "It ain't goin' to end like you think anyways," he told John. "Chust wait till I come back."

It was decided that Joseph Sherk and Sam Bricker were to start off for Pennsylvania on horseback the following Monday morning. At his first opportunity, Sam hurried to the barn to tell Menno about it. It was purely a business trip, he said, but he smiled as he patted Menno's white mane and whispered a name they both held dear. It was evident that Sam and Menno had secret business which would entail a visit to Hammer Creek—and Beccy.

Sunday came. The distressed people gathered as usual for worship. With tears in their eyes they prayed for the success of this expedition. Would God in His mercy incline the hearts of their friends in the homeland, so that they would come to their relief? Wisdom and favour with the people they invoked on behalf of Joseph and Sam that their case might not be weakened in the telling. Nor did they forget Robert Heasley, the man who had betrayed them. Oh that the great wonder-working God would strike his hard heart with His hammer of conviction, and would dissolve it into penitence, so that he might cry aloud for forgiveness and find rest for his sin-cursed soul. Weak and impotent they were of themselves, but they were the children of the mighty God. They had brought their case to Him; they were willing to leave it now in His hands; His will, not theirs, be done.

Fortified with these earnest petitions, Joseph Sherk and Sam Bricker started off early the next morning to do all that was humanly possible to help the Almighty perform a mighty miracle.

In all the history of the country there never were such melancholy days as those that visited the dwellers on the mortgaged Heasley Tract during the fall of 1803. The clouds hung thick and heavy, and rain fell for days at a time. The wind moaned in the trees; the sun refused to shine. A terrible gloom seemed to have fallen like a pall over all the land. The treachery of Robert Heasley filled their minds with despondency. The story of Sam's scandalous doings in York had leaked out, and now Heasley's perfidy was overshadowed by the garrulous Peter Potter and his equally successful methods. Robert Heasley! Peter Potter! The world was full of such rogues. Sam Bricker was nothing but a broken reed swaying in the wind. If by any chance he and Joseph should obtain the twenty thousand dollars, there was sure to be some unscrupulous man waiting to appropriate it before it reached either Heasley or his tract. So between the misfortunes that had actually befallen them and those which were bound to overtake them in the future, the people gave themselves up to deep despair.

But there was one person on the Tract who saw in this gloom the promise of better days. Annie Bricker had never been happy since the day she left Pennsylvania. She had never been a robust woman and she had not recovered from the mental and physical strain which the journey to Canada had occasioned. She longed for the homeland with an inexpressible yearning. She had "the homesick." Not even the geranium slips which Rachael had thrust into her hand at The Twenty had availed to ward it off. She hated Canada with an undying hatred, she declared. She would never be happy again until she could go back to her old home in Pennsylvania and live among the friends of her childhood.

With her homesickness, Annie was becoming "queer." At every opportunity she would wander off into the bush alone. John noticed and grew apprehensive. He followed her secretly one day to her retreat and watched her in a few moments of abandonment. On the summit of a little hill she had built a tower of refuge—not a rampart with battlements—but a little enclosure cleared of underbrush by her own hands and surrounded by a fence of her own making. There she had planted Rachael's geraniums, and there in the midst of her garden she had fashioned a little seat. Far below, the river flowed with many a graceful curve, beautiful in either direction. But Annie did not look to the north. Her eyes and her thoughts wandered with the water away to the south. She stretched out her arms towards the homeland; she lifted her eyes to the sky. Somewhere beyond that blue vault was God, but very inaccessible He seemed, very indifferent to her cry.

Every day the unhappy woman visited the spot, and poured out her soul to Pennsylvania and to God. Nor did she cease to visit her little garden sanctuary when at last it seemed as though her prayers might be answered. The frost killed her flowers; the brown leaves invaded her holy enclosure; the wind blew cold and strong; nature was buried beneath a blanket of snow; but the little ray of hope that had been kindled in her heart lived on. God had heard, and in His own good time He would answer her prayer.

But one day—it was near the end of January—Annie did not so much as think of her retreat on the hill-top. She couldn't think about anything all day long, except Little Johnny, who tossed and tumbled about in his bed, muttering all sorts of incoherent things in his delirium. The night before he had complained of a sore throat, and Annie had wrapped his stocking around his neck, patted his cheek and told him he would be better in the morning. But he got worse, and when at daybreak she looked into his throat, she saw that it was swollen and inflamed. There were two large, white spots.

"Dip-theria!" gasped John.

Annie sighed.

John staggered to the nearest chair and hid his face in his hands. Was it possible that he was going to lose Little Johnny, too?

"Don't let Moses and Noah get his breath," cried Annie, "and shove Leah's cradle a little off." Then she lapsed into a terrible silence. She refused to leave the sick-room, but wandered about dejectedly, tucking in the covers when the boy kicked them out, and bathing his face and hands with warm water.

"Let me do it," said John, but Annie did not hear. With face as white as any sheet, she hovered over the sick-bed and continued her silent ministry.

John had to dress the other children and prepare the breakfast. But when he tried to eat, the food stuck in his throat, and when he carried a plate to Annie, she pushed it away without a word.

If there was only something John could do to help—. There was. The sulphur! Why hadn't he thought of it before? He called all the children into the bedroom and came himself, bearing a shovelful of burning coals from the fireplace in one hand and a tin can in the other. He closed the door and commanded them all to open their mouths— wider—as wide as they possibly could. Noah and Moses sat side by side on the chest, looking like a pair of nestlings ready for a worm. Leah thought it was a game and she stretched her little mouth to its utmost capacity. Then the father dropped the yellow powder from the box, not into their waiting mouths but on the glowing coals. A blue smoke rose and pervaded the room.

Noah's eyes were bulging with wonder. He closed his little, disappointed mouth and opened it again to cry out; "What are you doin', pop?"

"Killin' the dip-theria."

"Dip-theria? What's that?"

"It's what will kill you, if we don't kill it," was the explanation John offered. He kept pouring the contents of the box upon the shovelful of fire.

"It's killin' me!" shrieked Moses, springing up from the chest and rushing madly about the room.

"Me, too!" gasped Noah, rubbing his eyes with his fists and coughing like to crack his little throat.

Leah didn't like this new game that they were playing, but she wasn't going to give up. She danced and pranced with the others about the room.

"Keep your mouths open," commanded John, continuing to feed the blue flame now and then with the contents of his magic box. "It'll soon go dead now."

Annie always blamed the sulphur as much as the diphtheria for the death of Little Johnny. The poor little fellow coughed away all his strength, she said. Day by day he grew weaker and weaker. The neighbours brought all their home-made remedies, and Annie poured them down his throat, but it was all of no avail. At the eleventh hour Christian Reichert came and charmed him. But the Angel of Death had already set His seal upon the boy. Little Johnny turned his face to the wall, and closed his eyes forever upon this weary world.

The grief of the parents knew no bounds. Little Johnny was the most precious lamb of their little fold. What fond hopes they had entertained for him! And now he was cold—dead. They must bury his body in this foreign, mortgage-cursed land. When in the spring they should turn their faces to the south, they must leave him there alone. That was the thought that wrung their hearts.

Young Sam Betzner came over to help dig the first grave on the Heasley Tract. Quite near the house they turned the sod, but Annie stopped them. She would show them, she said, the spot where his dear body must lie. Through the forest she led them to the hallowed enclosure on the hill. Then she sank into the little seat and watched the men dig a great, ugly, black hole in the ground. Her own grave, it seemed, to the disconsolate woman.

And there they buried all that was mortal of Little Johnny,—there where the river that flowed to the south murmured by and where the flowers would bloom again in the spring, though all who loved them would be far away. Only the birds would come, perhaps, and perch upon the seat, and sing a song over his poor, little, neglected grave.

In the weeks that followed a terrible epidemic spread throughout the land. It was as if a hideous monster, having tasted Little Johnny's blood, now stalked about seeking whom else it might devour. There was scarcely a family into which it did not push its hated presence, scarcely a home that it left without a grave. On every hand was heard the dismal wail of despair. It was more than the disheartened people could stand. Was God dead, or why had He forsaken them?

Into a world of deepest gloom the second Little Johnny Bricker was born. He was a puny child, not made to face the rigours of a Canadian winter. In the spring he would be stronger, the women said, trying to look cheerful for Annie's sake. But in less than a month they had to put his little body in a box and bury it beside the grave of the original Little Johnny, the brother whom he had never seen.

Annie's heart was all but broken. When the last guest had departed after the funeral, she wrapped herself in her great shawl and wandered off alone for the first time in months to her little garden graveyard on the hill. She stood beside the new-made graves, sobbed and sighed. How cold their little bodies must be with not even a blanket of snow to cover them. If she could only fold them to the warmth of her bosom. "Oh, God!" she cried, throwing an agonizing glance to the blue skies above and bursting into a torrent of tears. She dropped into the seat at the foot of the graves and buried her face in her hands, while her whole frame shook with pent-up emotion.

Suddenly she felt a presence. A voice sweet as an angel's was calling her name. A great peace overwhelmed her. Ah, God was still with her.

"Annie!"

She looked up and saw—not an angel—but John leaning over her. His great arm tightened around her shoulders. "You!" she exclaimed. "Is it chust you?"

John tried his best to console her. "It's hard, I know," he said, very softly.

Annie's head dropped on her husband's bosom. "You don't know how hard it is," she sobbed. "If I could only go, too—".

"You can, when your time comes, Annie," was the gentle reply.

"But I didn't want you to know," wailed Annie.

That was the trouble with Annie, John said. She tried to bear her troubles alone. If she would only let him share them. His own heart was breaking with grief; but above and beyond that he had a worry that was crushing him, a worry that Annie knew nothing about.

Annie started, and looked up into John's face with wondering, frightened eyes.

"It's you, Annie," he whispered. "I am afraid I might lose you, too. Then what would I do?"

Annie was quiet for a moment and then she said; "And I didn't even think about you, John." She dropped her head again on her husband's shoulder and let him draw her very close into the shelter of his arms. A strange glow warmed her heart. There beside the little graves she had found happiness—true happiness—such happiness as she had never before known in all her life.

111

Another month of the snow and ice of winter lay before the anxious dwellers on the Heasley Tract. To the gloom of sorrow was added the dread of starvation. The supplies which the provident women had stored away against the winter-time were getting low. For months they had been saving the parings of potatoes for planting in the spring, and now even the parings must go if they would save their lives. When things came to their worst they went to Coote's Paradise without any grist and begged for flour. They would pay when they could.

In April Joseph Sherk returned. One glance at his face and the last lingering hope died away. He had visited Franklin and Cumberland Counties, he said, calling upon all the wealthy men he knew, but with no success. They would not listen to his entreaties. Some had even laughed at their plight, though they claimed to wish them well. If they had money to throw away, why should they send it to Canada to enrich a man who had already proved himself a rogue? There were plenty of good causes in the United States, at their very doors. Better pack up and come to Pennsylvania, they advised. If they did, they should not want for sympathy and support.

"Where is Sam?" asked John Bricker, with a sigh. "Is he sick, mebbe?"

"Ach, Sam," replied Joseph. "He thinks he knows a man in Lancaster County that might help. Christian Eby is his name."

"He might," John allowed, "if she would leave him. But she won't. If Sam's went there, he'll take Eliza Hoffman and her farm, and we won't see him no more."

So every hope of help was abandoned, and preparations were made at once to leave the tract. Some determined to try their fortunes with the Moyers, the Kolbs, the Honsbergers, and the Albrights at The Twenty, while others were resolved to push farther into the wilds of Upper Canada. But the Brickers, the Betzners, the Sherks, and George Clemens chose to return to Pennsylvania. Early in the morning of the fifteenth of May they were to set out together for the homeland.

The conestogas were brought forth and drawn up before the houses and the packing began. But this time there was no happy, buoyant heart in all the company. The spirit of adventure was dead in them; they had failed.

On the thirteenth of May, just two days before the date set for the departure, two conestogas loaded to capacity drove up to John Bricker's door. They contained the families and all the worldly goods of Annie's two brothers, Daniel and Jacob Erb. They had come to settle, they said, preferably among their own people from the Hammer Creek community. The news of trouble on the Heasley Tract surprised them beyond measure. But they were not going back to Pennsylvania, not they. Weren't there other lands in Canada just as good as the Heasley Tract? They entreated John and Annie to stay in Canada, and offered to lend them money to start again in some other tract.

But John shook his head. No matter what were his own inclinations in the matter, he must think of Annie and her wishes. He must take her back home.

Annie acted very "queer" on that last day they were to spend in Canada. She scarcely spoke to her husband or to her brothers, but walked like a ghost among them. When evening came on, John saw her take the trail that led to her retreat on the hill. "Poor Annie," he thought, "she has the homesick so."

But Annie did not see the river that flowed to the south, did not stretch out her arms to the land of her birth. She stumbled into the little enclosure and fell prostrate between the two little mounds that marked the last resting-places of her children. She poured out her heart in tears and prayers.

John was anxious. He came and knelt beside her. He put his arm protectingly about her.

"Ach, John, I can't let them here," she wailed. "I can't go away and let them here."

John racked his brain for some consoling thought. They must mark the graves, he said. Some day, perhaps, they would come back and see them. But in his heart of hearts he knew that it was foolish talk. When morning dawned again they would turn their backs upon the Heasley Tract and the two little graves on the hill-top, never to see them again.

But the idea took hold of Annie's more sentimental nature. Yes, they must mark the graves, not with slabs of wood or stone—they were so cold and lifeless—but with something that would live and grow like her memories throughout the years. A young sapling was the very thing. They would plant it together between the graves. In time it would become a mighty oak tree. The more it stretched its limbs up towards the heavens, the deeper would it send its roots into the earth, until at last they would encircle the bodies of her children in place of their absent mother's arms.

To humour her, John planted the tree. But he was more anxious about Annie than he cared to confess. He was glad they were going back to Pennsylvania, and he hoped that when she got back among her friends, Annie would not have such "queer" thoughts.

CHAPTER X

No sooner was the frost out of the ground in the spring of 1804 than building operations were begun on the Hammer Creek homestead. The buildings already standing were numerous and commodious enough, one would have thought, to meet any emergency, but Hannes had long been meditating upon a proposition which would entail the erection of a new building, quite in a class by itself. And now he had decided to build it.

He had worked hard all his life, Hannes had. True, he had come by a large farm and a substantial home from his father, but it required much effort to maintain it. So much time had to be spent in the business of making a living and of skimping and saving for a possible rainy day that Hannes found very little time to really live. By living, he meant sitting down in the quiet of an evening and forgetting all the cares of his own life, as he read of the lives of the strange people of other lands, their history, and their customs. Hannes Eby would surely have been a great traveller and a profound scholar, except for the fact that he had been born a Pennsylvania Dutch farmer.

But the privileges that had been denied him, Hannes was determined to make possible for others. What education he had acquired, only with the greatest effort and sacrifice, he would put within easy reach of the generation that was growing up about him. The building which he was about to erect was to be his contribution to the great cause of public education, the first rural school in Lancaster County.

Old Christian Eby was delighted beyond words with the idea. He was proud of his family and intensely interested in any enterprise which they undertook for the public weal. Not even when the hands of the brethren had been laid upon Peter, his eldest son, in ordination to the bishopric had he found greater satisfaction than he did now when Hannes, his second, assumed this great responsibility in the interests of a cause which he believed to be—one of his "dumm" Eby notions, Nancy said—the handmaiden of religion.

Benj was now his father's chief concern, "der gle' Bench," the youngest and most beloved of all his sons. He was still young, not yet of age, slight of frame and quite unsuited physically to strenuous labour on the farm. Most of his time he spent in his father's cooperage, making barrels for a grist-mill in the neighbourhood. But that was only a temporary occupation, the old man hoped. Every day he prayed that this son of his, this Benjamin of his old age, might be constrained to enter the Christian ministry and eventually become a great bishop, whose name and fame should be handed down to future generations of Mennonites in that far-off country which an unkind fate had prevented him from seeing—Canada, the land of his dreams.

But Benj Eby had no intention of becoming a preacher—much less a bishop. What little inclination he had felt towards Canada had died away with the sound of the wagon-wheels when the Brickers had driven away into obscurity, and had never been heard of again. The height of Benj's ambition was to be a teacher in Hannes' new school, to marry presently—if Mary Brubacher would have him—and to settle down somewhere among his own people in the Hammer Creek community.

Old Christian hid his disappointment saying that "der gle' Bench" had chosen a noble calling, and one which might some day lead him into an even greater field of activity. He was glad to help pay the boy's salary and board him for nothing. But he refused to relinquish his great ambition for him. Not a day passed but he hoped and prayed in secret that God would in some mysterious way bring to fruition the seeds which he had endeavoured to plant in the boy's heart. Nevertheless, in this, as in all other things, the Lord's will be done.

So while Benj continued to work in the cooperage by day, he spent his evenings with his books. He was planning a course of study which would introduce the prospective pupils to the A.B.C.'s, and lead them by easy stages through the pleasant pastures of learning, until ultimately they should stand with him upon dizzy intellectual heights. A great responsibility, and a wonderful privilege, without a doubt, but at the same time a marvellous opportunity for self-advancement and culture.

But frequently Benj was not alone when he sat late into the night and studied at the kitchen table of the "doddy-house." Sometimes Beccy sat beside him and borrowed light from his candle. While he studied, she sewed. Scarcely a word was interchanged between them. What did Beccy care for "readin' and writin' and 'rithmetic?" Her thoughts were all of Sam. The two years of waiting were almost spent.

He would come for her soon, and when he did, he would find her and her "aus styer" ready.

The "aus styer" is the Pennsylvania Dutch name for an institution which enters into the experience of most young women contemplating matrimony. But while it often entails a display of costly china, cabinets of silver, and embroidered linens for the bride to take with her into her new home, to Beccy—poor, little orphaned Mennonite girl, as she was—it meant only a collection of hand-patched quilts, a few rag mats which her own hands and ingenuity had woven and a supply of homespun towels which she had made in anticipation of her marriage. Whenever she finished a piece, she packed it away in her little chest, an unpretentious piece of furniture which she cherished, partly because it had once belonged to her father, but mostly because it was the only thing she possessed in all the world that had not been bestowed upon her by the odious hand of charity. That little, cedar chest! When she looked at it and thought of Eliza Hoffman, she sighed—it was so insignificant in comparison with her wealth—but when she opened it and thought of Sam, no words could ever express the happiness that filled her heart and shone in her face.

When March drew to a close and still there was no word of Sam, Beccy could not help but be anxious. After all he might not come, might never come. He was dead, possibly, or worse still, dead to her. Perhaps he was tired of waiting and had found some other girl. Sam was such an impulsive young man.

All the time, although the girl did not dream it, Sam was hastening to her side. She sat one evening with Benj, putting the last stitches into a mat which could yet be squeezed into her chest. Not a word was spoken. All was quiet, save for the laboured breathing of the old people asleep in the adjoining room.

Suddenly the dog barked.

"What's that?" said Benj, starting up from his reading.

"It's him!" cried Beccy, dropping her needle in her excitement and quite forgetting to pick it up again.

"Who?"

"Sam!"

And Sam it was. No, he would not come in. He was on his way to Brickerville, but he had seen the light and he could not refrain from looking in for a minute. He wondered who would be up at that hour of the night and what they could possibly be doing.

Beccy flushed, and pushed the mat under the table. For her life she couldn't have told why she did it. Her tongue was tied so that she could not speak. A strange presentiment of trouble overcame her. Instinctively she knew that something was wrong, but she could only stare blankly at Sam.

Benj had pulled him in. The next minute Hannes and Lizzie, half-dressed, had joined the company. They plied Sam with innumerable questions that he could not have answered in a week.

If Sam thought he was going to satisfy their curiosity that evening with general assurances of the health and well-being of the Brickers, he did not know the Ebys. They begged him for the story of his adventures; they insisted, until at last he yielded. How they hung on his words as he tried to describe the Alleghanies, the arduous trekking through the forests with their conestogas, and the terror of the wild animals. How they opened their eyes with wonder as he told of the thundering Niagara, the giant growth of the timbers, the wealth of the rivers, and the marvellous fertility of soil. And how sympathetic they became when he tried to define that indescribable sensation of loneliness which none but pioneers can ever fully understand.

"Did Annie get the homesick, tell me that," demanded a woman's voice from behind the bedroom door. It was Nancy, of course, who was anxious to join in the conversation without the inconvenience of dressing.

Sam hesitated.

"If she's got it, it serves her right, and if she hasn't, I hope she gets it." She lifted the latch to emit this gust of opprobrium. "Has she got it, eh?"

Sam had to confess that Annie was suffering from that affliction.

The unsympathetic one cooed with satisfaction. "I told her so, but she wouldn't hear to it," she said. "You'll come that way, too, Beccy, do you hear?"

Beccy bit her lip. She wanted nothing so much in all the world as a place to hide her burning face. She stole a confused glance at Sam, but he was not even looking in her direction. Her heart gave a terrible thump. Couldn't they see that something was wrong?

"When are you goin' back, Sam?" asked Hannes. "The ploughin'."

"Yes," replied Sam, looking at the copper caps on the toes of his cow-hide boots.

"And then the sowin'," continued Hannes. "Or don't you have to sow at all in that wonderful Canada land? Does the potatoes chust grow hillfuls in the cellars without plantin'?"

Sam had nothing to say. Those copper toe-caps fascinated him. If he would, what a story he could tell of treasured potato parings and threatened starvation. But there was plenty of time for that.

Sam's hesitation did not escape Nancy's observation. "Mebbe you ain't goin' back at all," she suggested, thrusting her head out of the door and making a frantic effort at the same time to conceal her night-gown. "Have you got some sense by now? Did you come to stop, Sam?"

Sam swallowed a lump in his throat and said: "dunno."

"You dunno!" ejaculated Nancy, opening the door a little wider and filling the whole aperture with her portly white-clad figure. "You stop in bed, Christian Eby," she called back into the room, when the bed creaked suspiciously. "You'll ketch your death of cold. No, Sam ain't goin' back."

Sam did his best to protest, but he did not know what to say. He mumbled some incoherent thing without the least bit of assurance, and looked again at his boots. It was so unlike Sam.

"Eliza Hoffman ain't took yet," insinuated Nancy, "and look at the farms she's got."

Still Sam was speechless.

"But Beccy—" gasped Lizzie.

"Never you mind about Beccy," sniffed Nancy. "Her folks never did have nothin'—nothin' but debts."

"But her 'aus styer'—" persisted Lizzie. "It's all ready, and it's nice."

Beccy had stood all she could. She hid her face in her hands and rushed from the room. She did not stop until she reached her bed-room upstairs. There before her little cedar chest she fell, dropped her arms upon it, and sobbed as if her heart would break. In all her un-happy, orphaned life she had never endured such unutterable disappointment and chagrin. What a cruel world it was that had snatched her cup of happiness from her very lips and dashed it, and her, into a sea of despair.

It was not until the next morning at the breakfast table that the Eby family learned the real purpose of Sam's coming and were able to put a correct interpretation upon his strange behaviour. Hannes came over to the "doddy-house" and announced that there would be a meet-ing in the forenoon of the following day to listen to a financial proposition which Sam had come all the way from Canada to make.

"What did I say last night already, Christian?" broke in Nancy. "I said Sam's got trouble, and now we hear it's money trouble!"

Without so much as noticing the interruption, Hannes proceeded to relate how he had gone to the door with Sam the evening before and heard more of his cousin's experiences. It had been too late to learn all the particulars but this much he knew—the Mennonites had been cheated. The land which they had bought belonged to a tract of sixty thousand acres encumbered, as Sam had discovered, with a mortgage of twenty thousand dollars, and the landowner had promised a clear title to the land on condition that they should raise enough money to lift the mortgage.

Having given this information to his father's family, Hannes now set out on horseback to impart it to all the others of their religious circle. He did not return until he had obtained a promise from each head of a family to come to the meeting and discuss the matter. It certainly would be a unique, and it promised to be an eventful occasion.

"We must help them," said Christian Eby for the third time that morning before Nancy appeared to hear. The old man was so nervous and distraught that he could not sit still, but he kept bobbing back and forth in the kitchen and getting into everybody's way.

"And why must we help them?" said Nancy at length. "Tell me that."

"Well, we urged them to go," replied Christian, doggedly. "It's all our fault."

"Yours, you mean," snapped Nancy. "Didn't I do my best to get them dumm notions out of all your dumm heads? But no—I don't know nothin'—never nothin'."

Christian did not reply, but he continued to pace about the room.

"And you sicked Beccy on Sam, too, you did," the infuriated woman went on. "She's no woman for a poor man like Sam. And look at all the time she's wasted with that 'aus styer.'" She waved her arm dramatically as if to display a long procession of fruitless hours.

It was all too much for Christian. Before noon he had developed an affection of the stomach and had to be helped to bed. He was now fully persuaded that as chief instigator of this Canada movement, the blame lay unconditionally at his door, and if retribution could be made to the Brickers, he was the one to do it. He entreated Nancy to send for Sam, but she only shook her head. He tried to get out of bed to go to Brickerville himself, but this domineering wife of his shoved him back in again with her inexorable arm.

Next morning the old man was worse. He no longer had any inclination to get out of bed. Indeed, he was too weak to move. Nancy was concerned, but by no means displeased. She was profoundly thankful that this indisposition of Christian's was severe enough to preclude his attendance at the meeting. Providence was evidently conspiring with her to protect this whole-hearted, open-handed husband of hers from any possibility of financial support to the deep-laid schemes of improvident men.

From the bedroom window Nancy watched Sam Bricker and the other men gather for the meeting. She could hear them move the chairs in the front room of the big house, and sit down. They were singing, kneeling. Peter was leading in prayer. She could hear him telling the Lord that this was no ordinary meeting and that they wanted everything that was done in it to redound to His glory. They would leave it all in His hands, Whose they were and Whom they tried to serve.

Another shuffling of chairs announced that the time had come for Sam to speak. Nancy glanced at Christian. His eyes were closed; he was breathing heavily. On tiptoe she stole from the room and found her way to the kitchen of the big house. From that place of vantage she could not only hear but see all that was going on without the disadvantage of being seen.

Sam Bricker had stood up and was beginning his address. He was no orator, Nancy could see that, a man of action rather than of words, but for all that he had the sympathy of all his audience. Soon he forgot himself and his limitations, and thought only of the cause he represented. Expressive gestures came to his aid when words failed him, and no one so much as noticed the omission. His hearers seemed to feel the impact of even those words which he had not the power to speak.

It was a graphic picture the young man presented. From the day on which he had said good-bye to this his coming again, he had endured two long years of care and anxiety, privation and want. There were giants in the land. Prowling wolves and howling wild-cats were a terror by day, as well as by night. Famine had already stared them full in the face, and forest fires might at any moment destroy their hard-earned homes. But after all it was a goodly land. In the years to come it would be to their children's children a land flowing with milk and honey. The Heasley Tract comprised sixty thousand acres of the best land in Upper Canada. True, a mortgage hung over it like a pall, but even that would eventually, he predicted, prove a blessing in disguise. The land was cheap at three times twenty thousand dollars, and the British Government was an institution which could be depended upon, they knew by experience, to keep its sacred promise to the people called Mennonites. He challenged them to go up into the land, for they were well able to possess it. The Lord Jehovah would be with them as truly as He had been with the Israelites of old.

So far all was well, but Sam blundered at the strategic point. He was too innately honest to conceal any of the facts of the case. He told how the settlers on the Tract had appointed Joseph Sherk and himself to go and appeal to the people of Pennsylvania for help, how together they had gone from one community to another throughout Franklin and Cumberland Counties, but had met with nothing but disappointment and discouragement on every hand. In despair Joseph Sherk had returned to Canada, while he had come to Hammer Creek to make this final appeal for aid from his own friends and relationship.

Then the shrewd business heads began to wag ominously. They began to see the proposition in another light. They were asked to consider what others had judged a poor investment. Neither Sam Bricker nor his father had been a tower of financial strength in the community. The land was at best a tract of uncultivated soil, in a foreign country, and its owner had already proved himself a scoundrel. Their fathers and grandfathers had not bought land in that wise.

Even before the vote was taken, Sam knew that he had failed. He sat down with a heavy heart and listened to the trite words of Peter, the Bishop, offering on behalf of the Hammer Creek community to the dwellers on the Heasley Tract the consolation of their prayers.

Now Sam had been taught to believe that the fervent effectual prayer of a righteous man availeth much. That Peter was a righteous man there could be no doubt, but somehow he did not put a shred of confidence in his promised petitions. It was not prayers he had come from Canada to solicit. Away back on the Heasley Tract righteous men and true had for weeks been besieging the Throne of Grace with fervent prayers for his success. The last opportunity for the fulfilment of these prayers had passed, and they were still unanswered. What was the use of praying anyway? If God would not grant the earnest entreaties of an innocent, betrayed people, was He likely to heed the petitions offered as a compensation by one comparatively disinterested in their fulfilment?

But Sam was, as usual, too hasty in his judgments. Even at the eleventh hour the Lord did answer the prayers of His distressed people. The Bishop was about to pronounce the benediction when Hannes Eby gave a sign of dissent, walked to the front of the room and asked permission to say a few words on a subject that was near to the hearts of all of them.

Nancy pricked up her ears and wondered what was going to happen now.

Hannes then reached for his Bible on the shelf and turned the pages over until he found the words; "He that hath pity on the poor lendeth to the Lord, and that which he hath given, will He repay him again." This he announced as a sort of text, a pivot, upon which he wished to hang a few remarks.

"A sermon!" gasped Nancy. "Hannes ain't no preacher!"

But preacher or no, Hannes had a message to deliver. He did not think they had considered Sam's proposition in the right light. Instead of looking upon it as a mere speculation to enrich themselves, which in all likelihood it would not do, they ought, he thought, to regard it as their Christian duty to assist, if possible, their friends in distress. If it yielded them no financial profit, they would at least be doing their duty, an act which the Lord might in His own good time bless in a way none of them thought of. He would leave it to each man's conscience what he ought to do, but he felt constrained to express his own views on the matter. He hoped there were others who felt as he did.

A new light shone in Sam Bricker's face. His eyes sparkled with hope.

"I want to help our brethren in Canada. I feel it is my duty." It was Christian Eby who spoke. His voice was physically weak but morally defiant.

Nancy started to her feet. She saw her husband standing in the doorway, and she attempted to reach him by a circuitous route. But when she came to the spot where she thought he was, she saw him up in the midst of an enthusiastic crowd of men, away up near the front, and saying by so doing that he was willing to lend his money unto the Lord.

"Dumm!" muttered Nancy. "What won't that man do all yet, if I ain't there to stop him?" Once again in their long marital experience the tables had been turned, Nancy had been outwitted and the Eby stupidity prevailed. When the meeting was closed with a short prayer of thanksgiving, Christian Eby stood before her triumphantly waving a piece of paper in his hand. He read it to her later without a quaver in his voice: "Christian Eby, $,."

Nancy did not invite Sam to stay at the "doddy-house" for dinner; but he overlooked the little omission; helped himself to a plate

123

from the cupboard; and squeezed in beside Benj. In spite of his aunt's glowering face that met his eyes every time he looked up, he was hilariously happy. He joked about everything and kept Beccy's radiant face suffused with becoming blushes. He stayed for supper, too, not an invited but a tolerated guest, as far as Nancy was concerned. It seemed like old times, said Christian, who insisted that he was well enough to eat with the family. This was for him the happiest day in years.

In the evening when the different members of the family circle had retired one by one, Beccy was left alone with Sam.

"You don't want me to go yet, do you, Beccy?" said the happy lover.

Beccy smiled. "You know you durst stop so long as you otherwise can," she said, pointing to the door behind which their Aunt Nancy was probably at that moment pressing an eavesdropping ear. It was one of their little jokes, this ungracious permission of Nancy's that had brought them so much happiness.

They talked for a while in whispers, and then Sam said; "Fetch your shawl once, Beccy, I want to see how the old apple-tree looks."

Hand in hand they walked out into the garden and stood on the spot where the bench had held them on that memorable night when they had first confided to each other their love. Again the man's strong right arm encircled her shoulders, and again they renewed their plighted troth.

"It ain't grand, Sam—my 'aus styer,'" said Beccy. "Now if it was Eliza Hoffman—"

Sam pressed his hand gently over Beccy's mouth. "Eliza Hoffman," he scoffed, "who wants her and her 'aus styer'? I'm sick of her!"

"But Eliza is a nice girl," protested Beccy.

"Nobody wants her with all her farms, it seems," replied Sam.

Beccy reached up and buttoned Sam's coat a little tighter about his neck. "It's her own fault," she affirmed. "She won't take them. She wants you."

Sam made a gesture of impatience. "It's a good thing we are going so soon away," he said. "Till next week we must go."

"Ach, Sam," murmured Beccy, and she clung to this man whom she loved better than all the world beside.

They had moved slightly, and now around the corner of the house they saw low on the horizon a great, full-orbed moon. It was actually smiling at them, and nodding with approval. "Glad to see you two there again," it seemed to say. "My blessing on you both!"

Then Sam told Beccy what the moon had meant to him during the lonely hours of his absence from her. He never looked at it but it brought him sweet memories of a certain lovely girl at Hammer Creek. If it happened to be full, he stayed up half the night, living over again a certain, very happy experience.

Beccy tapped this amorous swain of hers on the arm and called him a silly boy.

A shadow of disappointment passed over Sam's face at this gentle reproof. "Why, I thought—" he started to say, and then he paused and looked foolish.

"What did you think, Sam?"

"I thought you was lookin' at it, too. It always felt like that."

Beccy tittered.

"So I was, Sam," she confessed. "Ain't we the pair of silly geese?"

When Sam told Beccy that within a week they were to be on their way to Canada, he had no idea of the difficulties that were yet to be encountered before he could set out with the twenty thousand dollars that were to bring deliverance to the anxious people on the Heasley Tract. Meeting after meeting had to be called to decide all sorts of perplexing questions that continued to crop up.

In the first place there was the matter of the division of the shares. With Christian's offer of $, as a basis, it was agreed that there were to be eight such shares. The maximum investment was fixed at one share, and the minimum at one eighth of a share. Benj Eby was detailed to keep the records and do the necessary ciphering.

By common consent the honour of being the agent of the new company fell to Sam Bricker, and to avoid the possibility of Heasley's refusing to grant him the five hundred acres of land as he had promised, Sam was to receive it from the new company. Daniel and Jacob Erb, Annie's brothers, who had only a few weeks before left for Canada, were named assistants. These three were to be jointly answerable for all the interests of the company.

But the most perplexing problem of all was how Sam Bricker was to get the twenty thousand dollars to its destination. There were no banking facilities between the two countries, and silver was the only standard of currency. After much discussion, it was finally decided that Sam Bricker must take the money with him in actual coins.

A certain unfortunate experience of his adventure in Little Muddy York invariably persisted in confronting Sam at the most inopportune moments. No sooner did he hear that he must be responsible for the safe conduct of twenty thousand dollars over hundreds of miles than he fancied he saw standing before him the elusive Peter Potter who had once relieved him of fifteen dollars. But not a word of this escaped his lips. It was only for a moment that he wavered. With all the confidence of his optimistic nature, he declared that if anyone took that money from him, it would be over his dead body.

Within a week, a light two-wheeled buggy was constructed for the express purpose of conveying Sam and the money to Canada. A "weggli," they called it. The women made hundreds of small linen sacks, each one capable of containing a hundred silver dollars. These they filled with the coins and packed—two hundred of them—into the hold of the "weggli." Since Beccy was to ride on Menno's back, the company provided another horse which was to carry Sam and the money and Beccy's little "aus styer" chest.

In spite of Nancy's opposition, Sam and Beccy were married at the Hammer Creek House in the presence of the entire community. Hannes' wife attended to the wedding repast—and it was a bountiful one—while Nancy rocked herself complacently in her chair and said Beccy would surely live to rue the day. She had a presentiment that nothing but misfortune awaited those who were not satisfied with the good things that the Lord had provided for them in the land of their fathers.

Beccy smiled indulgently. What had she to fear anywhere with Sam and Menno? Even in the hour of farewell she was happy. When after dinner the women crowded about the little bride to "give" her good-bye, mingling words of sympathy with their congratulations, her face was radiant with joy. The long avenue of the future looked wonderfully entrancing on this her wedding-day.

Meanwhile, out in the kitchen, the men were trying to persuade Sam to accept a bag of silver, a hundred dollars, which they had collected to pay him for his trouble in conveying their money to Robert Heasley. But Sam clasped his hands resolutely behind his back and refused to touch it. The five hundred acres which Heasley had promised him was all the recompense he wanted.

"But we want to pay you," persisted Hannes.

"Then give me—give me a cow."

"Give him two," cried Old Christian. "The best we've got."

So it came about that two sleek jerseys were led out of the stable at the Hammer Creek Farm, and tied to the back of the "weggli." Once more Sam's thoughts wandered back to Little Muddy York, Peter

Potter, and the fifteen-dollar muley, but this time he could scarcely refrain from chuckling.

So Sam and Beccy began their wedded life and their journey to the home that awaited them in Canada.

CHAPTER XI

Sam and Beccy encountered many difficulties on their way to Canada, but they were much too happy to notice them. No matter how dreary the day, or how weary the way, their thoughts were centred on their home in the heart of Upper Canada and the good news they were bringing to the neighbours. They would have a housewarming the first night, Sam decided, with a public exhibition of his house, his twenty thousand dollars and his Beccy. Sam had the sweet consciousness that he was returning to the Tract in something of the rôle of a conquering hero.

They reached The Twenty in safety, but stopped only long enough to introduce Beccy to the Moyers, and to open the lid of the "weggli" and show the hoard of silver that was to bring a great deliverance to the victims of Heasley's treachery. One meal was all they could stay, they said, and then they turned again to the west.

It was evening when at last they reached the Heasley Tract. Sam was determined to push on until they came to their future home, but as he neared John's shanty he could not withstand the impulse to let his brother into their glorious secret. He pointed out the place to Beccy from across the river. The house was dark and silent as death. But by the light of the moon Sam could discern two conestoga wagons standing in front of the house.

"What does that mean?" exclaimed Sam. He decided to cross the river to investigate.

"They're asleep," suggested Beccy, meaning, of course, John and Annie and the little Brickers.

"Yes, they are," replied Sam, when he had poked his nose into one of the wagons and discovered a coop of chickens with their heads under their wings. "There I've woke them up. How they do cackle! And the pigs is gruntin'. I don't know what you think, Beccy, but it looks to me a lot like movin'."

"Movin'!" exclaimed the little bride. "Why I thought I was the only one that's movin'!"

"So you are," said Sam. "John chust thinks he is. Wait once till he sees what we've got to show him, eh, Beccy."

A second conestoga stood near by, his own, if Sam could believe his eyes. He walked over to it and looked in.

"They're movin' me, too, Beccy," he announced. "Here's the bureau I made for you and the chairs and everything. It don't look much like a house-warmin' to-morrow night."

Beccy's heart sank. It was so different from what she had expected, this home coming.

Then some one called—John. He wanted to know who was there.

Sam nudged Beccy, disguised his voice as well as he could, and replied: "The devil." He was never tired of recalling his famous joke at Robert Heasley's expense.

"It's Sam!" cried Annie. "It's Sam come back! I know him at the voice."

"And Beccy!" added Sam's little wife joyously.

"Whatever!" exclaimed both John and Annie together, coming out of the darkness to welcome their unexpected guests. But before John could clasp Sam's hand in his own, his eyes fell upon his brother's very unique equipage. He stared at it so obviously that Sam laughed.

"What is it anyhow?"

"Ach," replied Sam, "it's chust such a little 'weggli.'"

John gaped. "You didn't——"

"Of course I did," said Sam, importantly. "Didn't I say I would? Come on over once and look in." He tossed Beccy's little "aus styer" chest to the ground, opened the lid of the money box and told John to thrust his hand in.

But John was a very cautious man. He didn't take chances. He demanded to know first what was inside that queer little wagon-box.

"It won't bite," laughed Beccy.

"And it's hard and round," added Sam, trying to create an atmosphere of mystery. "Will you give it up?"

"It ain't money," gasped Annie. "You don't mean it's the money."

Then Sam straightened himself up and said dramatically; "Twenty thousand silver dollars! Two hundred sacks and a hundred dollars in each! Didn't I say I'd fetch it over?"

"Ach, you, Sam," was all John could reply.

"You fetched something else along over," Beccy hastened to remind him.

"I went single away and I've come double back," said Sam, bowing before Beccy with mock solemnity. "Beccy is mine now."

But the young wife protested that she hadn't meant herself at all. Had Sam forgotten the present he had brought for John?

Sam's eyes sparkled in anticipation of another one of his jokes. "Not a present quite," he said. "It's more like a debt." He untied one of the jerseys and led her out before his brother's astonished gaze. Even in the pale light of the moon it was evident that this was no mean animal. "How's that for your fifteen dollars, John?" He slapped the cow's sleek flank. "You can have the best. That's for interest. Now we're square."

"No, we're not," said John, clasping Sam's hand and shaking it whole-heartedly. "I can never pay you—none of us ever can. We didn't think you could do it."

Then Sam laid aside his pride and his levity and paid a glowing tribute to the people at Hammer Creek. It was their money, he was only their trusted agent. If they were to search the world over, no such friends could ever be found as their own "Freundschaft" in the home-land.

At these words, Annie who had long been struggling with her distraught emotions, burst audibly into tears. She fled to Beccy's bosom for comfort.

Sam shook his head. This "homesick!" Was Annie never going to get over it? Was she always going to make life miserable not only for herself but for everyone about her? John had his sympathy.

"Poor Annie," said Beccy, patting the distressed woman on the back. "Do you want to go so bad?"

Instead of answering, Annie surprised everyone by suddenly breaking out into an uncontrollable fit of laughter.

"'Sterics!" exclaimed John, hurrying to Annie's side and taking her into his strong arms.

Sam looked on with mingled feelings. He made bold to suggest that if that was how Annie felt about it, John had better finish his packing and take her back to Pennsylvania. The sooner, the better.

"No! No!" cried Annie. "I don't want to go. I don't want to go—now."

"You're glad you don't have to go, ain't you, Annie?" said John.

Sam coughed to hide his lack of appreciation of these womanly emotions. These women! Did they ever know themselves, he wondered, what they did or didn't want?

"It would kill me to go now," said Annie, growing calmer and wiping her eyes. "I couldn't let them here—them graves."

It was Sam's turn to gape. "Graves!" he ejaculated.

"He went with the dip-theria," John hastened to explain.

"Who?"

"Little Johnny."

"And the other Little Johnny," added Annie. "He chust went."

"The new baby," interjected John. "He went only last week already."

"And not a month old," sobbed the disconsolate mother.

"Poor Annie!" said Beccy. "Of course she don't feel to go now."

Sam was beginning to understand as well as any man can ever understand the inconsistencies of womankind. His own heart was filled with tender emotion when he thought of Little Johnny. He suggested that, late as it was, they should all go together and visit the graves.

So up to the little Bricker God's-Acre Annie led the party. She showed them the little garden enclosure, the new-made mounds, and the tree which she and John had just planted. She tried to explain how she felt about it. She hoped they wouldn't think her foolish.

"It's a nice thought," said Beccy. "You will leave the tree grow, Annie?"

"If it will."

"It will. Why, Annie, you will be here to water it."

Sam and Beccy slept that night for the first time since their marriage under a roof. Annie's beds were all packed in the conestogas, but she had plenty of blankets which she spread out upon the floor. They slept very well on these shake-downs, so well, indeed, that the sun was up before anyone was astir.

The minute Sam was awake he pulled on his clothes, snatched something to eat, led Menno out of the stable, and started off to the north on the trail that led to the Betzner settlement. He was going to have a little visit with his old friend, Joseph Sherk, he said. Beccy smiled to herself. She knew that all the way over Sam had been planning that at their housewarming, this same Joseph was to have a seat in the front row while he presented to the astonished assembly the twenty thousand silver dollars in actual coin.

131

Joseph Sherk was packing the last of his household effects into his conestoga when Sam came up behind the wagon and lifted the canvas top from its fastenings. "Hello, Joe," he called. "Movin'?"

Sherk looked up, dropped the furniture and stared. "Sam Bricker!" he cried. "When did you come?"

"Last night," replied Sam, trying not to look too pleased with himself and life in general.

"Chust in time to drive your own wagon," observed Joseph. "Well, I'm glad Annie don't have to do it."

Sam laughed. "You'll see me and Beccy goin' by in it some time to-day," he said.

"Beccy!" exclaimed Sherk. "You didn't fetch her along over."

"That's what I did."

"But you ain't——you ain't goin' to stop here?"

"That's what I am."

Joseph Sherk was dumbfounded for the moment, then a light flashed in his eye. "You didn't——?" he gasped, "They didn't give it to you?"

"That's what they did," Sam replied. "Come on over to John's once and see it. Twenty thousand dollars in such a little 'weggli.'"

Joseph Sherk whistled his astonishment. "I don't believe you'd stop at nothin', Sam Bricker," he said.

"I don't stop till I'm done," returned Sam, a trifle boastfully, and he told his story.

"Well, you earned your five hundred acres," said Joseph Sherk. "That's all I've got to say." His wife at this moment appeared at the door of the house loaded with articles for packing. "Put them back, Lizzie," he called to her. "We ain't goin' for all. Sam Bricker fetched the money over."

"And Beccy," added Sam, waving his greeting to Joseph's wife. "After dinner I'll fetch her over." Then he hurried back to his treasures.

In the afternoon when Sam was driving Beccy and his conestoga and all his belongings to the humble shanty which he himself had not seen for many a long, eventful month, all the Betzner "Freundschaft" had gathered at the Sherks to greet him and to be introduced to Beccy. Such a handshaking as then ensued!

Old Sam Betzner, always ready with a pleasant remark, said Beccy was as good as a doctor. He had to thank her for a new lease on life. Until that morning he hadn't cared whether he lived or died.

"But it's Sam," protested Beccy, "I didn't do nothin'."

Old Sam Betzner blinked his eyes knowingly. "Don't you know yet there's always a woman at the back of everything?" he said. "What did Sam go over to Hammer Creek for, eh?"

"Why, the money."

"And not you?"

Beccy glanced at Sam, who could not conceal the fact that he was greatly pleased with this little dialogue.

"I was there," said the little wife, "and he took me."

Old Sam Betzner laughed merrily. "If you had been here on the Tract," he said, "Sam wouldn't bother much about Hammer Creek, I guess. He would 've come back, too, like Joe did, wouldn't you, Sam?"

Sam didn't care to commit himself on the question, and the episode ended, as it had begun, with the remark; "There's always a woman at the back of everything."

Then Grossmommy Betzner pushed herself into the foreground. She had stood back long enough, she said. She wanted to see the little "weggli" that Joseph had been telling her about—and the twenty million dollars.

"Million!" laughed her husband. "You make it big enough. It's twenty thousand dollars."

Grossmommy shrugged her shoulders. "It's all the same," she said.

"It's over to John's," Sam told her. "To-morrow I'll fetch it over with my new Jersey cow. I'll stop then and leave you look at them."

With this promise, Sam and Beccy were permitted to continue their journey. A few more miles along the bank of the river and they would be at home.

It was only a little, deserted log shanty, their home. The door stood open, but not in welcome. There were no blinds on the windows, no smoke curled upward from the chimney. It was nothing but an abandoned settler's shack surrounded by a patch of clearing in the midst of the virgin forest.

Sam felt instinctively that he must make some apology for it. "It's small, Beccy," he ventured, "after the Hammer Creek House. I thought the furniture would be all set."

But Beccy hushed him up. "Why, Sam, it's home!" she cried ecstatically. "Fetch the things in once and I'll set them where I want them all."

So they set to work, he carrying the furniture in, and she arranging it to suit her pleasure and convenience. Every time he brought in a load from the conestoga, he was singing blithely, while Beccy picked up the refrain and hummed it just an octave higher.

But when the furniture was all in and set, Sam did not seem altogether pleased with the room.

"What's wrong?" said Beccy, whose face was radiant with the new-found joy of homemaking.

"Looks small after Heasley's," Sam told her. "You ought to see the fine house he gave her."

"With other people's money—yours," sniffed Beccy. "Don't you know yet, Sam, that things don't make happiness? It's people—you and me."

Sam threw his arms about her impulsively and kissed her.

The very next day it looked as though their happy dream was to be shattered. A little seed of discord had sprouted in this new home of theirs. They had their first tiff.

Sam had been over at John's and had returned with the "weggli" and the cow, after a few minutes' stop at the Betzners' to show his treasures. As soon as he came into the house Beccy asked him where he intended to keep the money.

"Ach, we might chust as well let it out in the 'weggli,'" Sam had replied.

But Beccy was not at all satisfied with this arrangement. She insisted that it ought to be brought into the house and put under the bed in her little "aus styer" chest, now emptied of its contents.

Sam resisted but Beccy persisted and would give him no peace until he went to the barn and carried the money back to the house sack by sack. But he was not at all gracious about it. It was a "dumm" notion, he said.

"One of them that grows in the Eby dummheads?" Beccy flung at him. "I heard a lot about them back in Pennsylvany already."

That made Sam more impatient than ever. Had he married this wife of his to have her poke fun at him? He made another trip to the barn, dumped the nineteenth and twentieth sacks into the chest, and closed the lid with a bang. "There!" he said, dropping wearily into a chair, "Does that suit you? Is it the Betzners you are scared of?"

Beccy tried to explain that while she distrusted nobody, she thought it wise to take some precaution. The money was not theirs, but in their care. She would never sleep at night if she knew it was out in the barn.

Sam sat there glowering at her.

Then Beccy full of penitence came and dropped her head on Sam's shoulder. "We ain't goin' to fight, are we, Sam?" she whispered.

Sam pushed her away and told her it was for her to say.

"You mean you are always ready?" said Beccy. "Ach, Sam, it's the red hair. That always gives temper."

To be reminded of his besetting sin and his greatest physical affliction in the same breath was a trifle disconcerting to say the least, but Beccy immediately poured oil on his troubled spirits by enumerating some of her husband's good points. His energy, perseverance, and will power, quite made up for his hastiness of temper, she said; and anyway, red hair and temper notwithstanding, she loved him and would continue to love him to his dying day.

Sam, now mollified, let Beccy run her fingers through his fiery locks. "Will you love me, Beccy," he said, "no matter what happens?"

"No matter what happens," repeated the little wife, very solemnly.

"It don't give many women like you, Beccy," said Sam, drawing this prize of his to a seat on his knees.

So the first cloud on the horizon of their wedded life blew away.

In the days that followed visitors began to pour in from all sides, not only the usual Sunday visitors, but week-day visitors. The excuse they brought was that they wanted to see Beccy, to welcome her to the Heasley Tract. But no matter how animated the conversation, or how absorbed they were in Beccy's new "aus styer," there always came a time when someone voiced the curiosity of all in the suggestion that they "go along out and see once how the 'weggli' looks like." Then it was Sam's extreme pleasure to open Beccy's chest and show the sacks filled with precious treasure and then to lead the procession to the barn to inspect his "weggli." He was unconscionably proud of the queer, little vehicle. Nothing would ever induce him to sell it, he said. If he could leave nothing else to his children, they should at least inherit his good name and this, his most valued possession.

Two weeks passed by, and Sam decided that it was time to close the deal with Heasley. Daniel and Jacob Erb, who before Sam's return had set out towards the north in quest of other unencumbered tracts, were overtaken and apprised of the new duty their friends at Hammer Creek had imposed on them. Sam was very glad when he learned that they were willing to share his responsibility. By bitter experience he had proved that it was easy for some people to part with money at The Head of the Lake, as well as in Little Muddy York. But Sam had a plan up his sleeve whereby he and the Erbs could outwit a whole retinue of Heasleys and Peter Potters. Mr. Ridout, the registrar, would be their friend. They would drive straight to him and put the whole matter in his hands. Sam had every confidence that he, and Providence, would see them safely through their difficulties.

The plan was a good one, but when the day of execution came Sam was in the throes of a fever and much too ill even to think about going. Week after week the Erbs waited, hoping for Sam's recovery. But when the fever finally subsided, it left him too weak to do anything. Bitterly disappointed, he at last gave over his sacred charge to his assistants, counted and recounted the money with them, lent them his much-prized "weggli" for the trip, encouraged them with directions and valuable counsel, and sent them on their way to Mr. Ridout.

As soon as Sam was well enough, he found plenty of work on his "Bauerei." There was the ploughing to be done and the seeding, and a dozen other things that should be done as soon as he could find time to do them. The building of the spring-house, for instance. During his memorable visit to Pennsylvania, Sam had taken a few lessons in stone masonry, and now he was impatient to try his skill at it. He hauled load after load of barge stones from the river. With them he intended to build first a huge trough to hold barrels of the bright, sparkling water his spring afforded, and later, if he could contrive it, a little stone house to cover it. There Beccy was to keep her milk and butter. The young housewife was so pleased with the idea and so anxious to help that she left her kitchen day after day and went out to assist in this great enterprise.

But one day when she returned to the house after working for an hour or two with Sam, she was surprised to find that someone had entered her shanty during her absence. Everything was thrown about in the greatest confusion, every box opened and explored, the bed dismantled, the top torn off her tree-trunk table and her own little chest, the only real possession she had in all the world, smashed to kindling wood. Terrified and not a little indignant, Beccy rushed to the door and called loudly for Sam.

Sam lost his temper at once. He hopped about like a madman, vowing that he would not sleep until he had found the Indian that had done this mischief. He would level his wigwam to the ground.

"Sam!" cried Beccy, in alarm, "It's wicked to talk so!"

Sam didn't hear. He was off in pursuit of the malefactor.

"Sam!" Beccy called after him. "Come back, Sam! It was not an Indian at all!"

"You don't know nothing about it," he flung back at her over his shoulder.

"It was money they wanted—not the Indians. Ach, Sam, don't be so dumm!"

There was logic in what Beccy said, but Sam would not think of admitting it. He went over to the Betzner settlement in one direction, then to Christian Reichert's in the other and made inquiry, but they had seen nobody. He tramped the woods until he was almost exhausted, but he found no clue to the mystery. At last he came home and told Beccy that he was sure it must have been a white man.

"Do you think so?" replied Beccy, very sweetly and innocently. "And what did he want, Sam? Do you know that, too?"

Sam looked up rather sharply at this wife of his bosom, but not even a suspicion of a smile betrayed the fact that she was laughing at him. "The money," he told her in all seriousness.

"So?" said Beccy, with well-feigned surprise. "What a smart man you are, Sam, at finding things out!"

Sam beamed with pleasure, but the spirit of revenge still burned within him. He would keep his ears and eyes open, he vowed, and if he ever found out who was the culprit, he would not rest until he had paid him back in his own coin.

A few days later the Erbs returned with the "weggli." They said they had left the money with Mr. Ridout, the registrar, and they showed the receipt that he had given them for it.

"But where's the deed?" demanded Sam.

The Erbs explained that Heasley could not be located in York. Obviously, Mr. Ridout could not furnish deeds without Heasley's signature. But he would certainly be there in November, when the House would be in session. If they would come again at that time, he would be glad to attend to the matter.

Sam made a grimace of impatience. "Why didn't you go to his fine house at The Head of the Lake?" he wanted to know.

"We did," said Jacob.

"And wasn't he there?"

"No," said Daniel, the elder of the Erbs. "She didn't know where he was. She didn't keep no string of him, she said. Them were her very words."

Beccy's heart stood still. She shot a quick glance at Sam, and was relieved to find that he was still worrying about the deeds.

In November the Erbs went again to York, but once more they returned without the deeds. Ridout had the papers all ready for the signatures, but Heasley would not sign. He had made no such bargain, he declared. Sam Bricker was a confounded liar, and a fire-brand. If he thought he was going to get the finest tract in all Upper Canada for a song, he didn't know Robert Heasley. Let him come himself, like a man, and air his grievances in court.

Sam was so enraged at this message that he would have gone at once to The Head of the Lake but for a terrible snow-storm which blew up and blocked the roads beyond the possibility of getting through. Three times he started off, but each time he was compelled to return. At last Beccy persuaded him to wait until spring, when the Erbs would accompany him and strengthen his cause.

Very early in April, Sam and the Erbs started off for The Head of the Lake, and learning that Heasley was at Parliament, they continued their journey to York. They came upon their man, walking about in front of The Place of the Government with a number of other dignified Members of Parliament. But the sum of all their dignity did not save Heasley. Sam pounced upon him as a cat would seize a rat, and dragged him nilly-willy to the Registry-Office, where Mr. Ridout greeted him with an amused smile.

Heasley was more tractable on this occasion. It happened that at the time he was out of luck. Creditors were on his heels. Jim Wilson, his former partner, had compelled him with threats of exposure to buy over his share of the tract and on that very day the last payment of three thousand dollars was due. The mortgage on the tract was long overdue, but he hoped to have the time extended and was contemplating a lien on his house at The Head of the Lake to pay the interest for another year. Mr. Ridout assured him that the twenty thousand dollars was available at once. He reminded Heasley that he could not hope to sell any more land, at least to Mennonites, now that his duplicity had been discovered, and he predicted that if he persisted in refusing to live up to the bargain he had made, the name of Robert Heasley, Member of Parliament, would be a black mark on the page when in future years the young colony's history should be written.

Whether it was the appeal to the man's business acumen or to his reputation that prevailed could only be a matter for conjecture, but his promise to sign was a glorious fact. Mr. Ridout lost no time in presenting the document, a huge piece of parchment covered with line upon line of unintelligible writing, which the registrar construed to mean that Robert Heasley was transferring to Daniel and Jacob Erb, agents for the new company, all that parcel of land known as the Heasley Tract, and consisting of sixty thousand acres, more or less, in return for twenty thousand dollars of lawful money, the receipt of which was hereby acknowledged.

Heasley swore profusely and cursed Sam for a robber, but finally dipped his quill into the ink and signed his name. To the infinite relief of the Mennonites, he refused to remain in such contemptible society a minute longer than was necessary to secure his money, and hurried off to join his friends of importance at The Place of the Government.

Sam paid Mr. Ridout for his services and registered a copy of the deed in his office, but the original document he rolled up carefully and carried with him to the Heasley Tract.

During the summer that followed a surveyor was employed to draw up a plan of the Tract, dividing it into lots of approximately four hundred and fifty acres each, after marking the ground already occupied and Sam's five hundred acre reward. It was a laborious undertaking, and he worked at it all winter long. But when the roads were open in the spring, a copy of the plan together with a bundle of letters was sent by the hand of a trusted messenger to their friends and benefactors of the Hammer Creek community.

CHAPTER XII

When Sam Bricker left his friends in Pennsylvania with Beccy and the twenty thousand silver dollars, he had the good-will and confidence of all the shareholders of the company. But when winter came and went, and summer followed on the heels of spring for two years, and there was still no word of Sam or the money, a few of the more pessimistic ones began to show signs of dissatisfaction with their investment. Stories began to be circulated of Sam's unfortunate cupidity as a child; how on one occasion he had sold a chicken from his father's coop and withheld as a sort of commission part of the price; and how he had once worked for a neighbour without parental knowledge or consent, and had put his earnings in the family purse in his father's trousers pocket only after a very forceful reminder of his filial duty. Could it be possible that these seeds of iniquity sown in the child had sprouted in the man? The matter, they thought, would bear investigation.

But at last came the good news of the successful consummation of the bargain with Heasley, and the papers and letters confirmed the report. Then these wild rumours of Sam's youthful depravity were contradicted even by their perpetrators, and the Bricker reputation for honesty was sustained, even in the person of the youngest member of the family.

The Heasley Tract and its partition among the shareholders now became the one absorbing topic of conversation at Hammer Creek. The plan itself was something of a novelty which even those who were not financially interested felt it their privilege, if not their duty, to inspect. Of the sixty thousand acres nearly four thousand had already been allocated to the men who had bought land from Heasley. These were to receive clear titles to their lands. Sam Bricker was to have the five hundred acres, which everyone agreed he had abundantly earned. The surveyor had divided the rest of the land into plots of approximately four hundred and fifty acres each, and the great problem which now confronted the shareholders was to apportion the land. One share represented nearly seven thousand acres, a lordly estate rather than a farm. Of estates these quiet, unpretentious people knew little, but they had had enough experience in agriculture to realize what a herculean task it would be to evolve a farm out of even one-sixteenth of a share, representing, as it did, four hundred and fifty acres of un-tilled and heavily-wooded soil.

The Mennonites have one simple solution to all the perplexing problems of life. Whenever a troublesome question arises, they turn to their Bibles. If they cannot find any commandment or prohibition which meets the needs of the hour, they will review the whole story of God's dealings with men in the past with the hope of finding some precedent to follow. It is an infallible guide; it never fails them. Nor did it on this occasion. In both the Old and New Dispensations they found that when common property was to be divided, the people cast lots to learn what was the rightful possession of each. So was Canaan apportioned among the children of Israel. So was our Lord's cloak di-vided at the Crucifixion. Accordingly, slips of paper were prepared and numbered to correspond with the numbers assigned by the sur-veyor to the lots. These were then put into a box and carefully shuffled. The shareholders then cast themselves at the mercy of fate and allowed that blindfolded lady of the ages to determine what was to be their lawful possession. As no one knew anything whatever about the land, it proved a most amicable settlement of what might have been under ordinary circumstances a matter of much controversy.

The question of emigration to Canada now began to engage the attention of both old and young. Aged fathers had come into pos-session of large areas of land, which they were anxious to dispose of. Their sons were brought face to face with what appeared to be an op-portunity of a life time. It was a challenge that was being flung to them, and those who were not willing to accept it at once were deter-mined at least to investigate it. The question was looming up, too, before the young women. The time was coming when they would have to decide between John and the privations of Canada on one hand and Jacob and the comforts of Pennsylvania on the other.

The cooperage where Benj Eby spent so many hours of his early life was the scene of the most animated discussions on this all-absorbing subject. There the young men of the community gravitated from all directions when the day's work was done; and there late into the night for weeks at a time, they debated the momentous question. It was no mere problem propounded to provoke mental exercise, but a life issue, and they knew that when as old men they looked back over their lives, they would recall with satisfaction or regret the verdict they had passed then and there.

By the middle of April—that was in 1806—Benj Eby had reached a conclusion. The others might do as they pleased, but he was going to Canada on horseback that very spring to explore the land which his father had acquired. It did not require much persuasion to induce Henry and Jacob Brubacher to decide to go with him, with the understanding that whether they liked the country or not, they should all return together in the fall.

"You can get your 'aus styer' ready, Mary," said Benj to the girl of his choice, when he sat with her one evening on the front steps of the Brubacher homestead.

Mary cast her eyes down and blushed becomingly. "I thought it was chust you boys," she managed to say.

"We're comin' back till October," replied Benj, and in the most matter-of-fact tone imaginable he added; "Like as not you'll be goin' over with me soon after that."

Silence and a suffusion of blushes gave consent, and from that hour Mary Brubacher began to plan her "aus styer."

It was quite a different bit of drama that was enacted when Jacob Brubacher with much fear and trepidation took his heart in his hand and offered them both to Lizzie Eby.

"How soon will you be ready, Lizzie?" he asked, assuming that she would understand that he had come at last to invite her to embark with him on the sea of matrimonial bliss.

The object of his devotion tossed her pretty head. "Never!" she snapped. "If you go there, you can go alone!" She turned her back full upon him.

Jacob bit his lip. Was he going to allow this vexed Canada question to stand between him and the woman of his love? Bravely he began again; "I ain't goin' to stop, Lizzie—chust to see what like it is there." He paused a moment, hoping in vain for some sign of relenting, and then added weakly; "I won't like it, Lizzie, I know I won't."

But the irreconcilable one still stood with averted face, and in a voice which was surely exceedingly bellicose for one who belonged to a non-combatant race, she served an ultimatum. "You're not goin' at all. If you do, I'll throw you over——forever!"

It sounded very tragic, very final. It killed the long, last, lingering hope that Jacob entertained concerning Canada. Solemnly, as if at a funeral, he answered. "I won't go, Lizzie. I've changed my mind."

"Have you?" cooed the girl, turning to him a face wreathed in dimples and smiles. "You don't want to go, do you, Jacob?"

Jacob assured her that he didn't—now. With hopes renewed, he continued to press his suit. He wanted to know how soon she would be ready to marry him. But the provoking girl stuck her finger in her mouth and said she would have to ask her mother.

Everyone knew that Lizzie's mother was really at the bottom of the girl's refusal to countenance Jacob's going to Canada. But this fact did not take the sting out of the ridicule that all the community hurled at Jacob when he announced that he was not going to Canada after all. "You changed your mind," they said, derisively. "Why, Jacob, don't you know yet it's the women folks that does that?"

So Benj and Henry left Jacob, wished him well, and started off for Canada without him. They had a wonderful experience of adventure and exploration. The Brickers received them with open arms and introduced them to all their new friends. There was not a farm on the Heasley Tract that they did not visit and inspect, and everywhere they were most cordially received. By the time they had made their rounds, Benj at least was wildly enthusiastic. He declared that he would take back to Pennsylvania such a glowing account of the Heasley Tract and its people that a great flood of immigration was bound to follow. Certainly none of the shareholders of the new company would have any concern about the financial possibilities of their investment when they had heard what he had to say about Canada.

But these amateur explorers were not content to confine their attention merely to the Heasley Tract. Farther to the north they wandered and discovered a rich, fertile region, drained by a creek that meandered along, as if by its beauty alone it hoped to justify its existence.

"It's another Conestoga," said Benj, recalling the river which bore the waters of their own Hammer Creek to the great Susquehannah. He predicted that before long this tract would be the home of a great population, and the beautiful river would water the cattle of many farms.

"Another Pennsylvany," scoffed Henry Brubacher, who did not altogether share his companion's great enthusiasm for Canada.

When Benj came back to Pennsylvania in the fall he had some interesting news for Mary. He had fully decided that he would take her to Canada in the spring. One of the farms which had fallen by lot to his father had taken his fancy, and on it he had built a log house. Just three miles north and across the river from Sam Bricker's, he said it was, and Mary teasingly replied that she hoped he wouldn't be running over to see Sam every morning before breakfast.

But Benj was awake to other interests besides his own. He had sought out the owner of the tract to the north, and had entered into negotiations with him for the purchase of the valley of the charming river which he had named the Conestoga. He held out the prospect that when he should come again in the spring he would bring with him not only the price in silver coin, but also a group of settlers who would transform his forest into a community of smiling farms.

"And are you goin', too, Henry?" asked Jacob Brubacher, who had been drinking in all that Benj had to say about Canada and coming to the conclusion that he had won his Lizzie at a terrible cost.

But to the amazement of everybody Henry shook his head. He didn't "feel for goin' back," he said. Farming was so much easier in Pennsylvania.

"If you've got a farm," supplemented Jacob, who, as the elder of the two brothers, claimed as his birthright the Brubacher homestead.

Henry smiled a smile of superior wisdom. He wanted Jacob to understand that he wasn't dependent on him for a farm.

"Well, I don't know anybody that's goin' to give you one," replied Jacob, a trifle caustically.

"I do!" said Henry, bristling with perk importance. "Eliza Hoffman!"

The spring of 1807 witnessed a greater emigration to Canada from Pennsylvania than any previous season had seen. All over the countryside young men were fired with enthusiasm for the new enterprise and determined to go and seek their fortunes in the fabulous land to the north. There were young married people with little children, too young to understand the meaning of the excitement and too young to care. There were old men and women, grandparents, though still young enough in spirit to yearn to follow the gleam that beckoned them from behind the purple clouds of the west. It was as if a fever went stalking through the land seeking whom it might devour. Two men ploughed side by side in a field; one it took, the other it left. Two women ground their flour in the same kitchen; one it marked, the other was immune. It was no respecter of age or sex. Families were decimated and a great gulf fixed between those who were determined to go and those who resolved to stay, a gulf which would certainly grow wider and deeper each year of separation, until all ties of blood and friendship and propinquity which once had bound them together would be severed and broken—perhaps ultimately forgotten.

The Erb family was one that was divided on the great question of emigration, and no little hard feeling had been stirred up over it. Mary Brubacher's mother was an Erb and, as it happened, one of the most bitter opponents of all things Canadian. Hadn't she seen what Canada had done for her family? There was her sister Annie, John Bricker's wife, who had almost died of lonesomeness during those first awful years. Two of her children lay buried in a land where there were no doctors. And her brothers, Daniel and Jacob, what trouble and expense had they not endured going back and forth to York before they could obtain justice at the hands of one of the Members of the Parliament of Upper Canada. Rogues, those Canadians, all of them! And here was Mary dropping salt tears all over her "aus styer" because, like a dutiful mother, she kept warning her of the thorny path that lay before if she persisted in this mad idea of accompanying Benj Eby to Canada. Couldn't she find a young man who would give her a comfortable home in Pennsylvania?

But Mary wept in silence and plied her busy needle back and forth.

"It's one of them dumm Eby notions," stormed the mother of the Brubachers. "Old Christian got the start of it, and look at all the trouble he's made already. Tried to get your pop to go, too. I chust had to step on it."

Mary had a very vivid recollection of the family quarrels that had been enacted in her hearing in that very room over that same vexatious question.

"You're too good for Benj Eby and that wild country, Mary," continued her mother, trying persuasion where threats had failed. "You're a good girl. I can't complain about you unless it is when I think of you trailin' over there to Canada in a conestoga wagon with Benj Eby and his dumm notions."

But the chagrin that Mary was causing her mother paled into insignificance when her own parents, Grossdoddy and Grossmommy Erb, announced that they had made up their minds to go to Canada with Benj and Mary. They wanted to see Annie and Daniel and Jacob in their new surroundings, they said, while they were still in health and strength.

"But look how old you are!" argued the indignant daughter. "Canada is for young folks."

"Like Benj and Mary," replied Grossmommy, with a twinkle in her eye.

"And how old are we anyway?" said Grossdoddy, who seemed to have suddenly dropped twenty years from his age with the prospect of this new adventure.

"Seventy years old, both of you!" was the quick reply.

"No! no! Bevy," insisted the rejuvenated man, "we're seventy years young!" He threw his cane into the corner and pranced around like a man of half his years.

"Nancy has right," muttered Bevy Brubacher. "Dumm, all of them! There's no other word that can say it. They're dumm!"

Quite against her mother's wishes Mary was married to Benj Eby in the spring; and in spite of all she could do to prevent it, Grossdoddy and Grossmommy Erb stood by their resolution and threw upon the young couple the responsibility of their safe conduct to Canada.

Bevy was furious, irreconcilable, but she broke down in the hour of their departure, and wept bitter tears. One minute she clung to her parents, the next to her child. She couldn't give them up. They might as well be buried. She never expected to see or hear of them again.

Grossdoddy and Grossmommy were silent and tearful. They felt that Bevy had spoken the truth. But Mary was full of confidence and consolation. "Pretty soon you'll come over once and wisit us all," she whispered, pressing her mother to her breast for the last time. "It ain't so far as it was now that Beccy's went over on horseback." A wave of the hand, a few hot, blinding tears and the little woman who stood half way between youth and old age found herself in the midst of friends, yet forsaken and alone.

The honour of leading the procession fell to Benj Eby, and right glad he was that he had a new conestoga for the occasion. It was by far the largest company that had ever left Lancaster County for Canada, comprising as it did twelve conestogas and fifty souls. Never had a wealthier party, save one, set out on that long journey. In addition to an immense supply of provisions, household effects, and livestock, they had in their keeping a large, well-hooped barrel, in the bottom of which were packed in sacks of heavy canvas ten thousand silver dollars. Benj carried it in his wagon; for as a result of his enthusiastic description of the valley of the river which he had called the Conestoga, another company had been formed; and Benj had been appointed agent with commission to purchase that desirable property.

In the second wagon sitting at her husband's side behind two teams of heavy bay horses sat Susie Schneider—born Eby—Benj's sister. She looked quite as excited as she did on that Sunday in the long ago when Sam Bricker had come to the Hammer Creek House to show his "Schimmel" and had teased her about Josiah Schneider and his stiff-jointed bay horse. For more than ten years she had been climbing over the wagon wheels to open the gates for this man who had won her heart, if not the approval of her mother. And now she was on her way to Canada with him and five little Schneiders. They were going to start life all over again with a fresh coat of paint on their conestoga.

The journey was a memorable one because of the many misfortunes which befell the party. The almanac must have been misinformed about the weather, for although fair skies were predicted, incessant rains fell day after day, causing the rivers to swell and overflow their banks. The wagons were so heavily loaded as to retard greatly their progress, and the linen tops of the conestogas leaked water by the bucketful. So serious did matters become that the women and children were compelled to walk long distances, and for days at a time only six or seven miles were covered. One of Benj's horses took sick, rolled on the ground and threatened to die, an incident that held the party up for several days. When they had journeyed a dozen miles farther, they must needs be delayed again. During a game of quoits by the roadside, one of the young men had the misfortune to strike his brother on the head with a horseshoe. The latter was picked up for dead, but in time regained consciousness, only to learn that his panic-stricken brother had fled to the bush. Four days passed before the fugitive could be located and induced to return to the company. The crossing of the Niagara was always undertaken with no little apprehension, but this party of many misfortunes, essaying to cross it above the Falls, experienced, for the first time, a real danger. A terrible storm blew up quite suddenly when they were mid-stream, and drove one of the wagon-boats out of its course, so that it narrowly escaped being caught by the current and dashed to pieces over the wild cataract beyond.

There was joy without measure when at last The Twenty was reached, and the weary travellers were assured of rest and refreshment among people of their own kind. Nor were they in the least disappointed. The Kolbs, the Albrights, and the Honsbergers vied with the Moyers in opening to the strangers their homes and their hearts. The arrival was on Saturday night, a most opportune time, for both visitors and hosts could look forward to the rest and worship and friendly communion that characterized the crowning day of all the week.

147

On Sunday morning they were taken to the meeting-house which Levi Moyer had recently erected on a corner of his farm. A signal honour had come to Levi that very spring. He had just returned from a visit to Berks County where the brethren had laid their hands upon his head and created him a Bishop, the first Bishop of the Mennonite faith in Canada.

The service of the day left nothing to be desired. At least a hundred people had gathered from a radius of many miles to listen to the message that should fall from the good man's lips. The only discordant note was that uttered by little Aaron Schneider, one of Susie's numerous progeny. It was loud and shrill, but although it caused his parents much mortification at the time, it was later regarded as an unmistakable evidence of providential guidance.

In Pennsylvania Dutch communities the mother is alone responsible for the behaviour of all her little children during a religious service, no matter how numerous or how unmanageable the off-spring. So when the service was about to begin Susie led in three of her flock, arranging them by age on a bench near the door while she herself sat at one end of the row with her baby in her arms. Joseph, the father, was exerting his prerogative of sitting quite unhampered, except by the presence of his eldest son, among the adult males of the congregation on the opposite side of the meeting-house.

If ever there was a time when Susie was anxious that her children should behave well, it was in the presence of this great crowd of strangers. Both collectively and individually she had tried to impress them with the importance of the occasion. But her admonitions were quite unheeded when the young Schneiders perceived that they had an interested audience. Never in all their lives had they behaved so badly at worship. One dragged the music when he sang, and another echoed the intercessory groans of the Bishop during a lengthy season of prayer. When everybody had settled down to enjoy the sermon, little four-year-old Aaron insisted that he wanted a drink, and his older sister had to pilot him to the water-pail half way up the aisle. There the little fellow found a great deal of amusement in drinking with much sibilation from the dipper and then pouring the water that remained back into the pail with sounding dribbles. Susie was overcome with confusion, but she took what consolation she could find in the fact that neither was the Bishop disturbed in his discourse nor Josiah in the profundity of his meditation.

When at last Aaron was persuaded to return to his place, Susie lost no time in shifting the children about until the restless boy was at her side under the shadow of her strong right arm. She opened her "Windel-sack" and told him to help himself to the cookies which she had put there for just such an emergency as this. The child must have had a wonderfully digestive system if he ate only half as much as he dropped in crumbs upon the floor, but Susie was profoundly thankful that at least he was quiet. She put her arm about the little fellow, patted his little round stomach and whispered; "You're a good boy, Aaron. It don't go long now till the meetin' goes out."

Aaron looked up at his mother and smiled at these words of approbation and encouragement. The next minute he plunged his tiny hand into the maternal "Windel-sack" for another cookie. Then he began to whimper.

"Be still!" commanded Susie.

But Aaron had no intention of being still. He broke into a cry that proved beyond a shadow of a doubt that his lungs were as strong as his stomach. Susie handed her baby to Mary, who sat near by, and devoted her energies to Aaron, Josiah frowned perceptibly, and the Bishop dropped his voice and his discourse to beseech his audience to give him their undivided attention and to overlook what he was pleased to call "the snivelling of one of the lambs of the fold."

Aaron was quiet for a moment, but presently he burst out again more boisterously than ever. All the while Susie kept trying to find out what ailed him. Was there a pin sticking, perhaps?

"No-o-o," sobbed the child.

Or did it ache down there?

"No-o-o."

What was the matter then?

"Cookies is all!" Aaron shouted it out so that everyone had the satisfaction of knowing what was the cause that had produced so startling an effect.

With burning cheeks Susie seized the "Windel-sack" in one hand and Aaron in the other, and hurried out of doors.

The cookie-box was in the conestoga on the top of a pyramid of boxes so high that the children could not reach it. But when Susie climbed over the wagon-wheel to get it, she was amazed to discover that neither the cookie-box nor any other of her possessions was in its place. Everything had been thrown about topsy-turvy in the wagon-box, clothes, and provisions, tools and furniture in one conglomerate mass.

"Where's the cookies?" cried naughty Little Aaron, kicking impatiently against the wagon-wheel.

Susie did not answer. She had forgotten all about Aaron and the cookies. Her mind was full of questioning and conjecture.

Benj's wagon stood next to hers. Acting on a sudden impulse she went and looked into it. There before her astonished eyes she saw the mischief-maker, his head and shoulders lost in the depths of the money-barrel, his feet hidden in a litter of confusion. Very stealthily Susie climbed into the wagon, pounced upon the thief, secured him by the collar and shook him with all her might. She forced him to drop a large bag which he had been filling from the contents of the barrel, and helped him to turn out his pockets. Then confident that the fellow had nothing but what belonged to him, she let him go.

If the man was not strong, he had more agility than most men of twice his strength. He jumped from the wagon with a single bound, and like a hunted animal ran for shelter in the nearest woods.

Little Aaron stopped his kicking. His eyes fairly bulged with excitement. "Did he get the cookies?" was his great concern.

"Be still!" said Susie. "Let me think once."

She went back to her own conestoga, followed closely by Aaron, who had early learned the efficacy of importunity. She found the cookie-box, opened it, and soon the child was indulging himself in gluttonous dissipation.

Susie knew that she must think and act quickly. She decided that she would not sound an alarm but replace the money in the barrel, tidy the conestogas, and consult only with Benj and Mary. At the first opportunity she took her baby and led her brother out into the garden for a little private conversation.

Benj listened to the end of the story. He had only words of commendation for Susie. She had been very brave and very discreet, he said. Nothing could possibly be gained by circulating the report. It would only worry the good people at The Twenty, if they knew that this outrage had occurred under their hospitable vine and fig-tree. "What they don't know don't spite them" was a faithful saying and true, and quite applicable to this situation.

Susie agreed, but she insisted upon helping Benj count the money, and she admonished him to be more careful of his trust in the future. She didn't want him to have any such experience as Sam Bricker's memorable one with wrong and injustice in the person of Robert Heasley.

CHAPTER XIII

With the coming of Benj Eby and his party, there dawned a new day of expansion and development for the settlement on the Heasley Tract. The valley of the Conestoga to the north was opened up; and the trails which the Betzners and others had slashed through the forest only a few years before, soon became the great thorough-fares of the land.

More and more good roads were becoming a necessity. The Parliament at York decided to encourage the settlement of the Heasley Tract by improving the road through the bog known as the Beverley Swamp. It was a big undertaking. Great swaths of trees had to be cut down, the stumps removed from the road bed, and thrown up on either side. Then the trunks of the fallen trees were laid across the pathway and covered with clods of earth. But thirty miles of corduroy was a considerable stretch and progress was slow.

There was nothing slow, however, about the progress of a forest fire, when once it got a start and had a clear sweep through the land with a stiff gale blowing. Besides, the route of its swath was of no man's choosing, and utter desolation followed in its train. Like some hungry monster it howled and roared, seeking its prey where it would. People ran for their lives; buildings went down before it; cattle were consumed; and the season's crop ripe for harvest was licked up, so to speak, in a single, greedy gulp. The work of years was lost in a moment, and the helpless, penniless people were obliged to return to their ruined homes and climb the ladder of prosperity over again from the lowest rung.

Benj Eby's house narrowly escaped just such a conflagration when he and Mary were still upon their way to Canada. The fire started in a trackless cedar swamp to the north and west of Benj's settlement, and a strong wind blew it within a few rods of the little log house. The loss of timber was beyond all possible computation, but when Benj saw that his shanty was safe, he said that nothing else mattered very much.

On the borders of this dense cedar swamp there sprang up in the months that followed a colony of Ebys. Ebytown, Sam Bricker called it, and somehow the name stuck. Benj had brought over with him two young bachelor cousins of the same name, who evidently did not intend to remain long in that unhappy state. They began at once to build their houses, and there was much merriment at their expense and a great deal of speculation as to their matrimonial intentions when the houses neared completion and neither would give any definite information as to who was likely to inhabit them.

The fact of the matter was that the two young men were both casting amorous glances in the same direction. It was not to be wondered at, for Catherine Brech was a very beautiful girl of eighteen, bright, and vivacious enough to cause any bachelor's heart to palpitate. She, together with her widowed mother, two brothers, and a cousin named Esther Stauffer, had trekked their way from Lancaster County just a few weeks in advance of Benj Eby's party; had settled a little to the east of Sam Bricker's; and had immediately established friendly relations with their new neighbours.

George Clemens was the first to pay his court to the bewitching Catherine. To use his own expression, he hadn't been waiting with his mouth open all these years for nothing. Here at last was his lady-bug. He thought of her by day and dreamed of her by night. In less than a month he had invited her to "pop in." But Catherine was something of a coquette. She had caught a glimpse of the Ebys; she declined to give George a definite answer. It pleased her to keep him sitting upon expectant haunches while she flew about here and there under his admiring gaze exercising that essentially feminine prerogative of making up her mind.

With the arrival of the Ebys, poor George's hopes diminished appreciably. Benj Eby's cousins were likely fellows and quite susceptible to the charms of Catherine. George sat day after day, dejected but patient. At last, when he least expected it, came his great reward. She surprised him one day with a pair of soft brown eyes that spoke the language of the heart. She "popped." The quest was over, and George was delighted. Within a few weeks he had married her—not the adorable Catherine to be sure, but her cousin, Esther Stauffer.

Meanwhile, the Ebys were dividing their time between the Brechs and their new houses. Sam Bricker used to chuckle when he saw them pass by. One of them was Beccy's brother, Daniel, from whom years before Sam had purchased his horse Menno; the other, Amos Eby, was a younger man of splendid physique and strong personality, who had braved the opposition of all his father's family and thrown in his lot with the Canada party. If Daniel spent one evening with Catherine, Amos was sure to be there the next. Between the two of them, the girl was having a rather exciting time of it.

But her little flirtation came to a termination rather suddenly and unexpectedly when one evening, through some misunderstanding, both the suitors sauntered in, and Catherine was obliged to choose between them. She looked first at Daniel, then turned and gave her hand to Amos. Daniel put on his cap and made for the door, but Catherine called him back. She wanted to say that she was sorry she couldn't marry—both of them. Since Daniel couldn't be her husband, would he—perhaps—consider—becoming—her father? Widow Brech stood near by, beaming her willingness to acquiesce. Daniel was a prudent man. It did not take him long to discover that Catherine's mother was a woman after his own heart, and barring age, admirably suited in every way to be his wife. A double wedding was arranged and celebrated on Christmas Day, and two more knots were tied into the already badly-tangled Eby relationship.

The spring of 1808 saw the beginning of industrial development on the Heasley Tract, and Daniel and Jacob Erb were the men who had the foresight and enterprise to bring it about. They realized that long enough had the Mennonites travelled to Coote's Paradise whenever they wanted a few bushels of grain milled or a load of lumber cut. The day was coming—and coming soon—when these things would be done at home on the Tract, and the money would be kept within their own community. They investigated the question, deliberated, and speculated, and at last decided to build both a grist-mill and a saw-mill at the spot just below John Bricker's, where the power on the river was exceptionally strong. With much labour they erected the new buildings. They brought the equipment from York and started the mills running. From the very first day, the success of the new ventures was assured. The people realized that the mills were bound to enrich not only their proprietors but indirectly the entire community.

One day when the mills were running merrily, Daniel Erb, who was the miller, thrust his dusty head out of the window for a breath of the balmy spring air and saw a caravan of conestogas passing by. Five, he counted, and behind them rode a woman on horseback. Daniel could not forbear to shout and wave a friendly welcome.

Four conestogas returned his greeting and passed on their way, but the fifth stopped directly in front of the mill. "Is this the Heasley

Tract?" the driver called out, shaping his hand like a funnel to help the sound to carry.

Daniel nodded and smiled. He pointed not without pride to the sign over the door. "Erb's grist-mill," it read.

The driver seemed impressed and began to talk with the woman on horseback. No sooner did she see the sign than she became noticeably excited and in a shrill voice demanded to know where Daniel and Jacob Erb lived.

Daniel could scarcely believe his ears. "Why, Daniel—that's me!" he stammered.

The driver seemed satisfied, for he jumped from the wagon and began to jerk out from the back of his conestoga a small trunk, which he threw upon the ground. Then he shook hands with the woman on horseback, and climbed into his conestoga. "Wisiters" he cried to the astonished Daniel, as he gathered up his reins and told his horses to go on.

As Daniel lived, it was his sister Bevy Brubacher coming to visit him!

Right cordially the Erbs welcomed her, from Grossdoddy and Grossmommy to the little children, who now for the first time saw their Aunt Bevy in the flesh.

"And so you've come, too!" cried the overjoyed grandmother. "Pretty soon we'll all be here."

But Bevy made it very plain from the first that she had not come to stay. This was only a visit, three weeks at the most, if, indeed, she could endure it that long. If she couldn't, all she had to do was to leap into her saddle and join the first party that was going over to God's country, Pennsylvania.

Grossdoddy Erb laughed. If she had to depend upon conestogas returning to Pennsylvania, he thought the chances were good for a long visit.

"They come here," explained Grossmommy, "but they don't go back."

"Not even as far as Coote's Paradise, now that we've got the mills," added Daniel, who in spite of all the Mennonite discipline had to say against the ugly sin of pride, could not help feeling somewhat elated over the great achievement of the Erbs.

Jacob Erb and his family and Annie Bricker and hers were sent for, and there was a great family reunion that evening. The only thing that marred the occasion was the absence of Mary and Benj Eby, who were quite out of reach, being eight miles away. Bevy could not forgive Benj for the distance which he had put between Mary and her mother's people.

After all, it was Mary that Bevy Brubacher had come to see more than anyone else. She would give Daniel no peace on the following day until he closed up the mill for a few hours, packed her little trunk into his wagon and drove her to Ebytown. The news of her mother's arrival on the Tract had already come to Mary's ears, and she stood at the door with open arms to greet her. "So you did come for all!" she exclaimed. "You did come like I said you was to!"

"Ach, I thought I might chust as well," replied Bevy, loosening her bonnet-strings. "There ain't much to hold me there now— nothing but the graves."

Mary's face lit up with joy. "You'll stop here?" she cried, excitedly. "You'll stop here and live with me and Benj?"

But Bevy shook her head. It would never agree with her, she said. The air was so much sweeter over there. She wasn't going to give up her comfortable home in God's country, Pennsylvania, for such a wilderness as the Heasley Tract. This was only a visit. Three weeks, she would stay—four at the most.

"We'll talk about goin' home when that time comes," laughed Benj, who had come in from the fields to welcome his mother-in-law. "If you're like the rest of us, you won't want to go then."

Not the least feature in the cordiality of the welcome Benj and Mary accorded Bevy was the expectation of hearing news from the friends in the homeland. Mary's mother was scarcely seated in the only armchair in the house before Benj began to ply her with questions about his own people.

She had news about the family at the Hammer Creek House— bad news, although Bevy, being a very voluble woman, who knew better than to spoil a good story with a mournful tone, told it cheerfully enough. Old Christian Eby was no more. He had not been out of his bed since the day Benj and Mary drove away. Every morning found him a little weaker until finally on the last day of the year, he "went." Bevy verily believed that if Benj had remained at home like a dutiful son, his father would still be living.

It was a terrible blow, but Benj bore it bravely. He could find no words to reply.

"But you ought to see the big funeral he had," continued Bevy, beginning, as it were, a new chapter in her story. "Three hundred people almost, and they nearly all stopped for supper. Your pop had the friends though, queer and all as he was. But of course they all knew there'd be good eatin'."

Mary left her chair and went over and stood beside Benj. She laid a sympathizing hand on his shoulder. She determined to change the subject. "And is she good?" she inquired, referring of course to Nancy, and to her health rather than to her morals.

Bevy folded her hands across her stomach and looked very grave. She was a "widow-woman" herself, she said, and she knew how it felt to have something to say and nobody to say it to. She predicted that it would go hard with Nancy.

Benj was trying to picture his old home under these new conditions. He could see his father's arm chair—empty; his mother sitting beside it—alone.

"And there she sets all day," said Bevy, reading Benj's thoughts.

"Knittin'?" suggested Mary.

"No," replied Bevy. "She don't knit no more. Sometimes she thinks, but most of the time she chust sets." She had a feeling that Benj wanted her to be explicit about the matter.

"But Hannes goes often to see her," Benj was sure.

Bevy suddenly burst into a merry laugh. She had such a funny story to tell about Hannes and his new barn. He was making it just ninety-nine feet long so as not to offend Old Jonas Hoffman who had built one for Eliza and Henry Brubacher to the boasted length of one hundred feet. "But Nancy she wants him to make it a hundred and one. Says he's dumm if he don't."

"And of course Hannes won't."

"He won't hear to it," replied Bevy. "Nancy was gettin' madder and madder. I don't know how far it would 've went, but I stepped in."

"You!" exclaimed Mary. She could not understand why her mother should want to interfere with the affairs of the Ebys.

Bevy protested that she wasn't interfering, and if she were, hadn't she a right to, considering that one of the barns in question now belonged to her own son? All she did was to measure Henry's barn. There must have been some mistake about the measurements. It was only ninety-eight feet long.

"And now she's happy," said Mary. "But Hannes, what does he say? He ain't goin' to cut a piece off his, is he?"

Bevy's fat stomach shook with suppressed merriment. "He's in the secret," she smiled. "I lent one of his boots to measure with. Nobody can say it ain't a foot long."

With news and gossip, jokes and reminiscences, Bevy beguiled away the hours till bed-time. But she found time to intersperse a few inquiries about Sam Brickers. How many children had they? Two already! and red-heads, both of them! Did she ever! She was the last person in the world to want to say anything against Sam—it seemed as if he was almost in the "Freundschaft" since her sister was married to his brother—but she did hope that Beccy wouldn't live to rue the day when she "hitched-up" with Sam Bricker and that temper of his.

"Ach, Sam's all right," interposed Benj, ready as usual to defend his hero at whatever point he might be attacked. "If it wasn't for Sam Bricker, we'd all be settin' back in Pennsylvania."

"Where you ought to be with your own folks."

"He was pretty smart to fetch all them twenty thousand dollars over."

Benj was about to relate his own experience with transporting money—notably the incident at The Twenty—but Bevy would not listen. She felt moved to deliver a little tirade on the subject of temper in general and the Bricker variety in particular. "Temper is a sin," she declared. "It goes with the world, the flesh, and the devil. Us Mennonites dursn't give way to it. The Erbs don't, nor the Brubachers—much—but them Brickers, they have to fight it something awful. Chust look once at Nancy, your mom."

Benj flushed. For the first time in his life he felt that he had inherited some of the execrable Bricker temper. But he was an Eby, too, a very discreet young man who knew better than to pick a quarrel with his mother-in-law.

It was long past the usual hour for retiring when Benj carried Bevy's trunk into the front room, which Mary had converted temporarily into a bedroom for her mother. He had wished her good-night and pleasant dreams. Then he returned to the kitchen, threw himself wearily into the arm chair, and dropped his head upon his chest.

He had sat there for some time lost in thought when Bevy re-entered the room, half-dressed. In her hand she held a parcel wrapped with newspaper and tied securely with a heavy cord. "It's yours, Benj," she said, thrusting it into his hands, and hovering about him for some inexplicable reason.

"Mine?"

"Hannes said I was to fetch it along over to you," she explained. "It's a book by the feel of it, for all Hannes said it was your pop's will."

Benj took the parcel and laid it on the table without a word.

Bevy lingered for a time, consumed with curiosity, which Benj was determined should not be satisfied. When the silence was becoming oppressive, she ventured to remark that it was late and it, indicating the parcel, could wait until the morning.

Benj heard the inquisitive woman shuffle off to the bedroom, but he took the precaution of waiting until her laboured breathing assured him of no further interruption. Then he took the parcel reverently in his hands, undid the wrappings, and discovered the contents.

There was—he half expected it—his father's Bible! Its corners were crumpled and its pages thumb-marked, but it was to Benj the most sacred treasure in all the world. Did it not contain all the promises that had been his father's stay through all the vicissitudes of life? Had he not seen his father's tears fall upon the open pages, while the old man bore all his loved ones up before the Throne of God? And was Benjamin, the least of his sons, ever forgotten? Oh, no! More than for all the others his prayers ascended for "der gle' Bench" that he might be kept from the evil and grow up to be a blessing to the world.

He opened the sacred book. The pages fell apart naturally at the place where is recorded the story of Jacob's sons who went to Egypt in the days of famine to buy corn. He tried to read again the beautiful narrative that he knew so well, but tears filled his eyes, and dropped upon the already tear-stained page. What a heart of love his father had! How it must have yearned, as Jacob's did, over his son, Benjamin!

Overcome with reverence and sacred memories, Benj buried his face in his hands. His heart was melted to an infinite tenderness. Time had turned back twenty years in its flight and made him a child again—the happy child he used to be in his father's home at Hammer Creek.

Mary opened the door, stole to his side, and laid her hand upon his head. Then without a word she went back to bed and left him alone. Mary! He could not remember the time when she did not sympathize with his troubles, this sweetheart of his life.

A piece of paper fell from the table and fluttered to the floor. Benj stooped to pick it up.

His father's will! Benj and Susie were to share his Canadian lands, but that was not all. Attached to the bottom of the document was a sort of codicil written by his father's own hand, his last will and testament, and the only one in all the world who could execute it was Benjamin himself.

"My Bible to Benjamin, my son, with the prayer that he use it to preach the Gospel in Canada."

Yielding to an overwhelming impulse to escape somewhere, anywhere, Benj jumped up, opened the door and slipped out into the night. But when he looked up into the blue dome of heaven he knew that, go where he would, he could never out-run those myriads of twinkling stars that seemed to search his very soul. The eyes of God, his father used to say they were, watching visibly by night, but invisibly by day, the conduct of all little children.

But Benj wasn't going to be a preacher. He looked up into the galaxy of the heavens and said so.

Silently the stars twinkled on while Benj protested, now strongly, now weakly. A terrible warfare was going on within his soul. Hour after hour the battle waged unceasingly, indecisively. But with the first dawn of morning Benj was ready to fall upon his knees in utter exhaustion. He looked up into the heavens and cried as his father had taught him to do in the days of childhood: "Thou God, seest me!"

Then Benj realized that, like Jacob of old, he had wrestled with an angel until the breaking of the day. Humbly he claimed the patriarch's blessing. Then and there was vouchsafed to him a wonderful vision. He saw the Canada of the future, a land rich in resources and teeming with population. The wilderness had blossomed into a garden, and in the centre of it, at his very doors, where once an impenetrable cedar swamp had defied the ingress of man, he saw the belching chimneys of a great industrial city. Ah! what a task was his, to lay well the foundations of Christian citizenship in this new land of promise. A task, yes, but a worthy one, and withal a phenomenal privilege.

With a new aspect on life Benj returned to the house and announced that his father's prayers had at last prevailed. It was his intention to offer himself on the altar of the Christian ministry.

Mary was overjoyed. She declared that for years she had known that Benj was called to preach; that he would never be truly happy until he "gave himself up." She had been with him in spirit every hour of the night through which they had just passed. She knew the moment of his decision. Her one anxiety had been that perhaps she was unwittingly standing between him and his duty. "I thought mebbe I was a stumbling-block to you, Benj," she confessed.

"A stumblin'-block!" cried Mary's mother. "An Erb a stumblin'-block to a Eby! Such a dumm notion! Why, Mary, you're his steppin'-stone, ain't she, Benj?"

From his heart Benj declared she was. All that was good, and lovely, and true, and sweet; this and more, his Mary was to him.

"There now, what did I tell you?" cried Bevy Brubacher, complacent with exultation. "You always was too good for Benj Eby and this Canada, but now I see the hand of the Lord in it all. He ain't good enough for Pennsylvania, so the Lord sent him here in the bush, and you're to lift him up, Mary, you're to lift him up. Some day mebbe he'll be a credit to you."

Mary did her best to stay her mother's oratory and insults. "It's me that must climb up to him," she said.

"Well, anyway you don't have to go and tell him," rejoined the mother. "It don't do the men no good to hear how smart they all are." But whether she intended this speech to mollify Benj or to give her daughter a lesson out of her own matrimonial experience, Mary could only conjecture.

Time slipped by very quickly, very pleasantly, for Bevy Brubacher in her daughter's home. Before she realized it, three weeks had passed; and the fourth, the one of farewell, was drawing to a close. As yet she had visited no one but Mary, and not since the first week of her stay had she said anything about returning to God's country, Pennsylvania.

"It's five weeks to-day since you come," Benj reminded her one day.

Bevy looked up sharply. "You ain't gettin' tired of me, are you?"

"Not at all," Benj hastened to assure her. "But if I remember right, you didn't think you could stand it three weeks."

"But how was I to know that you was goin' to turn out to be a preacher?" retorted Bevy. "I can't go back there till I can tell them what like you can preach."

So two more weeks were added to Bevy's sojourn in the wilderness.

At last the Sunday came when Benj was to preach his first sermon. Old Sam Betzner's shanty was packed to the doors. And such a sermon as it was! Not even his brother Peter, the Bishop, had ever been known to preach like that. It was as if both preacher and people had turned their backs forever on the mundane things of life and had taken a pilgrimage to some lofty mountain-top of religious experience, there to enjoy a perpetual love-feast. They wanted to build a tabernacle and stay there with Moses and Elias—and Benj Eby. They crowded around him afterwards and told him how his words had moved them. Even Bevy declared that an angel could not have preached better.

"It was the Lord," replied Benj, quietly, refusing to be elated by their praises. "He told me what to say."

Another month went by. Bevy left the Ebys—but only temporarily—to visit for a time with her sister and brothers. She returned in time to welcome Mary's first baby, a boy with a pair of lusty lungs.

"We'll call him Isaac for his Grossdoddy Brubacher that was," said Bevy, and much as Benj had hoped to call him by the name of his own father, the woman had her way.

"And now pretty soon you'll go back to Pennsylvany, I guess," suggested Grossmommy Betzner, who had come to see the new baby. "You are here long already."

Bevy was aghast. "I can't go now," she said.

"And why not?"

"I can't go on horseback now," was the laughing reply, "Why, I'm a grossmommy!"

"It's chust an excuse," Grossmommy Betzner confided afterwards to her daughter, Lizzie Sherk. "She don't want to go. She feels for stopping here. If it wasn't for her man laying in the grave over there, she'd never go."

Whether there was any truth in this insinuation Bevy could never be induced to state definitely. But to judge by her actions, she was growing fonder of life in the wilderness than she cared to confess. Weeks grew into months and months lengthened into years before she had visited and re-visited all the "Freundschaft" to her satisfaction, and it was with many a backward glance that she mounted her horse and set forth in the spring of for God's country, Pennsylvania.

CHAPTER XIV

Towards the end of July, 1812, Little Aaron Schneider, who five years before had disturbed the meeting at The Twenty with his cries for more cookies, created another sensation by becoming alarmingly ill, so ill in fact that everyone feared that the time had come for Little Aaron to "go."

Just what ailed the child nobody knew. He seemed to be suffering from a complication of diseases with the symptoms of all the complaints listed in the almanac and a few others that the medicine makers had neglected to mention. Down the little patient's throat had been poured quarts of home-made remedies which the neighbours had brewed from native herbs for his benefit. He had been sweated and starved; rubbed and charmed. All that was humanly possible had been done. The child's life was now in the hands of God.

A very malicious sort of person it must have been, indeed, who in these days of anxiety would allude to the frequent deviations of the little sufferer from the narrow path of rectitude. Everyone knew, but no one remembered, how only two weeks before this terrible sickness had come upon him, the little fellow had ruined a set of good harness in the hope of satisfying a budding faculty for invention, or how the previous summer he had secretly sucked as many as ten eggs in the barn, when they were selling at six cents a dozen. These, and many other misdemeanours, were blotted out of the book of their remembrance; Little Aaron's sins were covered.

The time had come to speak only of the boy's virtues, the qualities which would entitle him to a place in the angel band in heaven. His father told how industrious he had been, helping with the chores both night and morning; a good boy, not at all destructive, or quarrelsome like others of his age, the best son an undeserving father ever had. But his mother kept thinking about how she was going to miss him, and her eyes filled with tears. She folded her hands in resignation over the top of her abdomen, and said; "The Lord giveth and The Lord taketh away; blessed be the name of the Lord."

Sam and Beccy Bricker had always been very fond of Little Aaron. He used to visit them every day on his way home from school, and the little Brickers looked forward with much expectation to his coming. It seemed as if he almost belonged to the family. And now he was sick, would probably never come again, and they were sad.

"I made some noodle soup for him," said Beccy one day when Sam brought home word that Susie and Josiah had despaired of his life. "Little Aaron was always great for noodles."

"Noodles!" grunted Sam. "He can't eat noodles now."

"And why not?" said Beccy. "Noodle soup is good for whatever you've got." She poured into a pail at least a quart of this panacea for all the ailments of humanity, and held it out to Sam. "Take it over to him once," she said, "and tell Susie I'll come till to-morrow if he's here yet."

Sam wasn't any too pleased about the errand, but he obediently put on his hat and carried the noodles to the Schneiders.

Little Aaron was still alive, but hovering between this world and the next. "He don't want to go," was the way Susie expressed his condition.

Sam presented the noodles which Beccy had sent, and then followed Susie into the bedroom, where the sick child lay upon what everyone feared would be his death-bed.

In the farthest corner of the room was the bed, and somewhere on the top of it was Little Aaron, elevated about half way up to the ceiling and quite invisible. The bed was a great four-poster with a huge straw tick supported by a net-work of ropes, and surmounted by a more billowy tick of feathers. On this lay the little patient, covered by numberless quilts of marvellous design and manufacture, and protected by a dark valance from draughts and the eyes of the curious.

Susie approached the bed on tiptoe, and quietly drew the curtains. The child was asleep. She motioned Sam to come and see him.

There lay the little fellow, white and haggard almost beyond recognition, a mere skeleton of his former self.

"Does he look natural?" said Susie, in a funereal whisper.

Sam shook his head.

The child moved, turned slowly on his side and opened his eyes.

"It's Sam Bricker, Aaron," said Susie. "He fetched some noodles along over. You like noodles, I know. Do you feel for some now?"

But Little Aaron turned his face impatiently to the wall. "I want water—cold water," he said, weakly. "I'm hot all over and my head aches me so."

Sam rushed to the kitchen and brought in a cup of cold water, but Susie brushed him aside unceremoniously enough. Was he crazy? The child must be kept hot for fear of a chill. She took the precaution at this moment to tuck a piece of flannel around his neck, lest a draught should reach him from the open door.

"Sometimes he gets wild," whispered the distressed mother, pulling the valance again to its accustomed place and preparing to leave the room. "I often wonder if he's goin' out of his head."

"I'm sure he will," replied Sam, "if you don't give him more air. That's what he needs—that and water."

At this moment a startled cry resounded through the room. Susie and Sam turned again to the bed. Aaron had jerked the valance aside, and he now sat bolt upright in the feathers with an avalanche of heavy quilts tumbling to the floor. His eyes were sparkling with excitement and fixed on some unseen object in another corner of the room. With his little white finger he pointed to this creature of his fancy. "Ketch him, mom," he cried.

The mother heaved a sigh and stooped to pick up the quilts.

"Give him water!" suggested Sam. "Cool him off!"

But Susie paid no attention. Gently but firmly, she tried to make the child lie down.

Still Aaron stared fixedly into the corner and shrieked in his delirium. "He's stealin', mom! He's at the cookies! Ketch him! Quick!"

A great tear fell from Susie's face and splashed on Little Aaron's flushed cheek. The child looked up questioningly. The delirium was gone and the little body fell back languidly among the feathers. Susie tucked in the quilts very securely and pulled the curtains once more. She motioned Sam from the room.

"All the time he thinks somebody is stealin'," explained the troubled mother, when she joined Sam a few minutes later in the kitchen.

"Funny," replied Sam, pulling his whiskers. "Did he perhaps see somebody stealin' once?"

"Only that time at The Twenty," said Susie.

"At The Twenty!" exclaimed Sam, pricking up his ears.

The cat was out of the bag. There was nothing for Susie to do but to relate, in part at least, the story that she and Benj had decided to keep to themselves. She explained that Aaron had been with her when she caught a man rummaging in Benj's conestoga. It must have made a wonderful impression on the child's mind, if he could remember it so vividly after five years.

Sam Bricker got up and paced the floor. His face was dark and foreboding, though Susie in her excitement did not notice. "What did he want—that man?" he demanded to know. "Not cookies!"

"The money," replied Susie. "Benj had it in such a barrel."

Sam fairly jumped. "He didn't get none?"

"Not a dollar!" Susie was glad to inform him. "I ketched him!"

"What like was he, Susie—this thief?"

Susie had at this moment her first hazy presentiment of danger, but she did not know what it was or how to avert it. She described the fellow as well as she could. A little man, she said he was, not a Mennonite.

Sam suddenly pounded his fist upon the table with such force that Susie bounced off her chair. "It's him!" he roared.

"Who?" cried Susie, in great distress. This black cloud of danger that she saw looming up was going to break over her head.

"Heasley! That scoundrel! That rogue! That thief! He was at our place, too!"

"At your place, Sam? You must be dreamin'."

"I was, but I've chust woke up."

"But when was he at your place, Sam?"

"When he smashed Beccy's chest. Now I'll smash him!"

He was gone. Like a madman he mounted his horse and rode away. Susie ran to the door and begged him to return for the pail that Beccy had sent with the noodles, but he did not hear. He had no ears for anything but what that devilish temper of his was urging him to do, no patience even with Menno, although he was straining every nerve to do his bidding.

Utterly bewildered, Susie went back to the kitchen, sat down at the table and buried her face in her hands. She was still there when Josiah came in and asked her what was the matter with Sam Bricker. He had seen him drive away acting like a lunatic.

"He's after Heasley!" said Susie. "He's goin' to smash him!"

Josiah didn't know what all the fuss was about. He thought the matter with Heasley had been settled years ago.

"So it was," replied Susie, "but Sam thinks he tried to steal from Benj at The Twenty." As Josiah had never heard the story, Susie had to tell it to him in detail.

Josiah was puzzled. "Heasley tried to steal perhaps," he said, "but did he get the money? No. Sam ought to be glad instead of mad."

"Ach, Josiah, you are a dummhead, too, for all you ain't an Eby," returned Susie. "Can't you see how Sam feels? But then you didn't have no trouble with Heasley like Sam did. He didn't come here either and smash our things like he did Beccy's chest. Her 'aus styer' chest, too, all she had in the world."

Josiah had no patience with either Sam Bricker or his logic. What proof had Sam, he wanted to know, that it was Heasley who had played the thief in either case? And if it was Heasley, what restitution could be demanded, when nothing had been lost? Was a man to have his head smashed because he was suspected of having smashed a trunk? Sam Bricker was nothing but a hot-head. There was no knowing where that ungovernable temper of his would lead him yet.

Susie either could not or would not follow her husband's argument. "I can't help but feel for Sam," she kept repeating, "and for Beccy."

"Well, it's all your fault," was all the consolation Josiah offered her. "What for did you have to tell him all you know? Mebbe it will learn you a lesson."

Susie said no more, but all night long as she sat at Aaron's bedside she thought about Sam Bricker, and mingled with her prayers for the recovery of the child were silent but fervent petitions that the man might be given grace and power to withstand this onset of his besetting sin.

166

CHAPTER XV

It was from Josiah Schneider that Beccy first learned the truth. He had come ostensibly to return the pail that Beccy had sent over with the noodles, but in reality to see if perchance Sam might have come to his senses and gone home. "Here's your dish," he had said, setting the pail on the table. "Where's Sam?"

"Sam?" Beccy looked at him anxiously with her large, blue, innocent eyes. "Why ain't he with the pail?"

Josiah was a stolid man of a stolid race. All he could do for a moment was frown. He was sorry for Beccy, but for the life of him, he didn't know how to show it. Bluntly he told her the truth; then stalked away, leaving the poor woman to cry her heart out alone on the kitchen table.

Beccy was left alone with her babies.

She had always feared for her husband's temper, but she expected to be at his side when the crisis should come. She had a way of managing him, even when he was in his pouts. If he had only come to her first instead of running off to the strange, unsympathetic world, she would have reasoned with him, persuaded him.

The next morning Susie came, her eyes red with tears and sleeplessness, and folded Beccy to her breast. She was utterly penitent. It was all her fault. If she had only thought. It had never entered into her stupid head that the thief might have been Heasley. She doubted if Beccy herself would have suspected it.

Beccy was sure she would.

"But," said Susie, anxious to defend her own lack of intuition, "your 'aus styer' chest, you never thought it was him that smashed that."

"I know it was," replied Beccy with conviction. "But I didn't leave Sam know it."

Susie was still unconvinced. "Did you see him do it?" she asked.

"No."

"I guess you saw him sneak out of the house, then?"

"No."

"Then how do you know it was him?"

Beccy could not explain the phenomenon, but of the fact there could be no question.

"You was always such a smart girl, Beccy," said Susie, in all sincerity. "I often used to wonder way back at Hammer Creek already how you got so many queer notions in your head. I chust wish now I had 've told you first."

Beccy could not but wish so too, but she refrained from saying so.

"Mebbe he'll come back yet," said Susie, growing more optimistic. "He might change his mind before he comes anywhere."

But Beccy shook her head. "It's not like Sam," she said. "If he starts something once, he don't stop till it's finished." A very good quality—sometimes—she thought, but like everything else, it had its disadvantages.

"He won't stop long away from you, Beccy," comforted Susie. "He's all the time sayin' it don't give many women like his Beccy."

With these and many other hopeful assurances, Susie turned to go. She was out of sight before it occurred to Beccy to inquire about Little Aaron. However, the sick boy would be no longer the chief figure in the public eye, as he had taken a turn for the better.

The news of Sam's furious outburst of temper had spread like wildfire throughout the community, and soon became the chief subject of conversation on the Heasley Tract. There was no excuse for Sam's conduct. It was foolish, extreme, sinful. The Lord would punish him in His own good time and in His own way. But while the men wagged their heads and said hard things about the husband, there was not one of them but had a kind thought for Beccy and the children. They sent her all sorts of consoling messages with the women, who came one by one to mingle their tears with the poor deserted and dejected wife.

Beccy could not understand why Benj did not come, or at least send some word of sympathy. Mary had been there and wept with her, but of Benj's feelings she had said nothing. Such friends as they had been, too, from earliest childhood. How Benj had idolized Sam—and now in the day of trouble, he had not even a word of consolation to offer. Beccy couldn't help but feel a little hurt about it. A little neglected, too.

He came at last one evening when it was growing dusk. Beccy had tucked the children into their beds, and had come to sit alone with her thoughts on the doorstep in the glorious twilight of the late summer. Then Benj stole silently to her side and sat down on the step with her.

"It's hard, Beccy," he said, presently. "You know I feel it, too."

Beccy dropped her head, and a great tear splashed on her folded hands. Thoughts too deep for utterance surged through her throbbing breast.

A lengthy pause ensued, and by-and-by Benj spoke again. "I have to do it, Beccy," he said. "It's in the rules."

Beccy started. She looked at Benj with sad, tearful eyes. "You ain't goin' to——?" She couldn't say the terrible words that she would have to use to express her thought.

Very gently Benj came to her aid. "He's set back," he said. "I had to. We can't have him in meetin' with thoughts like he has."

Beccy dropped her head again until her chin fell upon her heaving breast. Her eyes were blinded with tears that overflowed and coursed down her cheeks.

What could Benj do in the presence of sorrow like this? He laid a kindly hand upon her shoulder, he quoted a few passages from the Scriptures, and then he stole away as silently as he had come. He was glad enough that the terrible ordeal was over.

So another bitter ingredient was added to Beccy's cup of woe. Sam had been excommunicated. He was under the ban. By his own guilty life he had separated himself from Christ and His Church; he had enthroned the devil in the place of God in his heart and life. Unless he repented heartily of his wickedness, he must remain forever outside the fold. It would be Beccy's duty to teach her children to avoid their father, lest he should contaminate them and drag them in their innocence into the bog of sin in which he wallowed. A terrible breach separated Sam from all his loved ones, a breach which he himself had made and which he alone could span.

Harvest-time was approaching, and still Sam had not come. Beccy had never worked in the harvest-fields before, but there was no help for it this year. She took the scythe from its nail in the barn, and with a heavy heart, but a courageous one for all that, she went into the field to cut the ripened grain. She bound it, too, with her own hands, and garnered it in the barn.

The men had come repeatedly from the neighbouring farms to offer their assistance, but Beccy declined all their well-meant offers. She wanted no help, she said, so long as she could do it herself. While she had the strength, she would do Sam's work and her own. The time might yet come when she would have to call upon her friends for aid. If they would come then, they should not find her lacking in gratitude.

Quite suddenly and unexpectedly that time came, and a terrible day it was. Beccy threw up her hands and implored heaven to help. She could do nothing but wail. The last sheaf had been gathered in, and the brave little woman had just begun the threshing in her own feeble way, when a terrible scourge broke over the Bricker homestead, and left her penniless, hopeless, and homeless at the mercy of the neighbourhood.

It was one of those relentless forest fires that every now and then would swoop down upon the early settlers when they least expected it, consuming everything in its track, and leaving behind it nothing but a heap of black ruin. It came up so suddenly that Beccy did not see it until it literally knocked at her door. Frantically, she seized Baby Sophie and carried her, cradle and all, to the spring-house. Mary and Peter shrieked with terror and ran behind clutching at their mother's skirts. Beccy shoved them all in on the cold stone floor and threw a pailful of water on the wooden door, which alone stood between her helpless little ones and certain death.

The barn! Could she reach it? She must! She could hear the cow bellowing in agony, the horses neighing in alarm, the hens cackling with excitement. She saw the flames shoot from the roof, and the smoke curl from the windows. The "weggli!" She saw it, too, vividly, certainly, though not with physical eyes, Sam's most treasured possession. Not a moment now did she stop. Throwing her apron about her shoulders, she rushed towards the burning barn, she opened the door, she rescued the "weggli" from the very teeth of the fiery demon. With one hand on either shaft, she dragged it to the door of the spring-house, and turning it on its side, tugged at it until she got it safely indoors. Then she closed the door upon the flames, gathered her children in her arms, listened, and prayed.

Presently the roar and tumult of the flames passed by. They echoed in the distance. Her children were safe; as brands plucked from the burning, they had escaped with their lives.

A terrible scene of desolation greeted Beccy when she opened the door of the spring-house. A few charred pillars stood where the barn had been; a few frightened chickens that had fled from the scene of horror cackled in frantic protest. The horses and Sam's jersey cow, trapped in their stalls, had died a terrible death. Of the harvest nothing was left but a mass of smouldering grain and a cloud of dense, black smoke.

The house, fortunately, had come through the furnace of fire with some remnant of its identity. It could yet be saved, Beccy thought, though great tongues of fire still leaped forth through the holes in the roof and smoke belched from the windows. Trembling with emotion, Beccy carried a bucket of water to the kitchen door and tried to enter but a volley of smoke met her there and drove her back blinded and half-suffocated with smoke to her refuge in the spring-house.

"What is it, mom?" cried Peter, whose eyes were open wide as saucers with wonder and amazement.

Mary, who was two years older, knew, but she could not explain. She realized that it was her duty to keep Baby Sophie asleep to the terrors of an untoward world.

Utterly dejected and hopeless, Beccy prostrated herself before the little cradle, and sobbed as if her heart would break. It was the one piece of furniture that remained to her of her once happy home, the little cradle that Sam had made.

Mary, scarcely knowing what to do under these unusual circumstances, ceased rocking and stuck her thumb in her mouth. Presently she went to her mother's side, and bending down, whispered into her ear: "Don't cry, mom. You've got us yet."

"Of course I have," cried Beccy, gathering her dear ones about her.

Voices were heard outside. The neighbours had come; they were calling, "Beccy! Beccy!"

"Here she is!" shouted Peter, rushing to the door.

Benj Eby was there, and Josiah Schneider, and Beccy's own brother, Daniel; and soon there was gathered from far and near a great crowd of friends and relatives.

"Don't cry, Beccy," said Daniel, comfortingly. "We'll make it good, won't we, Benj?"

"Of course we will," replied Benj. "We'll have a bee, and before you know it, Beccy, you'll have a new house and barn."

"I'll fetch Sam's cow over," said John Bricker, when he came. "We never call her anything but Sam's cow anyway."

Tears of gratitude flowed down Beccy's cheeks, as she tried to express her thanks. "The good Lord put it into your hearts," she said. "He knows I can't help myself now."

The men worked hard, often leaving work that should have been done at home in order that they might come to Beccy's assistance. By the end of November, they had restored the Bricker buildings. With donations from her friends, Beccy was able to furnish her new home almost as well as the ruined one that Sam had made.

But no matter how kind her friends might be, life would never be the same again. There would always be an aching void. Beccy's very soul cried out for Sam! Sam! But all she heard, all she would ever hear, she feared, was a dismal, empty echo.

One morning when she was going to the barn as usual to do the chores, she saw, as if in apparition, Menno standing at the stable door with only a halter about his neck. Instantly her heart bounded for joy. Sam! Sam was back! But the horse had no rider. Sam was nowhere to be seen.

Anxiously, she hurried towards the stable. It was actually Menno; for he saw her coming and ran to meet her. He lowered his head for her embrace, frisked his tail for joy, but whinnied for sorrow. He was asking the same question as she: Where was Sam?

Beccy could tell at a glance that it had been many a long day since Menno had been with Sam; for the hair was worn off his hide where the heavy harness had rubbed. His mouth was sore, and his feet poorly shod. Menno had served a hard master, that was evident. Very gently she caressed the tangled mane, and led him into a stall in the barn.

Glad as Beccy was to see Menno, his coming emptied her heart of all hope of Sam's return. Nothing in the world could have persuaded Sam to part with Menno—nothing he could control. And what was there that Sam could not control? Death! Sam was dead. As Beccy expressed it, "He must 've went."

Towards the end of March there was a little rift in the clouds when a new member came to join the family circle, a bouncing boy with eyes as blue as the skies of heaven and hair as red and as curly as his father's.

"Too bad Beccy had to have him yet," said Annie Bricker to the other women, who had come to see the new arrival. "I'm sure she's got it hard enough without another bubby yet."

"Too bad," was the unanimous reply.

"But she don't think so, not her," continued Annie. "What do you think she wants to call him yet? Sam!"

"Sam?"

"Yes, Sam!"

Susie Schneider thought she could understand how Beccy felt about it. "Mebbe he'll grow up to be a comfort to her, poor thing," she said, "and I guess Beccy needs all the comfort she can get."

But when the excitement was over and the women had gone home leaving Beccy alone with her little ones, gloom settled down again upon the sorrowful woman and refused to be shaken. Loneliness, it seemed, was to be her lot in life. Her parents she could scarcely remember. Christian Eby, who had been both father and mother to her, had taken his journey to that far-off country from which no traveller has yet returned, and Sam, to whom she had given all her love, had left her in disgrace, without so much as a farewell. Nearly a year had passed since that terrible day. He had gone on the long journey, too, she was sure; but when or how she would probably never know. And here she was—alone—for the rest of her days, always alone.

Poor Beccy almost stumbled into that Slough of Despond known as self-pity. Indeed, she might have fallen hopelessly into it, but for her four tiny, helpless children who came to her rescue and pulled her out.

Mary, the eldest, was agitated about something. She pushed the kitchen door open with all the vehemence she could command and came to the court of law to lay her complaint. "Peter he slapped Sophie right at the nose and made the bleed come," she announced. With one hand she endeavoured to drag the young culprit before the tribunal of justice; with the other she led her little, sob-choked, bloody-nosed sister, the movements of whose tiny feet were still a constant worry to their youthful owner.

They came upon Beccy at a most inopportune moment when she had given vent to her emotions in tears. At the sight of their mother in such distress the children forgot both protestations and excuses. Their judge and lawgiver was herself in trouble. Could it be that someone had slapped her? With wondering eyes they stared at Beccy for a moment; then all three burst simultaneously into tears, and ran and hid their faces, if not their fears, in their mother's apron. It was for them all the darkest hour in all their life.

Beccy roused herself. Forgetting her worries, she turned to her children. Very tenderly she lifted little Sophie to her lap, and wiped her dirty face. She put her arm around Mary and Peter, and drew them both close to her breast. They must not quarrel, she said. The great God who had made them brother and sisters wanted them to love one another. They must promise not to quarrel and hurt one another any more.

They would be good, they promised, and Beccy smiled through her tears to hear them take their solemn vows.

The children went back to their play and soon forgot the occurrence, but the mother's heart was filled with a new joy. Alone in the world? Not Beccy Bricker with three small, helpless children clinging to her skirts; and another, the most helpless of all, crying in the cradle. She made up her mind then and there to think no more about her troubles, but to think and plan and work for her little ones—her's and Sam's.

When supper-time came, Mary brought the dishes and set the table. Never once since Sam had left had she neglected to set a plate for her father. But this evening Beccy said she was to put it back in the cupboard.

"Ain't he comin' ever?" asked the child with anxious, questioning eyes. She knew that there was some mystery about the sudden disappearance of the "doddy," but just what it was her young mind had not yet been able to fathom. "Ain't he comin' no more?"

"No," said Beccy. "He's went."

"We must have his funeral then," said Mary in the matter-of-fact, practical sort of way in which she had always heard her elders speak of the last sad rites.

Beccy turned her face away, and for a while she said nothing. But she determined to be brave. "No, Mary," she said. "He's had his funeral already."

"And we didn't go to it?"

"We couldn't, Mary," explained Beccy. "We don't know yet when it was." She suggested that when Mary should be old enough they would go together and see if they could find his grave. "Would you like that, Mary?"

"No," said the child, wonderingly. "I want my doddy!"

"Ach, Mary, so do I!" cried Beccy, pressing the child to her bosom. "Nobody knows how I want him!"

When evening came, Beccy heard the children lisp their prayers, and then she tucked them into their beds, kissing them all softly and patting their chubby little cheeks. She put the baby into his cradle and rocked him to sleep. But she could not leave her precious baby boy. "Sam, Sam," she cried from the depths of her burdened heart. "Little Sam." Her heart was full of tender memories and love. Full of happiness, too, the only happiness she would ever know, that of living and working for her helpless little ones. God was very good. He had not left her alone. Who could not be happy with such a family?

Presently she stole quietly from the room and went to the kitchen table. She reached for her mending.

Ah! Peter's stocking had a hole in the toe. Another in the heel. Such a boy! But some day he would be a good man, this same Peter; a preacher, perhaps, or a teacher. She must train him well, so that when his days were over people would say that the world was better because he had lived in it.

Sophie's little dress was stained with blood. There wasn't a clean one either. Perhaps she could shorten one of Mary's. Some day both Mary and Sophie would grow up to be useful women. Happy wives, she hoped. Here a sigh escaped Beccy, and instantly she coughed to hide it.

Little Sam, the most precious of them all. Here was his little night-gown, handed down from his elders, until now it was too old to mend. Well, he would soon outgrow it, and then the rag-bag. And what did the future hold for Little Sam? Just like his father, she intended that he should be. But he must learn to control his temper and live at peace with all men. What better could she wish for him?

Suddenly the little mother found herself enveloped by a pale, white light. With a start she looked up, and saw that a cloud had passed by, and through the window shone the moon in all its glory. "It's full!" she cried, joyfully. For a moment it seemed as though Sam sat by her side beneath the apple-tree with his arm across her shoulders. A blissful moment.

But the light in her eyes soon darkened, and another cloud hid the face of the moon. "Silly!" she muttered to herself as she folded up her mending. "The moon don't mean nothing to me now. Ach, Sam, I guess I am dumm like all the Ebys!"

175

CHAPTER XVI

Meanwhile, Sam Bricker was having the experience of his lifetime. He may have nurtured the most diabolical plots against his old enemy, Robert Heasley, but the occasion to carry them out always seemed to be lacking. A kind Providence was intervening, no doubt.

The first thirty miles of his journey were uneventful enough but, when Sam reached Coote's Paradise within a few miles of Heasley's palatial residence at The Head of the Lake, he discovered that the village was all agog about something. Old and middle-aged men stood about the streets in small groups arguing with much gesticulation, while around the village pump had congregated a number of young men, gaily dressed in red coats, for some fête, Sam supposed.

"Look at the Dutchman, will you," cried one. In an aside he whispered; "Come on, fellows, here's some fun!"

Sam's curiosity was aroused. It fairly burned within him. To satisfy it, he was willing to wish these young men of the world a solemn "Good-day."

"Good-day! good-day!" replied the wag, who seemed to be their leader. "Good-night, you had better say. Where are you goin', Dutchie?"

"To The Head of the Lake."

The impudent fellow made a grimace and said: "Take my advice and don't. They're full up over there. Better stay here and sleep with me."

It was a very kind offer from a strange young man and Sam accepted it gratefully.

"Never mind the thanks, old man," sputtered this prospective bed-fellow of Sam's. "I'm just Fred Frid, and no saint, but when I see a stranger I always take him in. Say, Dutchie, where did you get that horse?"

"Bought him."

The attention of the whole group was now centred on Menno. They stood all about him, patting his mane and commenting on his good points. A very wonderful horse, they thought he was.

"And how much would you take for him?"

Sam's extremely human heart was filled with pride. "He's not for sale," he said, loftily.

"Don't blame you at all, Dutchie," said the genial Fred Frid. "That horse is good enough for the General." He turned his back upon Sam and went through some contortions of face which must have been extremely diverting, for the crowd laughed uproariously.

Sam did not appreciate being held up to ridicule, and with his curiosity still unsatiated, he decided to forego the offer of a night's lodging and go his own way. But Fred Frid stopped him. "Didn't you come to fight, Dutchie?" he said. "Here we all thought you were coming to help us win the war."

"War!" gasped Sam.

"War," echoed Fred Frid.

"It can't be!" cried Sam.

"It can't be," mocked the impertinent Fred Frid. "But it is." Taking advantage of Sam's dismay, he turned to his pals and whispered; "Backwoods! Green as grass! Didn't even know there was a war! Never heard of the United States!"

Sam caught the last word. "The United States!" he ejaculated. "We ain't fightin' them, are we?" It was impossible, unthinkable. Could a man fight his own people, his parents, the friends of a lifetime? Could he raise his hand against those who had come to him in his hour of distress and lifted the pall that hung over his Canadian home?

"Sorry, Dutchie," said Fred Frid, "but they are all true, them thoughts you're thinkin'. Your crowd don't fancy this war much I guess. They're the kind that want to say 'Peace, Peace' when there ain't no peace. What's the use of foolin' yourself like that?"

Sam did not answer.

The talkative fellow continued his harangue. "But let the Yankees send one of them little foraging parties of theirs to the Heasley Tract and steal a few of your fat cattle, then you'd fight, I guess."

"We don't fight," said Sam, sullenly.

"Or if they would burn down your barn, or run off with your wife."

"We don't fight."

"So I've heard before," was the sarcastic reply. "Say, what's wrong with you? Ain't you got no red blood at all?"

"We don't need none," retorted Sam. "We don't have to fight. The law leaves us go free."

"Whew!" whistled Fred Frid. "Did you hear that, fellows? You and me must fight to save the skins of the likes of him."

Sam said not a word. He had taken his stand behind the solid wall of legislation. What did he care for the argument and the sneers of the world?

Again Sam made a move to go, but once more Fred Frid stopped him. He declared that he was going to go to the bottom of this injustice which he had just discovered. "Say, Dutchie," he said, "Who learnt you that little speech about not having to fight?"

"Dunno."

"You dunno? Well I guess there ain't much truth in it, then."

Sam tried to explain that it was one of the conditions under which his people had come to Pennsylvania years before, and he had unbounded faith that the British Parliament would live up to the promise it had made to the Mennonites.

"Tell your story to the Parliament at York," interrupted Fred Frid. "I don't give much for your chances. After all, that's the Parliament that counts here."

"I told it to Isaac Brock——"

"The General?" cried the soldiers all in a single breath. "Not him—the General—Sir Isaac Brock?"

"Yes, him."

"When?"

Sam related the incident and ended by saying; "He's a friend to me."

A titter passed through the crowd, and broke into a hearty laugh. "Say, Dutchie," said Fred Frid, after one of his inimitable grimaces, "do you happen to know that your friend Isaac is over at The Head of the Lake with our friend, Robert?"

"Not Robert Heasley?"

"Yes, him," replied Fred Frid, with mock solemnity. "He's the Colonel. He says he's our best friend, but we all know that's not the first lie he's told."

Sam could have confirmed the statement, but he cautiously decided to keep his own counsel. With this information which had just come to his ears, he was determined to go to The Head of the Lake that very evening to meet his friend and his enemy. It required not only Fred Frid but all the company of soldiers to dissuade him. It was useless, they said. The lateness of the hour and the lack of accommodation at The Head of the Lake made it advisable to wait till morning. They were going then themselves to join the regiment, and all aboard for Detroit.

So Sam slept that night, as arranged, with the loquacious Fred and stabled his horse in an empty stall, which his new friend said he was able to find for him in his uncle's stable. A very convenient as well as economical arrangement, it would appear.

But when he awoke in the morning his roommate was gone. In fact all the soldiers had gone. Sam rushed to the stable. Menno was gone! The stall was empty except for a big placard which ornamented the crib:

"Thanks for the fifteen dollars and the horse that money couldn't buy.

Your old friends,
Peter Potter and Fred Frid.

Peddlers of ideas to people that don't grow them."

Sam was prostrated with grief and rage. The horrid truth flashed upon his unsuspecting mind. Peter Potter and Fred Frid were one and the same person. Menno, the greatest treasure he possessed, was in the hands of this contemptible fellow, who under any name he might choose for himself would still be nothing but a scoundrel, the king's uniform notwithstanding.

It must have been the uniform that made Sam think of his friend Isaac Brock. If anyone could help him out of his dilemma, he could. And he would, Sam had every reason to believe.

But by the time Sam had reached The Head of the Lake, running and stumbling along as best he could, the General and his forces had set out for Long Point on Lake Erie, for the purpose of journeying by water to Detroit. Since daybreak they had been upon their way.

Like a drunken man Sam staggered about the street, scarcely knowing where he was going and too disheartened to care. The result was that he stumbled into another noteworthy adventure. He collided with an officer of such distinction that at his coming everyone else upon the street had stepped aside deferentially and saluted. But Sam did not even see him. The officer was a small man, and the impact proved a trifle too much for his equilibrium, so that although he did not fall, he succeeded in making himself look ridiculous. Sam hastened to apologize, but the aggrieved officer was too furious to listen.

He cursed Sam roundly for a fool; and then, his dignity restored, he strode off with steps which seemed somewhat too long for his fat, little body.

Sam was too much taken back to do anything but stare. Who was this man? His voice had a ring in it that he seemed to recognize, and in spite of his uniform, his figure looked familiar. His eyes he could not see, for they avoided his, but he had an impression that he had been not-looked-at in just that way at some time in his past experience.

"Who was he?" Sam ventured to inquire of one of the amused bystanders.

"Him? Why, the Colonel!" was the reply. "Colonel Heasley!"

"Little men need big hats," remarked the man's companion, with a cynical smile.

Sam tried to laugh, but the effort sounded very weak and hollow. The next minute he was walking up to Heasley's residence and asking the man who stood at the door wearing a breastplate consisting of two rows of large brass buttons, if he could see the Colonel.

"He's out," was the rather gruff reply.

"He chust came in. I saw him," replied Sam, with a note of persistency.

"Take my advice, young man," said the man behind the buttons. "The Colonel is out, and I don't know when he's coming back. If you are going to make a fuss about it, there's a nice dark hole in the cellar that I've got orders to run you into."

Poor Sam gasped. He staggered back to the road, and threw himself down upon the grass. The spirit of revenge consumed him. If it cost him his life, he was going to pay Heasley back. He would hurl him from his pedestal, expose his treachery, and heap shame and contumely upon his haughty head.

And here again Isaac Brock was the man who could help him. Brock was Heasley's superior officer, and had the right to take the Colonel to task for his dishonest dealing. There was no question in Sam's mind but that he would. Sam decided that all he had to do was to go to Detroit overland by way of Brant's Ford and tell his story. Brock would do the rest. Let Heasley and Fred Frid tremble in their great army boots.

So the irate man retraced his steps to Coote's Paradise, and set out for Brant's Ford. But the progress he was able to make was discouragingly slow. He was ten years older than he was on that memorable occasion when he had walked to York and back. He could not walk at that pace now. He had gone scarcely a score of miles when he became foot-sore. The weather was extremely hot, and the pools of water where he might bathe his weary feet were few and far between. Still he plodded along, resting only when totally exhausted. That indomitable will of his urged him on. It would bring him at last to the end of the journey.

After he had passed Brant's Ford, there began to come to Sam's ears rumours of war on the western frontier. Foraging parties from the American army were swooping down upon the Canadian farms and carrying back with them to the fortress at Detroit great stores of livestock and other provisions. There was no one to show any resistance. The young farmers had gone to join the army at Amherstburg, and only the old men remained with the women and the children. They could do nothing but shake their impotent fists and bemoan the cruelty of fate and the hellishness of war.

Mile after mile Sam trudged along by the power of his mighty will. As he approached his destination, his flagging hopes were revived by reports of a victorious battle. He saw the Union Jack waving over the citadel at Detroit. He saw redcoats everywhere, on both sides of the river. Brock had conquered his enemies; he would turn now and help Sam abase his. Full of assurance and confidence, Sam accosted a redcoat and asked to be conducted without delay to the General.

"General Proctor?"

"No. Isaac Brock."

"He's gone."

"Gone!" gasped Sam. "Where?"

"Niagara Peninsula," was the reply.

Disappointment in one form or another had been dogging Sam's footsteps for many a day, but this was the greatest he had yet experienced. Yet he braced himself remarkably well. He made a few fruitless inquiries about his horse Menno, and decided that he would not give up his quest, even if it meant that he must follow Brock to the ends of the earth.

The shortest route to the Niagara Peninsula was by way of the Talbot settlement near Lake Erie, and he chose that in preference to the more northerly route by which he had come. But the roads to the south were not so good, and with much walking Sam's shoes were wearing out. So weary of limb, and even of life, did the traveller often become that he wished he could lie down by the roadside and cease to be. But there was no cessation of the spirit of revenge which possessed him. It was that which kept him alive. It grew and flourished like the proverbial green bay tree in the midst of an arid and desolate land.

On one occasion Sam fell sick and lay down by the roadside to die. But a kind old woman took him into her home and nursed him as well as she knew how. Sam couldn't remember how long he stayed there, for he lay unconscious for days at a time on the borderland between two worlds. And after that he lost all track of time.

It was the thirst for vengeance that made him press on towards the east as soon as he was able to walk. The fall had come. Already the trees were bedecking themselves in the brilliant foliage of autumn. The nights were frosty and damp. It was a marvel how Sam in his weakened physical condition could endure such extremes of heat and cold as day and night presented. But he was no weakling, this Sam Bricker.

He came at last by strange routes to the region of the great Niagara River with its marvellous waterfall. A few miles, a day at the most, separated him from Isaac Brock. His day of vengeance was at hand.

The land was full of soldiers, and Sam was dimly conscious that they eyed him with suspicion. But he screwed up all the courage he possessed, put on a brave face and accosted one of them with the query as to where he might expect to find Isaac Brock.

The soldier stared in amazement, then shrugged his shoulders. "By the looks of you," he said, "you'll soon be with him."

"Take me to him," implored Sam.

The soldier smiled grimly. "If you happen to be an enemy," he said, "it will be my most agreeable duty."

He spoke in riddles, Sam thought. He begged him to speak more plainly.

The soldier complied with his request beyond the possibility of misapprehension. "He's dead!" he announced, boldly. "Dead!"

"Dead?" echoed Sam, weakly. At that moment every lingering hope of vengeance died within him. His shoulders dropped, his chest sank in. Blank despair seized him. No more chance of recovering his long-lost Menno; no hope of dislodging the traitorous Colonel Heasley and his brass buttons from his seat of power and dignity.

"He was killed in battle two days ago," the soldier was saying. "At Queenston Heights."

"He's livin' in style at The Head of the Lake," replied Sam, sullenly.

The soldier looked at him narrowly and indecisively for a moment and then said: "You heard about the battle, didn't you? You know how it went?"

"No," said Sam, "and I don't care. All I know is that him and justice is both dead."

"The man's crazy," muttered the soldier, as he turned upon his heel and went his way.

With a broken heart and a conviction that life was no longer worth living, Sam turned again to the west, and began to stumble along the road that led towards Beccy and home. He had thought of them both many, many times during his travels. There had even been moments when he had half a mind to leave the wicked old world with its Heasleys and its Fred Frids, and return to the quiet peace of the tract. But now it was too late. Shame had overcome him, a deep-seated, relentless shame that would not let him think of facing his friends upon the Heasley Tract again. If he could only slink out of sight—out of existence—somewhere, anywhere—he would never ask anything more of life. Weary and faint, he sank upon the grass of the roadside and longed for the sweet compassion of Death.

Now it happened that a good Samaritan passed that way that day, and seeing the bundle of rags and dejection on the roadside, stopped his horse and came to his relief.

Sam opened his wondering eyes and beheld—not the Angel of Death but—Levi Moyer!

The good man helped this sorry spectacle he had found into his wagon and told him he was going to take him to his home where his "woman," Rachael, would care for him until he was well.

"You don't ask my name?" said Sam.

"No matter," replied Levi. "If you need help, you are our friend."

"But I'm the devil!" cried Sam. His old-time joke had occurred to him again, but all the mirth and laughter had gone out of it. Sam felt that he was at least a very close relative of the demon of the lower world.

Levi turned and looked again at the queer man at his side. "You're not——" he gasped. "You can't be Sam Bricker!"

"That's who I used to be," was the reply.

It was the middle of October when the Moyers put Sam between the white sheets of their spare bed and undertook to restore him to his former self. It was a difficult task, for their patient was sick not only in body but in mind and spirit. Not a day passed but Rachael prepared some tempting dish, and Levi spent long hours at his side. Through all the long winter months they pulled the bed into the kitchen where it was warmer. But month after month went by, and Sam kept getting weaker and weaker.

"Best let Beccy know," advised Rachael.

"No! no!" pleaded Sam.

"Mebbe till spring you'll be well enough to go and tell her yourself," said Rachael, hopefully.

But when spring came, Sam's feeble life was still hanging as if by a single thread.

CHAPTER XVII

The war did not exert a very strong influence over the dwellers on the Heasley Tract. None of the marauding parties from the American army had invaded their farms, carrying away their cattle; no soldiers tramped through their grain fields. And yet they had to play their part in the great international struggle. An officer had come in the early spring and demanded that all the unmarried men on the tract should take their conestogas and their heavy horses and present themselves to Colonel Proctor at Detroit. He intimated that while the authorities were willing to concede the right of the Mennonites to exemption from actual fighting, they were not willing to excuse them from manual labour. They and their conestogas were needed to do the hauling. Having delivered his orders, he rode away again on the same day, and nothing more had been heard of him. A few weeks later thirteen young bachelors had left with their wagons for Detroit, and nothing more had been heard of them either.

And now there were rumours of a spy in the bush. Those who had seen him said he wore the garb of a Mennonite. He avoided the public roads and hobbled about in the bush on a cane. If anyone approached, he ran to a place of hiding. He kept himself alive, it was believed, with wild berries and grain that he stole from the stables. Gradually, but certainly, he was working his way towards the north.

Aaron Schneider thought it must have been the spy he met one day when he had strolled off into the bush to look for wild flowers. He saw him in the distance, limping along with great difficulty, but instead of running away as the fellow usually did when anyone approached, he actually hobbled towards him. The boy grew frightened, although he was ashamed to confess it. He was sure he had seen that spy before, but where he could not remember. He started to whistle to hide his fear.

The spy kept advancing nearer and nearer and presently he came up to a few yards from the spot where Aaron was stooping over a clump of flowers. "Sam Bricker lives somewhere around here, don't he?" he said.

"Sam Bricker?" said Aaron, trying to swallow a great lump that was forming in his throat. "He's went long already."

"Dead, you mean?"

"Might chust as well be," Aaron replied, growing bolder with each word he uttered. "She don't get no good of him."

"She ain't sick or nothing, is she?" the spy made bold to inquire.

"Ach, she's good enough," Aaron answered. He was glad indeed to see the fellow move off to the densest part of the bush. As soon as he was out of sight Aaron ran home to tell his father.

Josiah was disturbed about the matter. He scratched his head and puzzled his brain. "So he's after Sam Bricker, is he?" he said. "And what did you tell him, Aaron?"

The boy straightened himself up and said; "I told him that if Sam Bricker ain't dead, he might chust as well be. I didn't run away or nothing."

"That's right, Aaron," said the father. "You are a brave boy. You didn't do nothing. Why, you don't have to run for no spy. If you see him again, ask him once what his name is, and what he's got to hide."

Josiah went into the house at his first opportunity and told the story to Susie. "Why don't that spy come and ask me about Sam Bricker, that's what I want to know," he said. "I'd pretty soon tell him we don't want to hear no more about Sam Bricker and his wickedness."

"Josiah!" expostulated his wife, "that ain't right. Mebbe you don't want to see him again, for you was always none too thick with Sam, but Beccy does, and so do I."

Josiah had nothing more to say and stalked out to the barn.

In the afternoon of that same day, a beautiful one in early July, the same ragged old spy might have been seen limping his way up the path that led to Beccy's kitchen. Every few steps he turned and glanced about apprehensively on all sides. He stopped when he had reached the doorstep, wiped his eyes with his coat-sleeve and noiselessly lifted the latch.

Only the children were in the room. They stopped their play to stare at the intruder.

The man acted very strangely, so that the children continued to look at him wonderingly. He sank into a chair and sobbed like a child.

Presently he motioned Mary to him. "Don't you know me yet?" he asked, hungrily.

Mary shrank back, and because she did not know what else to do, she continued to rock the cradle with increased rapidity. Peter and Sophie stared hard at the newcomer for a moment, then scrambled up from the floor and stood, one at either end of the cradle, sucking their thumbs.

Children as they were, they knew that there must be something wrong with the man. He got up from his chair, staggered towards them, but fell into a second chair. All the while he kept his eyes fixed on the cradle, and its tiny occupant, who lay kicking and screaming with temper and surfeit of attention.

"Be still!" admonished Mary, rocking with astounding velocity.

The stranger looked at Mary, smiled weakly, and said; "How do you call the bubby?"

"Sam."

"Sam!" The man's face was radiant with joy. He stumbled over to the cradle; stopped its motion; and kneeling down before it, kissed Little Sam very tenderly on either cheek.

Mary was too much surprised to say anything. Even the baby stared in amazement.

"Where's die Mommy?" asked this strange, presuming man.

"Out in the barn."

Mary was glad enough to see him go, this man who asked so many questions and acted so strangely. She was not frightened, but she wondered who he was and why he was so sad. She had a feeling that her mother would know better what to do with him.

Out to the barn the man went. It was surprising how quickly he covered the ground. When he reached the door he paused, and wiped his eyes once more upon his coat-sleeve. Then he pushed the door open. Mary, who was watching from the kitchen window, saw him seize the sill for support and heard him utter a joyful cry.

"Menno!" he gasped.

The horse turned his head and neighed. Such a pricking of ears as there was, and frisking of tail.

Beccy heard the commotion, and came running to see what was the matter.

"Beccy!" cried Sam, rushing to meet her with extended arms.

"Sam! Sam! is it you. Ach Sam!"

They were all three together again. Sam stood in the middle with one arm around Beccy's shoulder and the other about Menno's neck, while tears of penitence and joy filled his eyes.

"You don't feel hard to me, Beccy?" he asked, as soon as he could command the words. "To think I went away and let you alone— you and Little Sam."

Beccy's head was on Sam's throbbing breast. She could feel his heart beat. She looked up into his dear, swimming, penitent eyes and said she had never been so happy in all her life. Her loneliness and sorrow had only helped her to appreciate this great joy that had so unexpectedly come to her. "Sorrow is for one alone, Sam," she said, "but happiness——"

"Happiness is for two," Sam finished the sentence for her. "I know that too, Beccy, but I didn't know how to say it."

Then the happy wife led her erring husband back to the bosom of his family. "It's your doddy come back, Mary!" she cried, joyfully. "Make the dishes on the table. Come here once, Peter. Don't you know him no more? Ain't Sophie growed, Sam?"

"And the bubby," said Sam, who couldn't keep his eyes off the little bundle of babyhood that was kicking and crowing in the cradle. "Who does he look like?"

"He's got Sam Bricker wrote all over him," replied Beccy, with a laugh. "Red hair and all." Of course Beccy knew that was what Sam wanted her to say.

After supper Beccy pushed Sam into the rocking-chair and the children crowded around, sitting on his knee and climbing over his back. He was a happy father again, so happy that he quite forgot his physical weakness. "Ach, Beccy," he cried. "This is chust like old times."

"We'll play horse like we used to," said Peter, recalling former days and clapping his chubby hands in high glee. He knew where the reins were, and the stick of wood that they always used as a bit. He pressed them into Sam's hands.

"I want to be a horse, too," cried Mary.

They made a splendid team. Sam tied the rope around his waist, and held the youngest of the Brickers on his lap, while Peter and Mary pranced about kicking, and neighing, and pulling on their bits, like regular thoroughbreds. Sophie had elected to be a dog, and she bobbed about the room running from one side of the team to the other, yelping quite as effectively as Hundlie did upon occasions.

"Let the bubby drive," demanded the children, forgetting for the moment that animals do not talk.

So Little Sam's baby fingers clasped the rope, while Sam's great horny ones held it securely. With one accord the driver and his horses and even little Hundlie joined merrily in a familiar ditty, something between a song and a recitation:

> Reite, reite Gaüle
> Zum Blockhaus.
> Dat gucke drei Bubbe 'raus.
> Einer spinnt Seide
> An're vickelt Weide
> Der an're macht ein gleine Rock
> Für mein gleine Zettelbuck.

Such a commotion as there was! The more the baby laughed, the oftener the horses reared up, and stamped their feet. And what a bark the funny little dog did have. It was a mercy there wasn't a runaway. But when they had careered all around the room, they came back again to the place where they had started, and Sam in the most realistic tone imaginable cried out: "Whoa! Whoa! Why here we are to home again!"

The romp over, Little Sam was consigned once more to his cradle and the other children prepared for bed. Beccy heard their prayers as usual, but to-night they insisted that Sam should hear them too, and tuck them into their beds. Having recovered their father, they intended to make use of him.

When Sam and Beccy closed the bedroom door and found themselves alone in the kitchen, a very serious conversation ensued.

Sam began it. "I'm not so bad with my temper like I was, Beccy," he said. "Levi Moyer learned me a lot."

"Levi Moyer!" exclaimed Beccy. "Was that where you was all the time?"

Then Sam had to give an account of himself. It was a long, sad story, but he had to explain how it happened that he lost his horse and came after much wandering to the home of the Moyers. He tried to shorten it, but Beccy insisted upon knowing even the minutest detail of the terrible experience that had aged her Sam ten years in a single twelve-month.

"It was all my temper," Sam told her. "Levi pretty nearly gave me up already, but at the end he made me see that I was wrong."

"God don't need your help to punish the wicked," said Beccy. "He says in the Bible He will do it His own self."

"That's what Levi said," corroborated Sam. "'Vengeance is Mine. I will repay, saith the Lord.'"

"And all the time you was runnin' after Heasley and that Fred Frid, they didn't even know how you felt. But you had to suffer though."

"Yes," said Sam. "Levi Moyer said I hurt myself more than I hurt them. I was very dumm, Beccy; I know it now."

Beccy was determined to drive the lesson home. "The Lord must of laughed a lot at you, Sam," she said. "Runnin' all over Canada tryin' to get people to help you, and never once askin' Him."

"And He was the only one that could," added Sam, shame-facedly. "That's chust what Levi was sayin'."

"And when you found Heasley, you didn't even know him. Ach, Sam, it looks to me like the Lord had a hand in that, too."

Sam looked at Beccy earnestly. "To think I had to go all the way to The Twenty to leave Levi Moyer tell me that," he said, "when my own Beccy could do it chust as well. It don't give many women like you, Beccy. It don't give many women like you."

Then Sam wanted to know about the fire, and Beccy gave a very graphic description of the terrible visitation. She did not forget to tell how the "weggli" was threatened.

Sam listened with bated breath. He could not wait until Beccy got to the end of her story to learn the fate of the historic vehicle. "It didn't burn, Beccy, that 'weggli'?" he asked.

"No," replied Beccy, with laughter in her eyes. "I saved it. I thought I might chust as well. You might want to sell it sometime."

Sam knew that Beccy was only teasing him; nevertheless he made haste to inform her once again that nothing in the world would ever induce him to part with that relic. It was more precious in his eyes than a hundred conestogas. First thing in the morning he was going out to have a look at it again.

They drifted then into the news of the community. Old Sam Betzner had "went," and Abraham Gingerich was "goin'," and George Clemens——

"He ain't, Beccy, not George Clemens!" gasped Sam.

"Not him," replied Beccy, "but all four bubbies, one followin' in the footsteps of the other. The cholera."

Sam's head dropped involuntarily upon his chest. "It's hard to understand," he told Beccy at length. "Four of George Clemens' took, and when Sam Bricker comes home where he should 've stopped, what does he find? All safe, and a new bubby into the bargain. Ach, Beccy, it's more than I deserve. Go and fetch the Good Book once; I must read where it says about the cup runnin' over. I could have wrote that psalm myself."

Beccy got the book and listened with a happy heart while Sam read. When he came to the words, "I will dwell in the house of the Lord forever," the little wife's face glowed with joy. But he had no sooner closed the book than all the joy faded in a trice, and an anxious expression took its place.

"What's wrong?" asked Sam, glancing apprehensively at her.

"Nothing," replied Beccy, smiling blandly. She meant of course that there was nothing she wanted to tell.

The fact of the matter was that in that moment of prophetic hope which marked the closing words of the psalm, there had flashed through Beccy's mind the realization that Sam wasn't going to get a chance to "dwell in the house of the Lord forever." He was set back; banned. He would receive a cool reception in every other house on the Heasley Tract.

Beccy had a fertile mind. It did not take her long to evolve a plan to meet the need of the hour. Sam must be received back into the fold. Moreover, he must never know how near he had come to being an outcast among his own people.

Sam was very tired and sleepy. His head had little more than touched the pillow when he fell asleep. Beccy waited until his heavy breathing grew into a sonorous snore. Then, quick as a flash, she jumped up and stole noiselessly from the house. Out to the barn she ran; and, leading Menno forth, she jumped into her saddle and rode away with all speed.

Three miles to the north she travelled, and came at last to Benj Eby's house. All was dark, but she had no compunction about rousing Benj from his sleep to tell him the good news of Sam's return. Her husband had come back, penitent and godly. The devil was no longer enthroned in his heart and life. She entreated Benj to lift the ban and bring the community in the evening of the next day to welcome the wanderer. Benj was glad to conspire with her to make Sam's return a matter of general rejoicing. She was to expect a great crowd at seven o'clock, he said. Then Beccy, delighted beyond words with this promise, rode back through the night and crept noiselessly to her place at the side of her sleeping husband.

Sam stirred. He put out his hand and felt for her. "Are you there, Beccy?" he asked.

"Yes," replied she, quite unable to suppress a smile, and glad for the cover of darkness. "Did you think I would run away?"

"No," said Sam, "but I wanted to be sure. It don't give many women like you, Beccy."

Next morning Sam was the most impatient creature imaginable. He seemed to expect that everybody in the neighbourhood was going to rush over before breakfast to see him. When the morning was nearly gone, and not even his brother John had put in an appearance, he did not know what to think of it.

"But," Beccy reminded him, "he don't know yet that you are to home."

"Then I must go and tell him once," said Sam. "Why didn't Little Aaron tell Josiah and Susie? They haven't so far to come."

"But you didn't tell Aaron who you was," argued Beccy. "Like as not he thought you was such a spy or whatever."

"I'm goin' to take Menno and go over to George Clemens's once," he said. "I must tell him how I feel about the cholera."

Beccy was at her wits' ends to dissuade him, but when she finally succeeded, he began to pace the floor like a lion in a cage.

"As far as I can see, Sam," said Beccy, "you ain't changed much yet for all."

Sam was heartily ashamed of his conduct, and came and sat down quietly and penitently at Beccy's side.

"Mebbe we'll have more wisiters yet than we have chairs for," his good wife said, hopefully.

No sooner had they got the children to bed after supper than Hundlie began to bark and a rumbling of wheels was heard.

"Somebody's comin'," cried Sam, springing up excitedly and opening the door.

They all came, and they all came together; the Brickers, the Ebys, the Schneiders, the Clemens's, the Betzners, and the Erbs, with a sprinkling of Bechtels, Gingerichs, and Reicherts. It was a marvel how they all squeezed into Beccy's little kitchen. Benj Eby was the spokesman. In the name of the meeting, he welcomed Sam back not only to the bosom of his family and to the circle of his "Freundschaft," but also to the spiritual brotherhood of the Mennonite faith.

Sam looked so puzzled that Beccy laughed outright, and reminded him of her prophecy that they would have more visitors than chairs. At this, everybody looked around to see how the crowd was being accommodated, and they laughed heartily at the numerous makeshifts.

"But how did you all know I was here?" Sam wanted to know.

"Beccy told us," they answered.

"Beccy!" exclaimed Sam, quite unable to solve the mystery. "Why she was all the time home."

"Except when you were sleepin'," laughed the mischievous Beccy. "How do you know what all I was doin' then?"

He didn't, of course; but by piecing together the remarks that followed, Sam got the story. His Beccy had been a brave woman; a heroine, he said. He did not even try to conceal the fact that he was inordinately proud of her.

"She learnt it off you, I think," said Joseph Sherk. "That time you and her fetched the money over."

This reference to Sam's historic journey afforded an opportunity for the host to conduct the party to the barn to see the "weggli" again. Once more the marvellous story of their deliverance was reviewed. Sam Bricker was the hero of the hour, and Beccy the heroine.

At intervals during the autumn of, there returned to the Heasley Tract by twos and threes the young men who had gone that spring to haul for Colonel Proctor at Detroit. They had driven away with horses and conestogas; but they came back on foot. All was lost, they said. They had escaped only with their lives. Twelve had returned; and they all had the same story. The last to come back reported that the unlucky thirteenth of their number, one Adam Shupe, had been caught by the Americans; they would never see him again. But their fears were unfounded; for, within a week, he came, wearing a broad grin on his face, and boasting about his unique experience. He had been summoned before the great General Harrison, he claimed, and examined. It was by no means as serious an ordeal as it sounded; for the general was very jolly and after a few minutes' conversation had dismissed him with his blessing and expressed a wish that the Canadians would send to the war more men of his type. This speech Adam was unsophisticated enough to construe into a compliment to himself and his people.

After this, the fortunes of war did not disturb the people of the Heasley Tract to any great extent. Rumours of battles came to their ears, but there was never at any time any real danger that the war would be carried into their quiet community. No more recruits were demanded; no more conestogas seemed to be required. As far as the Mennonites were concerned, the war was at an end.

For many months there had been ruminating in Benj's mind a plan which these peaceful times seemed to be ripening for execution.

Five years had passed since he became a preacher; and now, quite recently, he had been made a Bishop; but still the people were meeting
for worship in private houses under most cramped conditions. Benj's
ambition was to build a meeting-house where the people might gather
on Sundays from all over the Tract to hear the message that the Lord
should give him; and where the children might congregate on week
days, while he himself should teach them all he knew about the acquir-
ing of a liberal education.

Old Christian Eby's prayers were abundantly answered. The
meeting-house was built in due course, and "der gle' Bench" became
both preacher and teacher, the most earnest preacher and the most successful teacher of the first pioneer settlement in the interior of Upper
Canada.

Two years passed by before the news came of the close of the
war. Sam Bricker was ploughing one day in one of his new, well-
cultivated fields, when he saw a man in military uniform ride up before his door. His heart sank, presuming, of course, that more of the
young men of the community were to be pressed into service. Dropping his work, he came to investigate. "Ain't the war done yet?" was
his greeting.

"Yes, it's over at last," replied the soldier.

"And are we livin' in Canada or in the United States?" inquired
Sam.

The soldier seemed quite disgusted with the whole matter. Not
a single one of the disagreements that had caused the war, he said, had
been mentioned in the treaty. It was pretty much of a draw, with the
British winning by land, and the Americans on the Lakes. Things were
about as they had been; but, if he knew anything about warfare, the
Canadians were by all odds the best fighters of them all.

Sam was amused. "It looks like the Mennonites are right about
war after all," he said.

The soldier would not acknowledge it. He was a likely fellow
and fond of an argument. He could never understand the Mennonite
attitude on the question of war, he said. Did Sam mean to tell him that
if the enemy had come into the Heasley Tract and robbed them of everything their farms possessed, they would sit still and refuse to fight?

"Him that taketh away thy cloak forbid not to take thy coat
also," was Sam's reply.

"But if they should actually strike you, would you take it, and
say nothing?"

"Unto him that smiteth thee on the one cheek, offer also the other," said Sam.

"But suppose they killed your brother, your wife, you would hate them then?"

"We couldn't," replied Sam. "It says; 'Love your enemies, bless them that curse you, do good to them that hate you.'"

The soldier snorted his contempt. "A wishy-washy doctrine, that is, to be sure," he said. "Utterly impracticable."

"It was taught by the Saviour of the world," Sam reminded him.

The soldier was ready to change the subject. "You won't argue, Mr. Bricker," he said. "All you do is quote scripture." He paused, and then added quickly; "You don't seem to remember me."

Sam couldn't say that he did.

"Surely you haven't forgotten how I opened the gate for you and your cow at the tavern in York years ago."

Sam recalled at once not only the incident but also the man's name. "It's Mr. Wilson, not?" he cried. "You made me acquainted with the mortgage."

"Yes, but I couldn't make you believe it," laughed Wilson. "You kept urging me to get my head charmed."

"I thought you was crazy," said Sam, apologetically.

"So I was, I suppose," replied Wilson. "But I had had dealings with Heasley, too, and I was out for vengeance."

Vengeance! Sam recoiled at the word. His own fruitless quest for vengeance loomed up in his memory like a hateful dream. But for all that he couldn't help but feel a little inquisitive about Heasley. He allowed himself to inquire how things were with him.

"Same old Heasley," replied Wilson.

"But he's not rich like he was?" suggested Sam; who evidently had his own ideas about how Divine Justice was to be dealt out.

"He's one of the wicked that flourish," was Wilson's reply. "They don't all get their deserts, I have noticed."

The time had come at last for the soldier to state his errand. He had been sent, he said, to determine the losses sustained by the Mennonites during the war. The government was willing to pay five dollars a day to every man who had served with a two-horse team, and eight dollars a day if four horses had been used. Besides, full compensation was to be made to those who had sustained loss or damage to their horses and wagons.

Sam's face fairly glowed with pleasure. Once more he was to be the bearer of good news to his people.

"And this was a good excuse to pay you a visit," said Wilson. "I have wanted to come and see you—and the Tract—ever since that day when I heard you tell the story of the Mennonites."

Suddenly Sam's apparent lack of hospitality seemed to dawn upon him. He caught Wilson's hand and drew him towards the house. "You must come right in," he said. "No, the dog don't bite; and Beccy—why, you didn't see her yet, did you? She's—ach, I don't know right how to say it, but it don't give many women like my Beccy."

Also from Benediction Books ...
Wandering Between Two Worlds: Essays on Faith and Art
Anita Mathias
Benediction Books, 2007
152 pages
ISBN: 0955373700

Available from www.amazon.com, www.amazon.co.uk

In these wide-ranging lyrical essays, Anita Mathias writes, in lush, lovely prose, of her naughty Catholic childhood in Jamshedpur, India; her large, eccentric family in Mangalore, a sea-coast town converted by the Portuguese in the sixteenth century; her rebellion and atheism as a teenager in her Himalayan boarding school, run by German missionary nuns, St. Mary's Convent, Nainital; and her abrupt religious conversion after which she entered Mother Teresa's convent in Calcutta as a novice. Later rich, elegant essays explore the dualities of her life as a writer, mother, and Christian in the United States-- Domesticity and Art, Writing and Prayer, and the experience of being "an alien and stranger" as an immigrant in America, sensing the need for roots.

About the Author

Anita Mathias is the author of *Wandering Between Two Worlds: Essays on Faith and Art.* She has a B.A. and M.A. in English from Somerville College, Oxford University, and an M.A. in Creative Writing from the Ohio State University, USA. Anita won a National Endowment of the Arts fellowship in Creative Nonfiction in 1997. She lives in Oxford, England with her husband, Roy, and her daughters, Zoe and Irene.

Visit Anita at http://www.anitamathias.com, and on http://theoxfordchristian.blogspot.com, her Christian blog; http://wanderingbetweentwoworlds.blogspot.com/, her personal blog, and http://thegoodbooksblog.blogspot.com, her literary and writing blog.

The Church That Had Too Much
Anita Mathias
Benediction Books, 2010
52 pages
ISBN: 9781849026567

Available from www.amazon.com, www.amazon.co.uk

The Church That Had Too Much was very well-intentioned. She wanted to love God, she wanted to love people, but she was both hampered by her muchness and the abundance of her possessions, and beset by ambition, power struggles and snobbery. Read about the surprising way The Church That Had Too Much began to resolve her problems in this deceptively simple and enchanting fable.

About the Author

Anita Mathias is the author of *Wandering Between Two Worlds: Essays on Faith and Art.* She has a B.A. and M.A. in English from Somerville College, Oxford University, and an M.A. in Creative Writing from the Ohio State University, USA. Anita won a National Endowment of the Arts fellowship in Creative Nonfiction in 1997. She lives in Oxford, England with her husband, Roy, and her daughters, Zoe and Irene.

Visit Anita at http://www.anitamathias.com, and on http://theoxfordchristian.blogspot.com, her Christian blog; http://wanderingbetweentwoworlds.blogspot.com/, her personal blog, and http://thegoodbooksblog.blogspot.com, her literary and writing blog.